JONATHAN AMES

SEXUAL METAMORPHOSIS

Jonathan Ames is the author of *I Pass Like Night*, *The Extra Man*, *What's Not to Love?*, *My Less Than Secret Life*, and *Wake Up, Sir!* He is the winner of a Guggenheim Fellowship and lives in New York City, where he performs frequently as a storyteller in theaters and nightclubs. He is a recurring guest on the *Late Show with David Letterman*, and his books are being adapted for film and television. Ames has had one amateur boxing match, losing and fighting under the nickname "The Herring Wonder." Further information is available on his Web site at www.jonathanames.com.

ALSO BY JONATHAN AMES

I Pass Like Night
The Extra Man
What's Not to Love?
My Less Than Secret Life
Wake Up, Sir!

SEXUAL
METAMORPHOSIS

SEXUAL METAMORPHOSIS

An Anthology of
Transsexual Memoirs

EDITED BY
Jonathan Ames

VINTAGE BOOKS

A Division of Random House, Inc.

New York

A VINTAGE BOOKS ORIGINAL, APRIL 2005

Copyright © 2005 by Jonathan Ames

All rights reserved under International and Pan-American Copyright
Conventions. Published in the United States by Vintage Books, a division of
Random House, Inc., New York, and simultaneously in Canada by Random
House of Canada Limited, Toronto.

Vintage and colophon are registered trademarks of Random House, Inc.

Permissions acknowledgments can be found at the end of the book.

Cataloging-in-Publication Data for *Sexual Metamorphosis*
is on file at the Library of Congress.

ISBN 978-1-4000-3014-9

Book design by Fritz Metsch

www.vintagebooks.com

Printed in the United States of America

Contents

Introduction

My purpose is to tell of bodies which have been transformed into shapes of a different kind
— *Ovid*, Metamorphoses

IN OCTOBER of 1990, I took a trip to California. When I returned I flew into the Philadelphia airport. A friend picked me up. I was living in Princeton, New Jersey, at the time, and on our way home, my friend wanted to stop at a bar in New Hope, Pennsylvania. It was late, around eleven o'clock, and I was tired, but I didn't want to say no to my friend.

As we entered the bar, an older, very attractive woman took one look at me—a dramatic double take—and exclaimed, "Where have you been my whole life, baby? Look at those blond eyelashes!"

She then playfully took me into her arms and pressed me to her very lovely and substantial bosom. At the time, being youngish, I was still a breast man, and she was more than ideal in this department. She was a little old for me—in her early fifties—but she was very pretty, and coinciding with my youthful breast obsession, I did have a thing for older women, though more in theory than in practice. But here was a chance for some practice. So I was rather enthralled by this sexy, busty blond and was happy to have her hold me.

After about an hour at the bar, flirting and chatting with this beautiful woman, my friend, who had gathered me at the airport, wanted to leave, and so my new ladylove wrote down her name and number on a napkin. She too lived in the Princeton area and had come to the bar with some members of her theater troupe—she was an actress.

I called her a few times over the next few weeks and we spoke of getting together, but I was too scared to make a rendezvous. I had a girlfriend at the time and didn't want to be unfaithful, though I hadn't protested when the woman gathered me into her arms at the bar. Struggling with temptation, I finally threw away that napkin which bore the woman's number. I felt virtuous. I was a loyal boyfriend! Like most people, I'm good at lying to myself. Anyway, I never spoke to or saw the woman from the bar again.

Two years later, in 1992, the girl and I broke up and I moved to New York City. For a novel I wanted to write, I started doing a lot of "research" in Times Square. I did most of this research, though, at a bar called Sally's, which was right across the street from the *New York Times* building on Forty-third. It was a bar for pre-op transsexual prostitutes, and it has since been closed during the cleaning up of Times Square. I did manage to spend several years in that bar—research metamorphosed into a social life—and out of that time came my second novel, *The Extra Man*, which was published in 1998.

Since the publication of that novel, publishers sometimes send me books with sexual content with the hope that I might provide a book-jacket endorsement, and more times than not, I happily comply. Like most people, I enjoy books with sexual content.

In October of 2000, Temple University Press sent me such a book for a blurb. It was the memoir of a transsexual, Aleshia Brevard, and the book was titled, *The Woman I Was Not Born to Be.* I had never before read the memoir of a transsexual and her story was otherworldly—a Southern farm boy moves to San Francisco in the 1950s, becomes a Marilyn Monroe impersonator with such style that M.M. herself comes to a performance; then a few years later, so she can marry the love of her life, Brevard has a sex-change operation; the marriage doesn't go through, so Brevard moves to Los Angeles and becomes a

B-movie starlet, soap opera actress, and Playboy Bunny, and never once reveals her original gender to the Hollywood community.

And the whole time I read this book I was wondering why the name Aleshia Brevard was familiar to me, terribly familiar. Then I came to the end of the memoir and there was a mention by Ms. Brevard of being in a Princeton repertory company in the early 1990s. Suddenly, I had an eerie feeling why her name was known to me. Hadn't it been on a certain napkin with a phone number ten years before?

I dashed off an e-mail to the publicist at Temple University: *I'm going to write a blurb. I love the book. But there's something curious going on. I think I may have met Aleshia. Can you ask her if she recalls meeting me at a bar in New Hope, Pennsylvania, ten years ago?*

A few hours later, the publicist forwarded me a one-line e-mail from Aleshia Brevard. It read: *Where have you been, baby?*

———

WELL, ALESHIA's book, coupled with the publication around that time of Deirdre McCloskey's memoir, *Crossing* (an excerpt of which is included here, as well as an excerpt from Aleshia's memoir), sparked in me this idea that there was a whole rapidly growing body of literature that dealt with the subject of changing one's sex. Fortunately, I was spending that academic year, 2000–2001, at Indiana University, home of the Kinsey Institute, and making full use of the Kinsey library I began to read the memoirs of transsexuals and decided to put together this anthology. This book is by no means a perfect selection—no anthology with any organizing principle can make that claim—but I think it will provide an excellent introduction to the world of transsexuals, and it can lead, perhaps, to further reading and exploration.

I found the memoirs of transsexuals to be parallel in structure to that classic literary model—the bildungsroman, the coming-of-age novel. The basic outline of the transsexual memoir is as follows: A boy or girl very early on in life feels terribly uncomfortable in his or her gender role, and there is a sense that some terrible mistake has occurred, that he or she was meant to be the other sex. Attempts are made—by parents or society—to reform them, and they learn to repress their instincts as much as possible. Eventually—like the protagonist of the bildungsroman—they leave their home, their small world, and venture out, usually to a big city. There they begin to privately or publicly masquerade as the other sex, until eventually the masquerade goes beyond costume and posture and becomes permanent—especially in the latter part of the twentieth century with the advent of synthetic hormones and plastic and sex-change surgeries.

The third act to these stories—first act: gender-dysphoric childhood; second act: the move to the big city and the transformation—is the aftermath of the sex change. In most of the books I've read, whether it be female-to-male or male-to-female transsexuals, the writers will not proclaim that great happiness has been found or that all their problems are solved, but they all do seem to express this feeling that *they've done all they can*—penises removed, breasts implanted; penises constructed, breasts removed; myriad other surgeries; great physical and psychological suffering—and they have come, finally, to a place of self-acceptance and peace.

The books I've excerpted for this anthology have both a literary significance—the writing and the stories are remarkable—and a sociological significance—is it possible to say in the twenty-first century what is male or female? Has it ever been possible? Michel Foucault, in his introduction to *Herculine Barbin,* the eponymous memoir of a nineteenth-century French hermaphrodite, ponders Western man's seemingly narrow need for what he calls a *"true* sex"—a clear-cut classification and definition of a person's gender—and he wonders if man can't expand beyond his binary definitions of male and female.

He also writes in this introduction that the eighteenth century was somewhat "haunted" by the transvestite—it was in the 1700s that the Chevalier d'Eon stunned the world, appearing in the courts of Europe as a man and a woman, baffling all, and it was after d'Eon that the first term for transvestites was originated: *eonists*—and that the nineteenth century was haunted by the hermaphrodite. In both cases, it was because these figures—the transvestite and the hermaphrodite—forced a reexamination of what it meant to be male or female, and raised, too, that old literary question of appearance versus reality.

I'd like to add to Foucault's thesis that the twentieth century was haunted, for the same reasons, by the transsexual. Christine Jorgensen's sex-change operation in 1952 created headlines all over the world, and thirty years later the revelation that a James Bond girl—Caroline Cossey—had once been a boy created a furor that nearly destroyed Cossey's life. Excerpts from Jorgensen's memoir, *Christine Jorgensen: A Personal Autobiography,* and from Caroline Cossey's, *My Life,* can be found in the pages to come.

Transsexuals, seemingly as a rite of passage, undergo various levels of persecution and torment from the outside world—it is well established that people will attack what they don't understand, what scares them. And why are people scared of transsexuals? Because transsexuals shake up the order of things? Because they present people with an option that maybe they don't want to contemplate—that you can change who you are? But can you? I'm not going to answer such a question here—I couldn't anyway—but I do think the texts I've gathered here will force readers to contemplate the riddle of identity and self, because though the transsexual's quest is seemingly for their correct gender, it's also a journey to answer questions that haunt all people: Who am I? What am I?

I do want to say that of course not all people are "scared" of transsexuals; in fact, most people are wildly intrigued and fascinated. I think one of the sources of people's enormous curiosity about transsexuals—whether it manifests itself as fear or benign wonderment—is that nearly everyone at one time or another in their life wonders what it would be like to be the other sex, and these memoirs are accounts of people who dared to find out. Their stories, then, hold the appeal of an adventurer's tale: someone who has gone where you, the reader, will never go—the Amazon, Mount Everest, a change of sex—but you'd like to hear about it.

Transsexuals are groundbreakers, sexual adventurers, and as one pre-op transsexual said to me several years ago at Sally's, "We're the hippies of the nineties." And so the transsexual as a modern, latter-day twentieth-century figure—a sexual renegade, a chameleon, a creature out of myth alive in our time—has of course appealed to novelists. The authors Gore Vidal, Jerzy Kosinski, John Irving, and David Ebershoff, to name a few, have all had transsexual characters. David Ebershoff's award-winning book *The Danish Girl* is, interestingly enough, a re-creation of the long-out-of-print memoir *Man into Woman* by Lili Elbe, who I consider to be the very first "recorded" transsexual, having undergone an unusual surgery in 1931, a surgery that proved to be fatal. An excerpt from Elbe's book, *Man into Woman*, is included here.

I have also included a case history, the first-person account of "Joe" from Dr. Harry Benjamin's *The Transsexual Phenomenon*. Dr. Benjamin is the man who originated the word *transsexual*. He is the medical establishment's pioneer for sex-change surgery as a way to help those with the psychiatric condition of gender dysphoria. Whether or not this is a psychiatric condition or a physiological one (many transsexuals do have chromosomal and hormonal anomalies) or some kind of error of destiny—"I am a woman born in a man's body!" "I am a man born in a woman's body!"—is probably unanswerable. It is a mystery of the human condition, of human sexuality, but I think readers will find this question—why are some people so fiercely compelled to change their sex?—something they will ponder with great curiosity as they read through this book.

"Joe" is an autobiography of a female-to-male transsexual, and there are three other memoir excerpts in this anthology by female-to-male transsexuals—Mario Martino, Loren Cameron, and Mark Rees. F-to-M's, as they are sometimes referred to, are often in the shadow, publicity-wise anyway, of their male-to-female counterparts. This in itself is very interesting: the evolution from masculinity to femininity—to perhaps beauty itself—is perceived, I believe, as sexier and more glamorous and perhaps, too, more of an affront to nature than the blunting of female characteristics to achieve a male appearance. The act of going from male to female seems to cry out: Look at me! And the other seems to say: I want to live my life quietly and strongly as a male—stop looking at me!

The first chapter of this book is also, like the autobiography found in Benjamin's book, a case history—number 129 of Richard von Krafft-Ebing's famous nineteenth-century study of human sexuality, *Psychopathia Sexualis*. Case 129 is the autobiography—a letter written to Krafft-Ebing—by a Hungarian doctor who believed that he had changed overnight into a woman. And to momentarily bring up a separate but interesting literary issue, I think there's a strong chance that Franz Kafka's *The Metamorphosis* was in part inspired by Case 129. Kafka would have certainly been familiar with Krafft-Ebing's famous book and would have read it in German. Consider these lines from the Hungarian doctor's letter:

"But who could describe my fright when, on the next morning, I awoke and found myself feeling as if completely changed into a woman; and when, on standing and walking, I felt female genitals and breasts! When at last I raised myself out of bed, I felt that a complete transformation had taken place in me." Now compare this passage to the opening of Kafka's story: "When Gregor Samsa awoke from troubled dreams one morning, he had found that he had been transformed in his bed to an enormous vermin." Also, Krafft-Ebing introduced Case 129 with the following title: "Degree: Stage of Transition to *Metamorphosis* Sexualis Paranoia."

Ultimately, this Kafka–Krafft-Ebing connection is of interest to me, because as with all that you will read in this anthology, it touches upon the age-old story of becoming something else and its immovable place in our literature and in our psyches.

You will find that the memoir excerpts in this anthology are ordered chronologically and can be read as charting the perception of transsexuals over the last fifty years, as well as representing the various stages of transformation that transsexuals go through. What is also conveyed in these passages is the incredibly personal nature of these transformations, and I think you will find the stories of Lili Elbe, "Joe" Christine Jorgensen, Jan Morris, Mario Martino, Renée Richards, Caroline Cossey, Loren Cameron, Mark Rees, Deirdre McCloskey, Aleshia Brevard, Calpernia Sarah Addams, Donna Rose, and Jennifer Finney Boylan to be utterly beautiful, strange, funny, painful, and like little else you have read in your life.

Jonathan Ames
Brooklyn, NY
October 2004

PSYCHOPATHIA SEXUALIS

Richard von Krafft-Ebing

1886

Richard von Krafft-Ebing (1840–1902) was a German physician and neurologist. His Psychopathia Sexualis (1886), a pioneering collection of 237 case studies in sexual pathology, revolutionized the scientific understanding of sex, influencing Freud (a student of Krafft-Ebing's) and introducing the terms sadism, masochism, *and* fetishism.

In this excerpt, Case 129 is presented and is the autobiography of a patient who "feels like a woman in a man's form."

CASE 129. *Autobiography.* Born in Hungary in 1844, for many years I was the only child of my parents; for the other children died for the most part of general weakness. A brother of later birth is still living.

I come of a family in which nervous and mental diseases have been numerous. It is said that I was very pretty as a little child, with blond locks and transparent skin; very obedient, quiet and modest, so that I was taken everywhere in the society of ladies without any offense on my part.

With a very active imagination—my enemy through life—my talents developed rapidly. I could read and write at the age of four; my memory reaches back to my third year. I played with everything that fell into my hands—with leaden soldiers, or stones, or ribbons from a toy shop; but a machine for working in wood, that was given to me as a present, I did not like. I liked best to be at home with my mother, who was everything to me. I had two or three friends with whom I got on good-naturedly; but I liked to play with her sisters quite as well, who always treated me like a girl, which at first did not embarrass me. I must have already been on the road to become just like a girl; at least, I can still well remember how it was always said: "He is not intended for a boy." At this I tried to play the boy—imitated my companions in everything, and tried to surpass them in wildness. In this I succeeded. There was no tree or building too high for me to reach its top. I took great delight in soldiers. I avoided girls more, because I did not wish to play with their playthings; and it always annoyed me that they treated me so much like one of themselves.

In the society of mature people, however, I was always modest, and, also, always regarded with favor. Fantastic dreams about wild animals—which once drove me out of bed without waking me—frequently troubled me. I was always very simply but very elegantly dressed, and thus developed a taste for beautiful clothing. It seems peculiar to me that, from the time of my school days, I had a partiality for ladies' gloves, which I put on secretly as often as I could. Thus, when once my mother was about to give away a pair of gloves, I made great opposition to it, and told her, when she asked why I acted so, that I wanted them myself. I was laughed at; and from that time I took good care not to display my preference for female things. Yet my delight in them was very great. I took special pleasure in masquerade costumes—i.e., only in female attire. If I saw them, I envied their owners. What seemed to me the prettiest sight was two young men, beautifully dressed as white ladies, with masks on; and yet I would not have shown myself to others as a girl for anything; I was so afraid of being ridiculed. At school I worked very hard, and was always among the first. From childhood my parents taught me that duty came first; and they always set me an example. It was also a pleasure for me to attend school; for the teachers were kind, and the elder pupils did not plague the younger ones. We left my first home; for my father was compelled, on account of his business—which was dear to him—to separate from his family for a year. We moved to Germany. Here there was a stricter, rougher manner, partly in teachers and partly in pupils; and I was again ridiculed on account of my girlishness. My schoolmates went so far as to give a girl, who had exactly my features, my name, and me hers; so that I hated the girl. But I later came to be on terms of friendship with her after her marriage. My mother tried to dress me elegantly; but this was repugnant to me, because it made me the object of taunting. So, finally, I was delighted when I had correct trousers and coats. But with these came a new annoyance. They irritated my genitals, particularly when the cloth was rough; and the touch of tailors while measuring me, on account of their tickling, which almost convulsed me, was unendurable, particularly about the genitals. Then I had to practice gymnastics; and I simply could do nothing at all, or only indifferently the things that even girls can do easily. While bathing I was troubled by feeling ashamed to undress; but I liked to bathe. Until my twelfth year I had a great weakness in my back. I learned to swim late, but ultimately so well that I took long swims. At thirteen I had pubic hair, and was about six feet tall; but my face was feminine until my eighteenth year, when my beard came in abundance and gave me rest from resemblance to woman. An inguinal hernia that was acquired in my twelfth year, and cured when I was twenty, gave me much trouble, particularly in gymnastics. Besides, from my twelfth year on, I had, after sitting long, and particularly while working at night, an itching, burning and twitching, extending from the penis to my back, which the acts of sitting and standing increased, and which was made worse by catching cold. But I had no suspicion whatever that this could be connected with the genitals. Since none of my friends suffered in this way, it seemed strange to me; and it required the greatest patience to endure it, the more owing to the fact that my abdomen troubled me.

In *sexualibus* I was still perfectly innocent; but now, as at the age of twelve or thirteen, I had a definite feeling of preferring to be a young lady. A young lady's form was more pleasing to me; her quiet manner, her deportment, but particularly her attire, attracted me. But I was careful not to allow this to be noticed; and yet I am sure that I should not have shrunk from the castration knife, could I have thus attained my desire. If I had been asked to say why I preferred female attire, I could have said nothing more than that it attracted me powerfully; perhaps, also, I seemed to myself, on account of my uncommonly white skin, more like a girl. The skin of my face and hands, particularly, was very sensitive. Girls liked my society; and, though I should have preferred to have been with them constantly, I avoided them when I could; for I had to exaggerate in order not to appear feminine. In my heart I always envied them. I was particularly envious when one of my young girlfriends got long dresses and wore gloves and veils. When, at the age of fifteen, I was on a journey, a young lady, with whom I was boarding, proposed that I should mask as a lady and go out with her; but, owing to the fact that she was not alone, I did not acquiesce, much as I should have liked it. While on this journey, I was pleased at seeing boys in one city wearing blouses with short sleeves, and the arms bare. A lady elaborately dressed was like a goddess to me; and if even her hand touched me coldly I was happy and envious, and only too gladly would have put myself in her place in the beautiful garments and lovely form. Nevertheless, I studied assiduously, and passed through the Realschule and the gymnasium in nine years, passing a good final examination. I remember, when fifteen, having first expressed to a friend the wish to be a girl. In answer to his question, I could not give the reason why. At seventeen I got into fast society; I drank beer, smoked, and tried to joke with waiter girls. The latter liked my society, but they always treated me as if I wore petticoats. I could not take dancing lessons, they repelled me so; but if I could have gone as a mask, it would have been different. My friends loved me dearly; I hated only one, who seduced me into onanism. Shame on those days, which injured me for life! I practiced it quite frequently, but in it seemed to myself like a double man. I cannot describe the feeling; I think it was masculine, but mixed with feminine elements. I could not approach girls; I feared them, but they were not strange to me. They impressed me as being more like myself; I envied them. I would have denied myself all pleasures if, after my classes, at home I could have been a girl and thus have gone out. Crinoline and a smoothly fitting glove were my ideals. With every lady's gown I saw I fancied how I should feel in it—i.e., as a lady. I had no inclination toward men. But I remember that I was somewhat lovingly attached to a very handsome friend with a girl's face and dark hair, though I think I had no other wish than that we both might be girls.

At the high school I finally once had coitus; *hoc modo sensi, me libentius sub puella concubuisse et penem meum cum cunno mutatum maluisse.* To her astonishment, the girl had to treat me as a girl, and did it willingly; but she treated me as if I were she (she was still quite inexperienced, and, therefore, did not laugh at me).

When a student at times I was wild, but I always felt that I assumed this wildness as a mask. I drank and dueled, but I could not take lessons in dancing, because I was afraid of betraying myself. My friendships were close, but without other thoughts. It pleased me most to have a friend masked as a lady, or to study the ladies' costumes at a ball. I understood such things perfectly. Gradually I began to feel like a girl.

On account of unhappy circumstances, I twice attempted suicide. Without any cause I once did not sleep for fourteen days, had many hallucinations (visual and auditory at the same time), and was with both the living and the dead. The latter habit of thought remains. I also had a friend (a lady) who knew my hobby and put on my gloves for me; but she always looked upon me as a girl. Thus I understood women better than other men did, and in what they differed from men; so I was always treated *more feminarium*—as if they had found in me a female friend. On the whole, I could not endure obscenity, and indulged in it myself only out of braggadocio when it was necessary. I soon overcame my aversion to foul odors and blood, and even liked them. Only some things I could not look at without nausea. I was wanting in only one respect: I could not understand my own condition. I knew that I had feminine inclinations, but believed that I was a man. Yet I doubt whether, with the exception of the attempts at coitus, which never gave me pleasure (which I ascribe to onanism), I ever admired a woman without wishing I were she; or without asking myself whether I should not like to be the woman, or be in her attire. Obstetrics I learned with difficulty (I was ashamed for the exposed girls, and had a feeling of pity for them); and even now I have to overcome a feeling of fright in obstetrical cases; indeed, it has happened that I thought I felt the traction myself. After filling several positions successfully as a physician, I went through a military campaign as a volunteer surgeon. Riding, which, while a student, was painful to me, because in it the genitals had more of a feminine feeling, was difficult for me (it would have been easier in the female style).

Still, I always thought I was a man with obscure masculine feeling; and whenever I associated with ladies, I was still soon treated as an inexperienced lady. When I wore a uniform for the first time, I should have much preferred to have slipped into a lady's costume, with a veil; I was disturbed when the stately uniform attracted attention. In private practice I was successful in the three principal branches. Then I made another military campaign; and during this I came to understand my nature; for I think that, since the first ass ever made, no beast of burden has ever had to endure with so much patience as I have. Decorations were not wanting, but I was indifferent to them.

Thus I went through life, such as it was, never satisfied with myself, full of dissatisfaction with the world, and vacillating between sentimentality and a wildness that was for the most part affected.

My experience as a candidate for matrimony was very peculiar. I should have preferred not to marry, but family circumstances and practice forced me to it. I married an energetic, amiable lady, of a family in which female government was rampant. I was in love with her as much as one of us can be in love—i.e., what we love we love with our whole hearts, and live in it, even though we do not show it as much as a genuine man does. We love our brides with all the love of a woman, almost as a woman might love her bridegroom. But I cannot say this for myself; for I still believed that I was but a depressed man, who would come to himself, and find himself out by marriage. But, even on my marriage night, I felt that I was only a woman in man's form; *sub femina locum meum esse mihi visum est.* On the whole, we lived contented and happy, and for two years were childless. After a difficult pregnancy, during which time I lay at the point of death in the enemy's own country, my wife gave birth to our first boy in a difficult labor—a boy still afflicted with a melancholy nature. Then came a second, who is very quiet; a third, full of peculiarities; a fourth, a fifth; and all have the predisposition to neurasthenia. Since I always felt out of my own place, I went much in gay society; but I always worked as much as human strength would endure. I studied and operated; and I experimented with many drugs and methods of cure, always on myself. I left the regulation of the house to my wife, as she understood housekeeping very well. My marital duties I performed as well as I could, but without personal satisfaction. Since the first coitus, the masculine position in it has been repugnant, and also difficult for me. I should have much preferred to have the other *rôle.* When I had to deliver my wife, it almost broke my heart; for I knew how to appreciate her pain. Thus we lived long together, until severe gout drove me to various baths, and made me neurasthenic. At the same time, I became so anemic that every few months I had to take iron for some time; otherwise I would be almost chlorotic or hysterical, or both. Stenocardia often troubled me; then came unilateral cramps of chin, nose, neck and larynx; hemicrania and cramps of the diaphragm and chest muscles. For about three years I had a feeling as if the prostate were enlarged—a bearing-down feeling, as if giving birth to something; and also pain in the hips, constant pain in the back, and the like. Yet with the strength of despair, I fought against these complaints, which impressed me as being female or effeminate, until three years ago, when a severe attack of arthritis completely broke me down.

But before this terrible attack of gout occurred, in despair, to lessen the pain of gout, I had taken hot baths, as near the temperature of the body as possible. On one of these occasions it happened that I suddenly changed, and seemed to be near death. I sprang with all my remaining strength out of the bath; I had felt exactly like a woman with libido. This happened when the extract of Indian hemp came into vogue, and was highly prized. In a state of fear of a threatened attack of gout (feeling perfectly indifferent about life), I took three or four times the usual dose of it, and almost died of hashish poisoning. Convulsive laughter, a feeling of unheard-of strength and swiftness, a peculiar feeling in brain and eyes, millions of sparks streaming from the brain through the skin—all these feelings occurred. But I could not force myself to speak. All at once I saw myself a woman from my toes to my breast; I felt, as before while in the bath, that the genitals had shrunken, the pelvis broadened, the breasts swollen out; a feeling of unspeakable delight came over me. I closed my eyes, so that at least I did not see the face changed. My physician looked as if he had a gigantic potato instead of a head; my wife had the full moon on her thorax. And yet, I was strong enough to briefly record my will in my notebook when both left the room for a short time.

But who could describe my fright when, on the next morning, I awoke and found myself feeling as if completely changed into a woman; and when, on standing and walking, I felt vulva and mammae! When at last I raised myself out of bed, I felt that a complete transformation had taken place in me. During my illness a visitor said: "He is too patient for a man." And the visitor gave me a plant in bloom, which seemed strange, but pleased me. From that time I was patient, and would do nothing in a hurry; but I became tenacious, like a cat, though, at the same time, mild, forgiving and no longer bearing enmity—in short, I had a woman's disposition. During the last sickness I had many visual and auditory hallucinations—spoke with the dead, etc.; saw and heard familiar spirits; felt like a double person; but, while lying ill, I did not notice that the man in me had been extinguished. The change in my disposition was a piece of good fortune, for I had a stroke of paralysis which would certainly have killed me had I been of my former disposition; but now I was reconciled, for I no longer recognized myself. Owing to the fact that I still often confounded neurasthenic symptoms with the gout, I took many baths, until an itching of the skin, with the feeling of scabies, instead of being diminished, was so increased that I gave up all external treatment (I was made more and more anemic by the baths), and hardened myself as best I could. But the imperative female feeling remained, and became so strong that I wear only the mask of a man, and in everything else feel like a woman; and gradually I have lost memory of the former individuality. What was left of me by the gout, influenza ruined entirely.

Present condition: I am tall, slightly bald, and the beard is growing gray. I begin to stoop. Since having influenza I have lost about one-fourth of my strength. Owing to a valvular lesion, my face looks somewhat red; full beard; chronic conjunctivitis; more muscular than fat. The left foot seems to be developing varicose veins, and it often goes to sleep; but it is not really thickened, though it seems to be.

The mammary region, though small, swells out perceptibly. The abdomen is feminine in form; the feet are placed like a woman's, and the calves, etc., are feminine; and it is the same with arms and hands. I can wear ladies' hose and gloves 7½ to 7¾ in size. I also wear a corset without annoyance. My weight varies between 168 and 184 pounds. Urine without albumen or sugar, but it contains an excess of uric acid. But when there is not too much uric acid in it, it is clear, and almost as clear as water after any excitement. Bowels usually regular, but should they not be, then come all the symptoms of female constipation. Sleep is poor—for weeks at a time only of two or three hours' duration. Appetite quite good; but, on the whole, my stomach will not bear more than that of a strong woman, and reacts to irritating food with cutaneous eruption and burning in the urethra. The skin is white, and, for the most part, feels quite smooth; there has been unbearable cutaneous itching for the last two years; but during the last few weeks this has diminished, and is now present only in the popliteal spaces and on the scrotum.

Tendency to perspire. Perspiration was previous as good as wanting, but now there are all the odious peculiarities of the female perspiration, particularly about the lower part of the body; so that I have to keep myself cleaner than a woman (I perfume my handkerchief, and use perfumed soap and eau de cologne).

General feeling: I feel like a woman in a man's form; and even though I often am sensible of the man's form, yet it is always in a feminine sense. Thus, for example, I feel the penis as clitoris; the urethra as urethra and vaginal orifice, which always feels a little wet, even when it is actually dry; the scrotum as labia majora; in short, I always feel the vulva. And all that that means one alone can know who feels or has felt so. But the skin all over my body feels feminine; it receives all impressions, whether of touch, of warmth, or whether unfriendly, as feminine, and I have the sensations of a woman. I cannot go with bare hands, as both heat and cold trouble me.

When the time is past when we men are permitted to carry sun umbrellas, I have to endure great sensitiveness of the skin of my face, until sun umbrellas can again be used. On awakening in the morning, I am confused for a few moments, as if I were seeking for myself; then the imperative feeling of being a woman awakens. I feel the sense of the vulva (that one is there), and always greet the day with a soft or loud sigh; for I have fear again of the play that must be carried on throughout the day. I had to learn everything anew; the knife—apparatus, everything—has felt different for the last three years; and with the change of muscular sense I had to learn everything over again. I have been successful, and only the use of the saw and bone chisel are difficult; it is almost as if my strength were not quite sufficient. On the other hand, I have a keener sense of touch in working with the curette in the soft parts. It is unpleasant that, in examining ladies, I often feel their sensations; but this, indeed, does not repel them. The most unpleasant thing I experience is fetal movement. For a long time—several months—I was troubled by reading the thoughts of both sexes, and I still have to fight against it. I can endure it better with women; with men it is repugnant. Three years ago I had not yet consciously seen the world with a woman's eyes; this change in the relation of the eyes to the brain came almost suddenly, with violent headache. I was with a lady whose sexual feeling was reversed, when suddenly I saw her changed in the sense I now feel myself—*viz.*, she as man—and I felt myself a woman in contrast, with her; so that I left her with ill-concealed vexation. At that time she had not yet come to understand her own condition perfectly.

Since then, all my sensory impressions are as if they were feminine in form and relation. The cerebral system almost immediately adjusted itself to the vegetative, so that all my ailments were manifested in a feminine way. The sensitiveness of all nerves, particularly that of the auditory and olfactory and trigeminal, increased to a condition of nervousness. If only a window slammed, I was frightened inwardly; for a man dare not tremble at such things. If food is not absolutely fresh, I perceive a cadaverous odor. I could never depend on the trigeminus; for the pain would jump whimsically from one branch of it to another; from a tooth to an eye. But, since my transformation, I bear toothache and migraine more easily, and have less feeling of fear with stenocardia. It seems to me a strange fact that I feel myself to be a fearful, weak being, and yet, when danger threatens, I am rather cool and collected, and this is true in dangerous operations. The stomach rebels against the slightest indiscretion (in female diet) that is committed without thought of the female nature, either by ructus or other symptoms; but particularly against abuse of alcoholics. The indisposition after intoxication that a man who feels like a woman experiences is much worse than any a student could get up. It seems to me almost as if one's feeling like a woman were entirely controlled by the vegetative system.

Small as my nipples are, they demand room, and I feel as though the pelvis were female; and it is the same puberty the nipples swelled and pained. On this account, the white shirt, the waistcoat and the coat trouble me. I feel as though the pelvis were female; and it is the same with the anus and nates. At first the sense of a female abdomen was troublesome to me; for it cannot bear trousers, and it always possesses or induces the feminine feeling. I also have the imperative feeling of a waist. It is as if I were robbed of my own skin, and put in a woman's skin that fitted me perfectly, but which felt everything as if it covered a woman; and whose sensations passed through the man's body, and exterminated the masculine element. The testes, even though not atrophied or degenerated, are still no longer testes, and often cause me pain, with the feeling that they belong in the abdomen, and should be fastened there; and their mobility often bothers me.

Every four weeks, at the time of the full moon, I have the *molimen* of a woman for five days, physically and mentally, only I do not bleed; but I have the feeling of a loss of fluid; a feeling that the genitals and abdomen are (internally) swollen. A very pleasant period comes when, afterward and later in the interval of a day or two, the physiological desire for procreation comes, which with all power permeates the woman. My whole body is then filled with this sensation, as an immersed piece of sugar is filled with water, or as full as a soaked sponge. It is like this: first, a woman longing for love, and then, for a man; and, in fact, the desire, as it seems to me, is more a longing to be possessed than a wish for coitus. The intense natural instinct or the feminine concupiscence overcomes the feeling of modesty, so that indirectly coitus is desired. I have never felt coitus in a masculine way more than three times in my life; and even if it were so in general, I was always indifferent about it. But, during the last three years, I have experienced it passively, like a woman; in fact, oftentimes with the feeling of feminine ejaculation; and I always feel that I am impregnated. I am always fatigued as a woman is after it, and often feel ill, as a man never does. Sometimes it caused me such great pleasure that there is nothing with which I can compare it; it is the most blissful and powerful feeling in the world; at that moment the woman is simply a vulva that has devoured the whole person.

During the last three years I have never lost for an instant the feeling of being a woman, and now, owing to habit, this is no longer annoying to me, though during this period I have felt debased; for a man could endure to feel like a woman without a desire for enjoyment; but when desires come, the happiness ceases! Then come the burning, the heat, the feeling of turgor of the genitals (when the penis is not in a state of erection the genitals do not play any part). In case of intense desire, the feeling of sucking in the vagina and vulva is really terrible—a hellish pain of lust hardly to be endured. If I then have opportunity to perform coitus, it is better; but, owing to the defective sense of being possessed by the other, it does not afford complete satisfaction; the feeling of sterility comes with its weight of shame, added to the feeling of passive copulation and injured modesty. I seem almost like a prostitute. Reason does not give any help; the imperative feeling of femininity dominates and rules everything. The difficulty in carrying on one's occupation, under such circumstances, is easily appreciated; but it is possible to force oneself to it. Of course, it is almost impossible to sit, walk or lie down; at least, any one of these cannot be endured long; and with the constant touch of the trousers, etc., it is unendurable.

Marriage then, except during coitus, where the man has to feel himself a woman, is like two women living together, one of whom regards herself as in the mask of a man. If the periodical *molimina* fail to occur, then come the feelings of pregnancy or of sexual satiety, which a man never experiences, but which take possession of the whole being, just as the feeling of femininity does, and are repugnant in themselves; and, therefore, I gladly welcome the regular *molimina* again. When erotic dreams or ideas occur, I see myself in the form I have as a woman, and see erected organs presenting. Since the anus feels feminine, it would not be hard to become a passive pederast; only positive religious command prevents it, as all other deterrent ideas would be overcome. Since such conditions are repugnant, as they would be to anyone, I have a desire to be sexless, or to make myself sexless. If I had been single, I should long ago have taken leave of testes, scrotum and penis.

Of what use is female pleasure, when one does not conceive? What good comes from excitation of female love, when one has only a wife for gratification, even though copulation is felt as though it were with a man? What a terrible feeling of shame is caused by the feminine perspiration! How the feeling for dress and ornament lowers a man! Even in his changed form, even when he can no longer recall the masculine sexual feeling, he would not wish to be forced to feel like a woman. He still knows very well that, heretofore, he did not constantly feel sexually; that he was merely a human being uninfluenced by sex. Now, suddenly, he has to regard his former individuality as a mask, and constantly feel like a woman, only having a change when, every four weeks, he has his periodical sickness, and in the intervals his insatiable female desire. If he could but awake without immediately being forced to feel like a woman! At last he longs for a moment in which he might raise his mask; but that moment does not come. He can only find amelioration of his misery when he can put on some bit of female attire or finery, an undergarment, etc.; for he dare not go about as a woman. To be compelled to fulfill all the duties of a calling with the feeling of being a woman costumed as a man, and to see no end of it, is no trifle. Religion alone saves from a great lapse; but it does not prevent the pain when temptation affects the man who feels as a woman; and so it must be felt and endured! When a respectable man who enjoys an unusual degree of public confidence, and possesses authority, must go about with his vulva—imaginary though it be; when one, leaving his arduous daily task, is compelled to examine the toilette of the first lady he meets, and criticize her with feminine eyes, and to read her thoughts in her face; when a journal of fashions possesses an interest equal to that of a scientific work (I felt this as a child); when one must conceal his condition from his wife, whose thoughts, the moment he feels like a woman, he can read in her face, while it becomes perfectly clear to her that he has changed in body and soul—what must all this be? The misery caused by the feminine gentleness that must be overcome? Oftentimes, of course, when I am away alone, it is possible to live for a time more like a woman; for example, to wear female attire, especially at night, to keep gloves on, or to wear a veil or a mask in my room, so that thus there is rest from excessive libido. But when the feminine feeling has once gained an entrance, it imperatively demands recognition. It is often satisfied with a moderate concession, such as the wearing of a bracelet above the cuff; but it imperatively demands some concession. My only happiness is to see myself dressed as a woman without a feeling of shame; indeed, when my face is veiled or masked, I prefer it so, and thus think of myself. Like every one of Fashion's fools, I have a taste for the prevailing mode, so greatly am I transformed. To become accustomed to the thought of feeling only like a woman, and only to remember the previous manner of thought to a certain extent in contrast with it, and, at the same time, to express oneself as a man, requires a long time and an infinite amount of persistence.

Nevertheless, in spite of everything, it will happen that I betray myself by some expression of feminine feeling, either in *sexualibus*, when I say that I feel so and so, expressing what a man without the female feeling cannot know; or when I accidentally betray that female attire is my talent. Before women, of course, this does not amount to anything; for a woman is greatly flattered when a man understands something of her matters; but this must not be displayed to my own wife. How frightened I once was when my wife said to a friend that I had great taste in ladies' dress! How a haughty, stylish lady was astonished when, as she was about to make a great error in the education of her little daughter, I described to her in writing and verbally all the feminine feelings! To be sure, I lied to her, saying that my knowledge had been gleaned from letters. But her confidence in me is as great as ever; and the child, who was on the road to insanity, is rational and happy. She had confessed all the feminine inclinations as sins; now she knows what, as a girl, she must bear and control by will and religion; and she feels that she is human. Both ladies would laugh heartily if they knew that I had only drawn on my own sad experience. I must also add that I now have a finer sense of temperature, and, besides, a sense of the elasticity of the skin and tension of the intestines, etc., in patients, that was unknown to me before; that in operations and autopsies, poisonous fluids more readily penetrate my (uninjured) skin. Every autopsy causes me pain; examination of a prostitute, or a woman having a discharge, a cancerous odor, or the like, is actually repugnant to me. In all respects I am now under the influence of antipathy and sympathy, from the sense of color to my judgment of a person. Women usually see in each other the periodical sexual disposition; and, therefore, a lady wears a veil, if she is not always accustomed to wear one, and usually she perfumes herself, even though it be only with handkerchief or gloves; for her olfactory sense in relation to her own sex is intense. Odors have an incredible effect on the female organism; thus, for example, the odors of violets and roses quiet me, while others disgust me; and with ylang-ylang I cannot contain myself for sexual excitement. Contact with a woman seems homogeneous to me; coitus with my wife seems possible to me because she is somewhat masculine, and has a firm skin; and yet it is more an *amor lesbicus.*

Besides, I always feel passive. Often at night, when I cannot sleep for excitement, it is finally accomplished, *si femora mea distensa habeo, sicti mulier cum viro concumbens,* or if I lie on my side; but an arm or the bedclothing must not touch the mammae, or there is no sleep; and there must be no pressure on the abdomen. I sleep best in a chemise and night robe, and with gloves on; for my hands easily get cold. I am also comfortable in female drawers and petticoats, because they do not touch the genitals. I liked female dresses best when crinolines were worn. Female dresses do not annoy the feminine-feeling man; for he, like every woman, feels them as belonging to his person, and not as something foreign.

My dearest associate is a lady suffering with neurasthenia, who, since her last confinement, feels like a man, but who, since I explained these feelings to her, *coitu abstinet* as much as possible, a thing I, as a husband, dare not do. She, by her example, helps me to endure my condition. She has a most perfect memory of the female feelings, and has often given me good advice. Were she a man and I a young girl I should seek to win her; for her I should be glad to endure the fate of a woman. But her present appearance is quite different from what it formerly was. She is a very elegantly dressed gentleman, notwithstanding bosom and hair; she also speaks quickly and concisely, and no longer takes pleasure in the things that please me. She has a kind of melancholy dissatisfaction with the world, but she bears her fate worthily and with resignation, finding her comfort only in religion and the fulfillment of her duty. At the time of the menses, she almost dies. She no longer likes female society and conversation, and has no liking for delicacies.

A youthful friend felt like a girl from the very first, and had inclinations towards the male sex. His sister had the opposite condition; and when the uterus demanded its right, and she saw herself as a loving woman in spite of her masculinity, she cut the matter short, and committed suicide by drowning.

Since complete effemination, the principal changes I have observed in myself are:

1. The constant feeling of being a woman from top to toe.
2. The constant feeling of having female genitals.
3. The periodicity of the monthly *molimina*.
4. The regular occurrence of female desire, though not directed to any particular man.
5. The passive female feeling in coitus.
6. After that, the feeling of impregnation.
7. The female feeling in thought of coitus.
8. At the sight of women, the feeling of being of their kind, and the feminine interest in them.

9. At the sight of men, the feminine interest in them.
10. At the sight of children, the same feeling.
11. The changed disposition and much greater patience.
12. The final resignation to my fate, for which I have nothing to thank but positive religion; without it I should have long ago committed suicide.

To be a man and to be compelled to feel that *chaque femme est futuée ou elle désire d'etre* is hard to endure.

MAN INTO WOMAN

Lili Elbe

EDITED BY NIELS HOYER

1933

Lili Elbe was born Einar Wegener in Denmark, where she became a well-known painter in the 1920s. Shortly after her first surgery (1930), her marriage to a more prominent painter, Gerda Wegener, was invalidated by the king of Denmark. A second surgery, the implantation of ovaries, led to her death.

Man into Woman *contains changed names ("Andreas Sparre" = Einar Wegener; "Grete Sparre" = Gerda Wegener) and was assembled posthumously from Lili's diaries and letters, but is presented to the reader as a true account.*

Also, the excerpt included here from Chapter 13 of Man into Woman *is written by Grete Sparre/Gerda Wegener.*

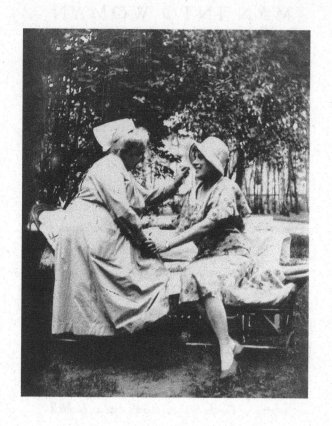

from Chapter 3

Dear Christian,

You have not heard from me for a long time, because I have
been able to tell you nothing good about Lili. From time to
time I have been examined by several doctors, but without
result. Throughout they prescribed sedative remedies, which
left me no better nor wiser than I was before. For I want to
know what is happening to me, even if it hurts. After consult-
ing with Grete,* Elena took me to one of her personal
acquaintances, who received me three hours before he was
leaving Paris. Then something happened which sounds almost
like a miracle! I had a consultation with the famous surgeon
and woman's doctor Professor Werner Kreutz, of Dresden.
Strangely enough, he resembled you. He examined me a long
time, and then declared that my case was so rare that only one
similar case had been known up till now. He added that in the
condition in which I am at present, I could hardly be regarded
as a living creature, because the ray treatment had been a great
mistake, especially as it had not been preceded by microscopical examination. Now he fears that this treatment in the dark
may have destroyed my organs—male as well as female. Con-
sequently, he wants me to go to Berlin as quickly as possible
for the purpose of a microscopical examination.

Some time afterwards he will operate on me himself. He
wants to remove the dead (and formerly imperfect) male

*His wife.

organs, and to restore the female organs with new and fresh material. *Then it will be Lili who will survive!*

Her weak girl's body will then be able to develop, and she will feel as young as her new and fresh organs. Dear Christian, I am now sitting here and weeping like a child while I am writing you these lines. It seems so like a miracle that I dare not believe it. One thing, however, consoles me—that were it otherwise I must soon die. Grete and I believe we are dreaming, and are fearful of waking. It is too wonderful to think that Lili will be able to live, and that she will be the happiest girl in the world—and that this ghastly nightmare of my life is drawing to an end. This wretched comedy as a man! Without Grete I should have thrown up the sponge long ago. But in these dark days I have had a fresh opportunity of seeing what a splendid girl she is . . . she is an angel. Overexertions, her own sufferings, have left her unscathed. She has contrived to work for two, now that I am no longer worth much. I do what I am able, of course, and have exhibited and sold with success in all the important salons. But now all this is over. I am no longer fit for anything. I am like a wretched grub which is waiting to become a butterfly. The operation is urgent, and the doctor would like me to proceed to Berlin immediately, as some twenty days must elapse between the first examination and the operation. And I must be in Dresden on the day he is ready to create Lili. He will send me medicine, which I am to take, in order to support the internal organs and thereby keep me alive until then. For practical reasons I begged for some delay, and I told him that I should prefer so to arrange matters as to proceed to Berlin via Copenhagen, as I wanted first to hold an exhibition in Denmark. I would then proceed from Berlin to Dresden at the beginning of April.

This does not particularly please the doctor; but he understood that I had suggested this for practical reasons.

Now, I do not know whether it is due to excitement, but my condition has worsened to such an extent that I no longer feel able to make preparations for an exhibition and attend to everything it involves—I realize that I have no time to lose.

Hence, I want your help.

Will you lend me the money for the operation and the stay in the nursing home? I do not know how much it will cost. I only know that Elena has so arranged it that the professor is taking an exceptionally low fee. Out of consideration for Grete I dare not take money from our savings; the less so as our trip to Rome and my illness has cost us so much.

I—or we—have deposited many pictures with Messrs. Heyman and Haslund, of Copenhagen, and I estimate their value to be between seven and ten thousand kronen. I do not, however, know what the operation will cost, but I estimate it will come to between four and five thousand kronen in all. I give you all these pictures in Denmark by way of security in the event of my death—and in any event. If the affair turns out badly, the pictures can be sold, and if it turns out well, we can soon repay you the money. Our earning powers are good, and we have many large orders.

Tell no one except my sister anything of the contents of this letter, and be good enough to let me know what you decide as quickly as possible, first by telegram and then by letter.

It is only because I have the feeling that death is on my track that I send you this letter. Up till now I have never incurred debts in any quarter. Warmest greetings to you and the sister from Grete and

Andreas.

from Chapter 8

SO LILI and I continued to live our double life, and no one, neither the "initiated" nor myself, saw in this anything else than a pleasant kind of distraction and entertainment, a kind of artists' caprice, neither more nor less. We were as little perturbed at the obviously growing distinction, of an emotional kind, which increasingly manifested itself between the mystical girl and myself; nor did anyone take any serious notice of the delicate changes which gradually became perceptible in my physical form.

But something had been silently preparing in *me*.

One evening I said suddenly to Grete:

"Really I cannot imagine what existence would be like if Lili should one day vanish forever, or if she should no longer look young and beautiful. Then she would no longer have any justification for living at all."

Grete at first looked at me, astonished. Then she nodded and said in her calm, thoughtful way: "It is strange that you have mentioned something which has been on my mind a good deal lately. In recent months I have felt prickings of conscience because I was, to a certain extent, the cause of creating Lili, of enticing her out of you, and thus becoming responsible for a disharmony in you which reveals itself most distinctly on those days when Lili does not appear."

I was thunderstruck at Grete's words. It was as if she had held up a mirror in front of me.

"It often happens," she continued excitedly, "that when she poses for me as a model a strange feeling comes over me that it is *she* whom I am creating and forming rather than the girl whom I am representing on my canvas. Sometimes it seems to me that here is something which is stronger than we are, something which makes us powerless and will thrust us aside, as if, indeed, it wanted to be revenged on us for having played with it."

Grete broke off. Tears stood in her eyes. "We have come to a steep part of the road, and I don't know where we shall find foothold," she cried. I tried to calm her; but I scarcely succeeded, at least, not at once. I spoke and she listened to me. "What you say is all so terribly true. And the most dangerous thing of all is that I feel it is Lili, just Lili, who forms the bond between us which has lasted all these years. I do not believe I could survive her."

Grete interrupted me to say that she had very often thought exactly the same, as Lili embodied our common youth and joy in life. She sobbed: "Sometimes I wonder what life would be without her."

We stared at each other, deeply moved by this mutual confession, which had been provoked by many, many weeks of secret brooding.

"At any rate, I cannot imagine," Grete went on, "what it would be like for us without Lili. We must not lose her. If she should suddenly vanish, it would seem like a murder."

"The more so as I cannot help feeling that she is on the verge of becoming more vigorous than I am," I said uneasily.

from Chapter 13

I WAS still sitting with closed eyes when suddenly the door of the operating theater was flung open and Werner Kreutz was standing in front of me . . . still in the india-rubber apron. His gait was tired. He held out both his hands and gave me a broad, benevolent smile. I only heard his words: "Everything has passed off well." I clasped both his hands. And I could only stammer: "I thank you."

Not until a few hours later did I learn what had happened inside. To find words in which to put it is unspeakably difficult. A whole human life which I shared with another floats before me as I write these words. A human being who was born a man, who was my husband, my friend, my comrade—

has now become a woman, a complete woman. And this human being was never intended to be anything but a woman. Like a sacrificial animal he has been dragged along with me for years until this German doctor brought him help! And today this human being has lain here bleeding under the knife of his helper. His body was opened, and disclosed a state of things which the craziest imagination would hardly have considered possible. The body of this human being contained stunted and withered ovaries which were not able to develop because an inscrutable Fate had also given him the others, the male germ glands. This secret of existing as a double being, hitherto divined by no doctor, has only been unveiled today, after Werner Kreutz had guessed at its existence in Paris, and like a wizard deciphered it.

"I can find no other words with which to express my meaning. And now this poor creature, so heavily handicapped by Fate, has had removed from its body what had formed such an obstacle, thus enabling it now to develop as its blood had dictated for years, namely, as a woman, and it has been equipped with unimpaired female germ glands from another, a strange and quite young creature. Then this tortured body was sewn up again, and now nothing more is left, not a particle is left of my life's comrade and fellow wayfarer—Andreas. He is the dead brother of Lili, who now lives, of the woman who has shared flesh and blood with him for almost a lifetime.

But the thought which haunts me is that though Andreas may now be extinguished, and though Lili may have risen like a phoenix from the ashes, yet in the world outside Andreas is still living in the eyes of the law, and I am his wife. Who is capable of grasping this horror, this fantastic idea, this unique happening? She whom it concerns most nearly, Lili, is still lying lulled in the mists of merciful morphia.

What will life now bring her? Will the miracle of the doctor, the miracle of his art, be great and strong enough to be perpetuated in Lili's life? All of us have been instruments of this fate. I not least. For it was I who many years ago enticed Lili out of Andreas, in wanton play, as a chance masquerade! And it was I who continued playing this game with Andreas, until what had been play became earnest, most mysteriously earnest. But I must not think of this now; I cannot help thinking of the one person who never really believed in Andreas, but only in Lili, Lili's most intimate friend, Claude Lejeune. What will he think when he sees her again?

from Chapter 20

I FEEL like a bridge builder. But it is a strange bridge that I am building. I stand on one of the banks, which is the present day. There I have driven in the first pile. And I must build it clear across to the other bank, which often I cannot see at all and sometimes only vaguely, and now and then in a dream. And then I often do not know whether the other bank is the past or the future. Frequently the question plagues me: Have I had only a past, or have I had no past at all? Or have I only a future without a past?

I have found a new friend who wants to help me to collect and collate the loose leaves of my confession. Many years ago he knew Andreas slightly. He can hardly recall him now. He can remember his eyes, and in my eyes he has found this recollection. He is a German, and I am glad of the chance of talking German with him here.

He told me that when I went to see him for the first time, before I entered the room, he felt somewhat afraid of me, as if he might perhaps feel a repugnance towards me, especially as shortly before he had again glanced at some photographs of Andreas. When I was in his presence, so he told me, every doubt was dissipated, every doubt of my proper existence. He only saw the woman in me, and when he thought of Andreas, or spoke to me about Andreas, he saw and felt a person beside me or behind me.

He gave me a new German translation of the Bible. The first volume. *The Book of the Beginning* was the title, and I read in it many times the words:

> And the earth was without form, and void; and darkness was upon the face of the deep. And the Spirit of God moved upon the face of the waters.

Is it presumptuous of me, whenever I think of my beginning, always to hear these words, the music of this verse, sounding in my ears?

———

I OFTEN give the loose leaves of my diary to my German friend to read. I ask him to tell me whenever I am obscure, and then a word from him encourages me to proceed. He understands my strange feeling about building this bridge in the dark.

Grete has returned from Italy. She is radiantly happy, and I rejoice in her happiness.

She is now living with me, as we need no longer be afraid of going out together. I am not nervous anymore. No one takes any notice of me in the streets.

We talked through many long nights. We talked nearly always of the life that was now coming for her and for me. She was also able to help me out of the difficulties which I encountered so often when writing down my confessions. She always knew the answer.

She talked a lot about Feruzzi. They wanted to marry without delay, and Grete said that her home would then always be my home. Feruzzi knew everything and said that he would always be my friend and protector. And Grete declared that we were so closely bound together that she could not imagine herself away from me for long.

She kept speaking to me in this strain. Then she would say laughingly that I was not only her sister, but also her big grown-up daughter. I had to promise her that I would go to her and Feruzzi soon after their marriage. Feruzzi, too, would welcome me like a grown-up daughter. How happy these words made me!

THE
TRANSSEXUAL
PHENOMENON

Harry Benjamin, M.D.

1966

Harry Benjamin, the preeminent figure in the transsexual medical field during the 1960s, popularized the term transsexual *with the publication of* The Transsexual Phenomenon *(1966). The following excerpt from Benjamin's book is the autobiography of "Joe," a female-to-male transsexual who was a patient of Benjamin's.*

LEGALLY AND otherwise, to the extent that is possible, I am now a man. For seven years I have been married to Helen, with whom I lived for three years before the legal wedlock became possible. As I write this now, in 1965, I think I have been long enough "transformed" to say with confidence that there will be no regrets, no wish ever to return to the unhappy life I now have left behind.

I cannot believe that my wish to be a man resulted from anything done by my parents during either my infancy or early childhood. The craving to wear the clothing of boys, to play with boys' playthings, to be a tomboy, and so on was all my own doing.

Never did my parents indicate they wanted a boy instead of a girl. There was nothing unusual in my home environment, and my life at home and at school was average, like that of others in a similar social condition. I was sent to private schools for girls, had psychiatric help, and, as a woman, I married twice. But nothing could shake my personal conviction that I wasn't born to be a woman, and nothing could ever change my longing and desire to be a male. No known treatment could efface my desire or change my mind, from my first consciousness of that desire as a very young child on up to the present!

More than eight years ago, as a result of hormone injections given by an understanding physician, my voice dropped to a deeper, husky male pitch. This started a few days after administration of the hormone solution. I never menstruated again after the first few injections. Before that, I had had a history of very irregular menses. Later, I underwent surgery to reduce the size of my breasts so that they resembled those of a male. My breasts had always been very small. Still later, I had the complete hysterectomy I felt to be necessary. In spite of the anatomical limitations, my sex life now is a satisfying one.

Before the hormone injections I had no body hair other than that considered normal for a woman. Nor did I have facial hair. However, this rapidly changed, and my heavy growth of body hair conveniently covers and hides the small scars from the breast surgery. Facial hair developed and grew to the point where I am obliged to shave daily. As a result of the hormone injections there was also a change in the distribution of fatty tissues in buttocks, thighs, and other body areas where women normally are padded. In other words, my body took on contours like those of the male physique.

While taking the hormones and effecting this transformation I continued to reside in a rather small, semirural community in Texas. After Helen joined me there, we continued to live in this same community during the whole of the transforming process. After my birth certificate had been changed, Helen and I married. Everything was accomplished through perfectly legitimate channels, with no publicity, either in our hometown or in the city of my birth.

All the members of both of our families are aware of my before-and-after situation and have shown and voiced an understanding acceptance, while admittedly more than a little amazed at my changeover. We now live elsewhere, but we continue to go back to visit our former community. And we find we are still accepted there by friends, acquaintances, and businesspeople with "no questions asked," no "raised eyebrows," or anything of the sort despite the change I underwent in my appearance and my adoption of complete male attire.

Today, among old friends who are "in the know," Helen and I are as warmly accepted as any normal married couple. We participate in every phase of social life, including sports. I am perfectly at ease in swim trunks with the upper torso exposed, and just as much at ease on the dance floor with my own or another man's wife.

Hard to believe though it may be, there isn't a person I know, among either family members or friends, who hasn't approved of my transformation. Not one has been lost because of it. As for myself, I truly feel that at last I have achieved my rightful station in life, my birthright formerly denied me through some strange quirk of nature and now restored to me by what I regard as the *miracle* of endocrinology.

I no longer have the haunting frustrations which kept me very nervous and on edge and which were inclined to make me impulsive and immature. I have lost a great deal of my former shyness, which apparently was nothing more than a defense mechanism used as a protective veneer at a time when I was completely confused and lost in a world where I seemed unable to find a place. Now that I *have* found my place in life I am eternally grateful to science for having carved out this niche for me; and especially to those physicians and surgeons who "took my hand" and led me out of the abyss in which I had been wandering for a great part of my life.

———

I WAS born in 1920 in a New England city of moderate size and was one of four daughters. My father, a salesman, was away from home a good bit of the time while I was growing up, and Mother mostly raised us. From earliest childhood I demonstrated two major traits that have stayed with me always: a preference for things masculine, and a great love of animals.

As a very small child I refused to play with dolls and demanded as toys, instead, stuffed animals and, later, electric trains. (When it came time for me to have a bicycle, I held out for, and finally got, a boy's bike instead of a girl's.) I especially liked dogs and cats but was never permitted to have a pet since Father disliked animals. From age three up to around eleven, I would play at being a dog—crawling on all fours, growling, demanding to be "fed," and so on.

When I was five or six I used to play baseball and other boys' games with a playmate, George, who was about my own age. One day, as a matter of curiosity, we went "off to the bushes" to compare our sex organs. This curiosity had been with me for some time, since I knew I was a girl but wondered why I wasn't a boy and what physically made the difference between girls and boys. Learning about that difference, I got the impression that I, perhaps, had just "grown short," and trying to produce for myself a penis like George's I would tie little strings to my vaginal labia and try to stretch them down with the hope that they would finally grow into a penis. I would often cry, looking for the answer to why I wasn't a boy, since I was aware I had all the traits of a boy but not the right physical attributes. Something seemed all wrong somewhere, but as a child I could find no answer to the puzzle.

At age five I started kindergarten and, while I tried to dress like a boy when at home, had to wear girls' clothing when at school. I chose my playmates usually from among children who were not my schoolmates; and they, seeing me dressed like a boy, would ask me whether I was a boy or a girl. Then I would answer: "Boy," and they often accepted me as such. In "playing house," I took the role of the husband; and, playing "doctor and nurse," I was always the doctor. When my father was away I would dress in his clothing, parading around the house in his wardrobe, even to the shoes.

At about age seven, my mother bought me boys' rather than girls' clothing. During weekdays I generally wore overalls and shirts, but on Sundays I was permitted to wear a white shirt and tie and duck pants in and out of the house and around town. I even dressed as a boy when attending birthday parties given by childhood friends. Dressing in boys' attire was always sanctioned by my mother and grandfather. Father, on the rare occasions when he was home, accepted my dressing as a boy, most likely because it was agreed to by the others. I had to dress as a girl only on school days and hated school for that reason.

Father being away so much, he took no great interest in my sisters or myself and, for the most part, left our upbringing to my mother. Yet we were always a closely knit family and lived in a tranquil, convivial atmosphere. My mother and grandfather were staunch supporters of our (Protestant) church, and we children went to Sunday school regularly. Holidays always found the family together and were festive occasions.

All sports pleased me and I learned to swim and ice-skate at an early age. Twice, my uncle helped me acquire pets. The first were guinea pigs, which I hid in his barn, but they were killed by rats. Later there was a dog, but my father made me get rid of him. Much, much later, I had two other dogs, but one ran away and the other was run over. I had no other pets until I was "on my own."

At age nine, my parents enrolled me in a private coeducational school. There I was able to take manual training instead of the cooking and similar classes offered for girls. Because of ear trouble, I usually did poorly in school and brought home bad report cards. Then Father would punish me, call me "dumb," and tell me what a "good-for-nothing" I was. My poor performance and the scoldings from my father continued after I entered a public school. The happiest times were spent with my uncle, fishing, hunting, camping, and roaming through the woods. Being out-of-doors was my chief delight, and dressed in shorts or jeans I also played ball and went fishing. Other diversions I enjoyed were the making of puppets, riding my boy's bike, and raising some mice in the cellar in a cage I had constructed.

At fourteen, because I had done so badly with my studies, I was sent to a private girls' school and also received special tutoring in the summer. I enjoyed riding horseback, but otherwise did about as badly as usual. It was at this school, when I was sixteen, that I developed my first "crush" on a girl. There was some necking and petting but nothing I considered sexual. I had just become aware of my "difference" and attraction to my own sex and feared making any sexual approach that might be rejected.

At the age of seventeen I was enrolled at another girls' boarding school, rooming with two girls. As always I avoided groups and had just a few close friends, mainly because of shyness and feelings of inferiority. With a girl who lived on another floor of my dormitory I established a very close and inseparable friendship. During our friendship this girl, Cathy, and I indulged in much "petting" and "necking" but there were no sexual relations. The following year, Cathy and I were allowed to room together, which surprised me, since I was sure the dean knew of my homosexual inclinations. There was proof of this in the hours the dean spent lecturing me on the subject of Cathy's and my relationship. These lectures only made me withdraw into myself all the more, convinced by now I was a freak. This feeling about myself troubled me greatly, so that I constantly wrestled with myself in an effort to subjugate my desires. I was additionally miserable because the school had a kind of uniform that made it impossible for me to wear boys' clothes.

In my eighteenth year, though we still roomed together, Cathy and I were good friends but my desire for her had largely subsided. Meantime, since it was the custom of the school to assign the old girls to assist a newcomer in making an adjustment to the school's routine, I was charged with looking after Karen. At first I disliked her, then became so smitten with her I was beside myself. She was extremely affectionate, not at all quiet and shy as I was, but active and mischievous, and I followed her blindly in breaking all sorts of regulations. It was with Karen that I first experienced passionate sexual contact, leading to a year that became a nightmare of punishments and threats. It was the first time for both of us, and we did just about everything in the way of sex, discovering all the methods for ourselves without benefit of previous experience or reading.

Karen invited me, during the summer, to spend two weeks of my vacation at her home. While I was there, the nature of our love and sex relationship became obvious to her parents. The result was that Karen did not return to school, where we had planned to be roommates, and once back home I never heard from her again although I wrote to her repeatedly. Then Karen's mother wrote to my mother, saying she'd have me put into an institution if I tried to see, call, or write to Karen. Sheer fright, bewilderment, and the knowledge I could never see Karen again left me emotionally torn to pieces.

During my senior year I roomed alone, avoided everyone, and was desperately trying to come to terms with myself and to figure things out. I graduated with barely passing marks and then, at my mother's insistence, was enrolled in some special classes in music composition, for which I seemed to have some talent. I accepted this with great reluctance and would have much preferred to study the training and care of animals—something my family refused to hear of.

My musical studies lasted for only a few months, and both at home and at school I was miserable. Dad was constantly picking on me, and I started cutting classes in order to go hiking. When home, I stayed in my room as much as I could. Especially I hated mealtimes, when Dad would belittle me at the dinner table. I begged to be sent away to school—anything to get away from home. Instead, when all my truancy came to light, I was scolded until I became mentally and physically sick. Then I was sent to a psychiatrist, which made me feel that Mom, my supposed ally, had turned against me and was trying to pry into my desires and troubles. I suspected the psychiatrist was relaying to her all that I told him, which made me withdraw even more into my shell. Finally things got so bad that I worked out a scheme to marry a boy who had always liked me, and who I knew would make it possible for me to move back where I could be close to my uncle. I had always felt, and feel it now, that my beloved pal Uncle Pete wasn't fooled about me and fully sensed and condoned my desire to be a boy rather than a girl. He was the one, in fact, who started everyone calling me Jo, which I—and, I think, he—knew really ought to be spelled *Joe*.

My plan was successful and Jack, my childhood friend, and I were married with all the usual ceremony. It was at least ten days after the start of our so-called honeymoon before I could muster up courage to let Jack consummate the marriage. Unlike most girls, I had never allowed a boy to become promiscuous with me. I loathed any contact in that way, with boys. I had thought that maybe, if I married and were "free," I could somehow adjust to the role of wife. Fortunately, Jack was a patient, unaggressive boy. If he hadn't been, I'd have fled in self-defense. I found intercourse most distasteful in every way and only performed the marital act twice during our marriage. The second time it happened, I discovered I was pregnant. I then miscarried, in about the third month, but said nothing about that or the pregnancy to Jack. Shortly afterward I left him and a little while later he joined the navy.

During the next few years I had several close friendships with women, for the most part platonic. Then, falling in with a fast crowd, I started to do a good bit of drinking and partying. This had disastrous results, since on one occasion I was evidently drugged and awakened to find myself in bed with a male member of our crowd, a fellow named Johnny. As a consequence of this mishap once again I found myself pregnant. To do the right thing by the expected child, Johnny and I were married. Less than four months later, I miscarried for the second time. And, a few months after that, I secured a divorce from what had been only a marriage of convenience. My experience with the second pregnancy was one of the reasons why I so strongly wanted the complete hysterectomy I finally achieved some years later.

It wasn't until I was almost twenty-six that I met for the first time, so far as I know, other people of my kind. Up to that time, I had never realized that there were hundreds and hundreds of homosexuals, like myself. Even in meeting them, however, I never felt that I was in quite the same category. I felt that somehow my "personality" differed in some important way from theirs. As time went on, I was introduced to more and more of them but did not particularly seek their company or solicit their friendship, since I was too busy planning, building, and working. I had moved, by this time, to the Southwest and started in the business of raising purebred cattle.

In this business, which prospered, I designed my own barns and equipment and was active in various groups of persons with similar interests. I met a young woman named Barbara, and after a while she came to live with me and help me around the place. Our sexual relations were fairly infrequent and consisted only of my using my fingers on her. I never allowed her to reciprocate. There were times, even so, when I'd become aroused to the point that I would experience an orgasm. But Barbara proved to be a heavy drinker and would embarrass me in front of groups of friends. Sometimes, in one of her many drunken stupors, she would beat me unmercifully, but I could never strike her in either retaliation or self-defense. If it hadn't been for some unusual circumstances, I never would have chosen her for a companion in the first place.

Barbara and I stayed together for several years, and then, while traveling cross-country together, I met Helen, a friend of Barbara's, who eventually became my wife. After returning home I began a correspondence with Helen, meanwhile having more and more trouble with Barbara because of her addiction to alcohol. I had given up drinking altogether, hoping this would lead Barbara to do the same, but nothing availed. As a result, I suffered a complete physical collapse and had to be hospitalized with a nervous breakdown. Barbara returned to her home in the East, marking the end of an affair that had raised havoc in my life.

During my recovery period I met the Carters, who gave me much help and moral support. They were homosexuals, and Doris (Mrs. Carter) accompanied me to Hawaii for a much-needed vacation. She and her husband were married solely as a matter of convenience, and it soon became clear that Doris was in love with me—an emotion I could not fully return. She wanted sex with me and was the aggressor. She insisted I "go down" on her. I found all lovemaking with her distasteful and would beg off at every opportunity. However, Doris was a good companion and was kind to me.

On returning to this country I again met Helen and still found her extremely desirable. But she was accompanied at the time by a girlfriend and had, I presumed, "affiliations." Since I would not try to encroach on someone else's relationship, not too much came of the meeting with Helen.

Also there was another girl, Ann, who was in love with me. I was the first woman she had ever been attracted to. One night she asked me to make love to her, and I found that I also wanted this. Our only means of sex was "dyking," from which we derived mutual satisfaction. She came and lived with me for a month, but then she got drunk one night and beat me, when I asked her to leave. I'd had quite enough of that already.

Another brief love affair also ended badly, and I found that my thoughts turned increasingly to Helen, with whom I kept up a correspondence. Finally I visited her, found her to be free and willing to return my affection, and brought her back to live with me. I stayed at her home for a time, met almost all the members of her family, and found them prepared to accept our relationship. No one attempted to alter her decision to begin what we hoped would be a lifelong companionship.

Helen and I find ourselves to be completely compatible in every phase of our lives together. We did not enter into our relationship precipitously but took time, through daily correspondence at great length, to learn as much about each other as we possibly could, while apart. We are now inseparable and experience mutual enjoyment in our constant comradeship. We respect each other's personal desires and pursuits, and neither encroaches upon the individuality of the other. We have no wish to make each other over.

We feel that we are both adult enough to know what we want of each other, not by demand, but rather by mutual consent, and what to expect of life in general. We are both well aware of our responsibilities to our families and to society and we have no wish to defy the conventions of society if we can possibly comply with them without snuffing out our own justifiable existence. Mutually, we have learned that neither of us has any preference for congregating with homosexuals to the exclusion of normal people. On the contrary, while we count a few high-caliber homosexuals among our friends, we prefer the normalcies of life and want to be accepted in circles of normal society, enjoying the same pursuits and pleasures without calling attention to the fact that we are "queers" trying to invade the world of normal people. As our situation is now, the living of a normal life is not always easy and sometimes we are in a position where we are the subjects of eyebrow raising and may overhear the speculations as to who and "what" we are.*

---

*The patient is of course writing previous to her sex conversion and change of legal status to that of male.

In my case, there is the embarrassment of being in public places and not quite knowing what restroom facilities to make use of. In using a men's room, when dressed in male attire, I subject myself to possible apprehension as a "male impersonator." In using a women's room, other women there might possibly regard me as a man invading their privacy. So, in this regard, I have always an insoluble and potentially dangerous problem. Other difficulties too might arise. Were I to be stopped while driving, for instance, I would have to display a license with a woman's name although appearing to be a man. Yet, on the rare occasions when I wear female attire because of absolute necessity, I feel inwardly that I am masquerading as a woman. I never have this feeling of impersonation when I am dressed as a man. Rather, I feel comfortable and as if living in tune with what has been part and parcel of me all my life and has been so accepted by my family and is now accepted by most of my friends and acquaintances.

In our sexual relations Helen and I have run the gamut of homosexual acts, not in the sense of experiencing variety but in the sense of expressing our love as we are able and wish to express it. We are not sexual thrill seekers, nor do we attempt to arouse each other for the sake of sex and sex alone. It is just a part of our entire lives together, and totally an expression of love. It is our mutual desire to be legally married in the future and not have to continue this fraudulent, homosexual pose as husband and wife, but eventually to live in the peace and acceptance of connubial happiness and as normal people.

In probing my life and my mind and the intense desire I have to achieve masculinity, I feel I have never dressed as a man just to flaunt my deviation or for any other reason except that to dress and behave as a man is natural for me, while to try to live any other way gives me always the feeling of being an impostor. I fully realize that should I achieve the possible measure of masculinity there would be many problems to face. However, I have given all this much more than an average great deal of thought—thought concerning not only my own well-being, but also the effect on my family and those close to them. I would have to protect these people from the consequences of my transformation, by banishing myself from their lives, or else by concocting some explanation that others would find acceptable.

As I reflect upon all this I recall how my mother, through my childhood years, was often criticized and questioned for sanctioning my pose as a boy, since she expressly permitted me to wear boys' attire and yet, on occasion, when demanded, contrarily plunged me into feminine attire. I would not assume now that she was merely appeasing my wish to play at being a boy, but that perhaps, without my knowledge (which I gained so late in life), she *knew*, better than I, that I *was a boy*, by nature if not so physically endowed. I have always felt, too, that my uncle accepted me as a nephew rather than a niece, since it was he who nicknamed me "Joe" and who made of me much more a boy companion on our hunting and fishing trips than a niece. I believe that Uncle Pete very clearly saw through my first marriage as an escapist measure rather than a true marriage, and yet condoned it with perhaps a "crossed fingers" attitude as to its eventual success and permanency in the guise of a normal marriage. As I think back to the day of that first marriage, I suppose that even then he *knew* it would fail, and yet, perhaps, *hoped* that somehow it wouldn't. I feel he must have been completely noncommital, in a most unexpected and broad-minded way. Whatever the explanation, Uncle Pete was *always* most understanding.

All through my life, all through the knowing and being with every woman I have known, I have always wanted to be in a socially accepted category. I have always wanted to pursue the normal aspects of life without the stigma of being an invader of normal avenues. Yet naturally my social life as I have felt obliged to pursue it has been warped to some extent by my homosexuality. I like men as companions, or to deal with in business, but loathe them when they pursue me as a woman, whether as suitors or as lovers. I have always felt that the natural thing would be for men to accept me as one of their own kind, and it has seemed unnatural whenever they showed interest in me as a woman.

Looking back over the years I recall how, when I was about ten years old, my uncle surprised me by making the remark, "Joe, don't you think you're too young to be shaving?" He had evidently guessed that I had been using his shaving equipment and he cautioned me about its effect on my complexion as a girl, implying that I was too good-looking to be taking such chances. His wise words, even though I was young at the time, penetrated and, as far as I recall, I refrained from shaving anymore for a long while. Over the last ten years or so, I have resumed the shaving to remove a light fuzz that appears on my face. Here again, realizing that I am forced to play a dual role, I shave at times in order to enhance my masculine appearance and as a protection for myself when appearing in masculine attire; and yet, at the same time, heed my uncle's warning that I might eventually make a monstrosity of myself if I continued to do so regularly.

Although Mother had fortified me with complete sex information when I was about fourteen years old and had explained the mysteries of menstruation to me, from that time on I *prayed* repeatedly that by some miracle or stroke of good fortune I would never menstruate. However, when I did, at the age of eighteen, I cried bitterly to the point of making myself sick over the emotional upset it caused in me. In spite of Mother's warnings about not going swimming or engaging in sports while I was menstruating, I did all these things, and did them especially so that people would not suspect I had the curse. It was, in my estimation, a denial of the fact that I had it.

As far as the knowledge Mother gave me about sexual intercourse was concerned, it repulsed me even to think of myself as ever being on the receiving end of intercourse, as a woman. On the contrary, since the age of five, and up through the present, I have always had a strong desire to have a penis and have envied all men because they have one and I do not. I have always envied a man's physique and wished so strongly that I had the same wide shoulders and narrow hips instead of my own womanish broad hips and bucket bottom!

As far as the thought had occurred of my ever being in the position of having to bear children as a woman, I absolutely abhorred the idea and considered myself to have been singularly blessed when I had the miscarriages during my two unfortunate marriages. It seemed to me a stroke of Fate, particularly since I had done nothing to induce them! When I knew I was pregnant I had seriously thought about killing myself rather than face a future of being a mother rather than a father. I gave no thought to having abortions, as the easy way out, since I knew with my conscience that I was to blame for getting myself into the stupid situations of becoming pregnant and that I had no right to destroy the lives of unborn babies.

These foregoing mixed emotions over the things I have mentioned have existed throughout my entire life, causing me to search and experience great conflict within myself in an effort to reason them out and reconcile myself to the fact that I should not let my problems dominate my life to the point where I would be frustrated and unable to accomplish anything worthwhile. As I have grown older I have been able somewhat better to deal with my inner turmoil and not to become so upset as I did when a child. Yet, fundamentally, I know that the mixed emotions still exist and will always exist until they are untangled by some means or other. The writing I do now seems to me to be, in a sense, the bringing up and revealing of secret things that at times I have almost tried to deny to myself. I did this in the hope that by the denial I could become a happier person. I never really felt that anyone could understand such mixed emotions, not even a doctor, and therefore never revealed them, partly because of a fear that they would be thought of as some peculiar obsession that might even place me in the classification of a mentally unbalanced person.

Now that I *have* found an understanding doctor, I am able to speak. And again Fate seems to have intervened on my behalf in leading me to such a doctor through my acquaintanceship with June (a male transsexual), who gave me my first hint that the sex change possible for males might also have its counterpart for the female.

In my thoughts concerning a transformation, I would naturally desire that every measure be taken (even including surgery, if necessary) to give me all the physical attributes of a man to the inclusion of the sex organ, growth of beard, deeper voice, and all. However, if it must be that I will have to settle for less then I still would desire as many of the attributes as could be given me, even if this does not include the sex organ of a male. In my so-called daydreaming, I have often visualized the satisfaction I would derive from possessing a penis and in being able to perform normal intercourse with a woman rather than engage in homosexual acts. Even such daydreams have made me a bit happier.

Despite this, I have never in my homosexual relationships resorted to the use of a dildo or artificial organ as a means of substituting for the penis that I do not possess. To me, that seems a pretty poor substitute and would involve too much kidding oneself. On the other hand, I have always been grateful for the fact that the women I have been associated with have accepted me as I am, and have been satisfied with homosexual relations with me in the only manner in which I am able to perform sex acts because of my limitations.

In the matter of considering having a hysterectomy, I have always envied women who have had cause to have them for medical reasons; and, in a certain sense, I have wished that I could have one for some minor reason. But again here I argued it out with myself, fully knowing I had no reason that I could fully convey to someone else, and here again the question arose, "What doctor is going to perform this operation when he can see no apparent reason for doing it?" Then, too, it seemed to me an incomplete solution to my problem, since a hysterectomy would not in itself help me to achieve complete masculinity but would only serve to eliminate my menstrual cycle and prevent any chance of pregnancy. I understand that a hysterectomy of convenience would seem to some a mutilation of my body serving no sensible purpose. Yet I feel that this is something I require, and want it, especially if it will contribute toward my achieving masculinization.

Finally, I would like to stress again how deep and strong has always been my desire to be a normal person and to be accepted as such by others. This goes back as far as I can remember. The irresistible desire I have had to dress and represent myself as a man has forced me, sometimes, to go to gay bars and similar places. Yet these do not appeal to me otherwise, and I think of them as being gathering places for low-caliber homosexuals who are frustrated and confused and have only the capacity or tendency to seek the company of other unfortunates or dissolute persons like themselves. I do not personally approve of the looseness of living that the general run of homosexuals engage in as they seek the superficial and meaningless pleasures of life, or try to lose themselves in nightly rounds of excessive drinking or promiscuous sex orgies with countless others that they encounter in their wanderings. It is not because my sympathies are not with them, but rather because I feel there are only a rare few who work toward achieving successful careers and who earn the respect of other people in their communities. It is my feeling that, homosexual or not, one should strive to make something of oneself and to walk the better roads of life rather than the crooked paths.

Now that I seem to stand at the beginning of the course of treatments that may bring me to my always hoped-for transformation, I have behind me a great deal of thought and other preparation for what is to come. I have read whatever scientific literature I could find in order to have as full an understanding as possible of what is possible in my case. I have considered all the implications of my action not only for myself but for others, especially my family. I am wholly convinced that my decision is the right one and am willing to accept to the last detail the diagnosis and treatment offered me by a doctor whom I trust.

CHRISTINE JORGENSEN: A PERSONAL AUTOBIOGRAPHY

Christine Jorgensen

1967

Christine Jorgensen (1927–1989) was born George Jorgensen in the United States, where she was a professional photographer. Upon returning home from Denmark after her 1952 surgery—one of the first forty surgeries on record—Christine earned unexpected celebrity and notoriety across the United States, maintaining popularity for the rest of her life.

from Chapter 18

ALTHOUGH SOME moments of February 13, 1953, are lost in a fog of faulty memory, there are others indelibly etched in my mind. If the sequence of events is not completely clear, the emotional leftovers remain. I remember that I was frightened and bewildered and I wondered why Irmy and our escort had left me so abruptly to face the ordeal alone.

I started to traverse what seemed to me was my last mile. There was a good deal of shouting and jostling as the crowd pushed against the ropes that marked off "quarantine walk," an area that separated the arriving passengers until their vaccination certificates had been validated. Three or four men crawled through the ropes, including Henry Wall, a friend who had come to greet Irmy. Almost immediately they were called to the United States Health Office at the airport, and had to submit to a smallpox vaccination on the spot.

I was rushed through the routine of customs inspection and then ushered through a long hallway into a small press-room jammed with reporters, photographers, and a huge battery of blinding floodlights. It seemed to me more like a battlefield with flashbulbs popping, photographers shouting instructions, and reporters lobbing questions from the firing line. I tried to smile and answer as best I could, but I knew I was ill equipped for that kind of exchange. Furthermore, the questions weren't designed to make me feel particularly poised or at ease. "Where did you get the fur coat?" "How about a cheesecake shot, Christine?" "How does it feel to be home?" "Do you expect to marry?" "What are you going to do now?" "Do you think Europeans understand sex problems better than Americans do?"

The hot lights were stifling, I was still wearing a heavy fur coat, and I was physically uncomfortable and plainly rattled under the emotional tensions. Finally, in an effort to break up the session and escape, I said, "Ladies and gentlemen, thank you very much for coming, but I think this is really too much."

That comment was quoted at great length in the press. At the time, it may have sounded like a lack of cooperation, but its real implication was simple and straightforward. I truly did think the attention I was receiving was out of proportion to my importance to the world in general, and that the Christine Jorgensen story had already been magnified to a point of hysteria.

Some months later, I was told by Ben White, the *Daily News* reporter who had written the original scoop in December of 1952, that the Jorgensen story had lain on his desk for a week before he decided to use it. Apparently, at that time, a lurid sex scandal involving the trial of a wealthy playboy had run its course, the public was beginning to lose interest, and the *Daily News* was looking for another "sensation" to take its place, in order to boost its circulation. In a sense, then, my notoriety was a matter of chance.

Whatever that coincidence, the press interview on my arrival home was a reality that had to be faced. Finally, the session was over and Irmy and the *American Weekly* representatives began herding me toward an exit and a waiting car. Suddenly, in the crowd, I recognized the familiar and smiling face of Madeleine Miller, my ex-boss from RKO Pathe News, who had come to welcome me home and wish me well. At that moment, in the frightening crush of people, it was a heart-warming sight.

Once settled in the car, I asked to be taken to my sister's home on Long Island, but the *American Weekly* staff had already arranged to take me to the Carlyle Hotel in Manhattan, to keep me "incommunicado" until after the series started on the following Sunday. I balked in no uncertain terms, but when I realized we were being followed by other newsmen, I knew I'd only be involving Dolly and her family even more, so I agreed, reluctantly.

Approaching the hotel, we drove around in circles trying to elude the newsmen without success, and Irmy and I made a dash for the front door. Without stopping at the desk to register, she pushed me toward a waiting elevator, and turned to confront the pursuing reporters herself. The operator asked, "What floor, please?" Realizing that I didn't know what floor, I said, "Just up!" It seemed ridiculous when I found myself on the top floor of a strange hotel, waiting in a deserted corridor, but eventually I was rescued and escorted to a suite reserved for me under a fictitious name.

With all of the attendant excitement and tensions of the day, I decided I wanted a drink, and Irmy suggested a Bloody Mary. I wasn't sure what that was, though the name was intriguing and, at that point, rubbing alcohol would have been welcome. When the drinks arrived, I found I didn't care for the combination of vodka and tomato juice, and as a result I doubt if I had more than a sip or two.

At any rate, my mind was on other things, and by then I had no intention of staying imprisoned at the hotel. Above all, I wanted some rest and privacy. I called Dolly and arranged to have my brother-in-law drive in from Long Island to pick me up. Irmy agreed to stay on at the hotel to keep up the pretense that I was still in residence. Bill finally arrived, and we sneaked out of the hotel through a side entrance undetected by the enemy and fled to the seclusion of their home.

For the next few days the newspapers had a field day and, once again, I was making headlines. My arrival was fully reported, sometimes in a friendly and sometimes hostile way:

what I wore, what I said, what I looked like, my behavior, all with varying degrees of accuracy.

"Christine tosses off Bloody Mary, just like a real guy!"

"Fur collar, pearl earrings set off her beauty."

"Christine, by George!"

"Chris back home, perfect little lady."

"Christine teeters on high heels, leaving the plane."

"Christine conducted herself with dignity."

"Christine ill at ease."

"An artistically minded reporter who trailed her to the swank Carlyle Hotel, reported that Christine probably will not seek work modeling bras."

"MDs Rule Chris 100 Percent Woman!"

"Judge Wonders is Chris Real George."

"Christine is Certified as Legal Woman."

As I remember, the only paper that reported my return with any degree of conservatism was the *New York Times*, which carried a brief column containing a few pertinent facts and lived up to its motto: "All the news that's fit to print."

However, one news release that did have basis in fact was from the *New York Daily Mirror*, datelined Copenhagen, February 18, 1953.

DENMARK CURBS CHRIS SURGERY. (INS) A top-ranking medical informant said today the Danish government has turned down appeals from more than three hundred persons—over half of them Americans—for transformation operations. The informant, familiar with the series of treatments and operations performed on Christine Jorgensen, said the requests for similar surgery and treatment were denied because the Danish minister of justice had decided to limit treatment of future cases to Danes.

Looking back on it, I can understand why some of the misconceptions have prevailed and how they got an early start. Except for my arrival in the United States, the *American Weekly* editors were determined to keep other newsmen in the dark to protect the exclusivity of the article series, a precaution that was understandable even then. Unable to reach me and gather the real facts, rival newspapers proceeded to enlarge on the slightest item to keep the Jorgensen story moving before the public. If I sneezed, it was duly reported as an event. Perhaps the controversies would have been minimized had the information been shared equally.

However, I hoped the *American Weekly* series would clarify some of that information for the public, and I knew that everything possible had been done to make it a fair and truthful presentation. In a later edition of *Editor & Publisher*, a trade paper for the publishing business, an article appeared outlining some of the aims and preparations of the *American Weekly* editors:

Numerous editorial problems had to be faced. Both the editor and associate publisher of *American Weekly* were determined that the material be presented with complete accuracy and good taste. They visualized it, not as a sensationalized bit of erotica, but as the courageous fight of a desperately unhappy person with the fortitude to overcome a seemingly hopeless obstacle.

Their staff writer, Irmis Johnson, was so instructed. She was told to obtain unassailable verification for every statement in the story and to have each article read and approved by the doctors who had accomplished Christine's transformation. Complete documentation was in the *American Weekly*'s files before the story began appearing. It enabled the magazine effectively to silence

a number of unfounded rumors that were later circu-
lated.

Steps were also taken, with the cooperation of Miss
Jorgensen and her parents, who had joined her in
Europe with the aid of the *American Weekly,* to make
sure that no rival publication could usurp any part of
her life story or obtain unauthorized pictures.

The circulation increases that resulted were the greatest in the memory of circulators and were sustained
throughout the series.

The *American Weekly* series was translated into fourteen
languages and distributed throughout seventy countries.

Mom and Dad returned to the United States two days
after my arrival, and went immediately to their home in the
Bronx. Still unable to locate me, the press began to badger my
parents and, again, they became the victims of the curious and
the die-hard reporters. I stayed in hiding at Dolly's, getting
acquainted with my new niece, who had been born in my
absence. At the time, Dolly was expecting her second child,
another lovely daughter, born two months later.

By then, I realized that some satisfactory arrangement
would have to be made to ensure my family's security and
peace of mind and, therefore, decided to sell our old home and
leave the Bronx after twenty-six years. We rented a cottage on
Long Island Sound, a few miles from Dolly's, and stayed there
to rest and rally our forces, pending the time when I could buy
suitable property and build a home.

I soon found some property in Massapequa, Long Island,
that appealed to all of us, plans got under way for the building,
and Dad contracted the house himself. The word got around
that the Jorgensens were building a home and, for a time, the
vacant lot became a stellar attraction. Sunday afternoons were
particularly busy, and in the early building stages, people

drove by slowly and photographed the empty hole in the ground or the lone bulldozer. One family even brought a picnic lunch and spent a whole afternoon at the site. Later, when the building was finished, we often saw people scanning the windows through binoculars from the opposite side of the street.

During that period, Mom and Dad and I spent some of the time reading and sorting some twenty thousand letters I had received since early December, some from countries I'd never heard of. Letters were delivered to me merely addressed: "Christine Jorgensen, United States of America," and one arrived with no other address than "Copenhagen, Germany." I could only marvel at the ingenuity of the postal department.

The letters ran the gamut of human emotions and responses, and I suppose are typical of those received by people who find themselves in the public eye. Most of them were laudatory, expressing interest and encouragement, some of them were hostile and threatening, a few were obscene. It was interesting to find that many of the congratulatory letters were sent to my parents. Also, there was the usual sprinkling of anonymous letters, a practice that's always puzzled me, for if a person has the courage to state a conviction, then surely he must have the courage to sign his name to it.

Some of the letters, sent from all corners of the world, were from disturbed people who felt they suffered in much the same way as I had, and pathetically asked for help and counsel. I was deeply touched by these, and although many of the problems were unrelated to mine, I seemed to represent some sort of guidepost for accomplishment. Even though I was ill equipped to advise anybody, I tried to answer some of those poignant pleas.

At least one of the letters I received from that period, however, was to net me a lasting friendship, for it introduced Dr. Harry Benjamin, one of America's most distinguished endocrinologists and sex pathologists. I had no way of knowing then that I would become the subject of many of his medical papers, or that our meeting would influence his exhaustive study of transsexualism, published some thirteen years later.

Dear Miss Jorgensen:

These lines are written to you in the interest of some of my patients and naturally also of those whose emotional problem nobody understands better than you do.

Frankly, I am worried over the effect your story and publicity may have in some instances. I had a few rather frantic phone calls and letters recently. Therefore, I would be grateful to you if you would tell me how you are handling the innumerable communications that undoubtedly came to you. Don't they all indicate hopefulness yet utter frustration?

In my many years of practice of sexology and endocrinology, problems similar to yours have been brought to me frequently. I need not tell you how profoundly disturbed some of these people are. Naturally, they identify themselves with you. Can I tell them that you will answer their pleas with a personal note, a friendly noncommittal form letter perhaps, but—for psychological reasons—bearing your signature? That would help enormously. Or have you formulated another plan? Can I be of assistance? If so please feel free to call on me.

Most sincerely and earnestly yours,
Harry Benjamin, M.D.

Shortly after I received that letter, I set up a meeting with Dr. Benjamin at the home of his good friend, the author

Tiffany Thayer. We discussed cases similar to mine, and the problems of answering some of my correspondence. That was the beginning of our great friendship, inspired by mutual interests and his own particular brand of graciousness and charm. It was at our first meeting, too, that he told me Dr. Alfred Kinsey had indicated interest in interviewing me, and would request a conference in the near future.

During my first weeks on Long Island, I bought a car and, as my driver's license had expired in my absence, I went to the Motor Vehicle Bureau to take the driver's tests and have it renewed. I was met by a flood of reporters and photographers, and again became the subject of headlines. Although I didn't think that was a particularly newsworthy event, one newspaper called it "another step in her famous career," reasoning which escapes me to this day. Apparently, the slightest excuse was used to fill up newspaper space. Even Dolly was drawn into the incident, and I was beginning to get a firsthand idea of the demands made on my family.

". . . [This] reporter was sitting with Christine's sister yesterday, while the he-turned-she was taking a driver's license test. The sister, a pleasant woman who has been striving for anonymity, made small talk . . . but absolutely refused to talk about Christine. She wouldn't even tell the reporter her name. . . ."

Soon after my arrival, I began meeting friends and relatives, and found that this experience, which I'd somehow dreaded, was, for the most part, not really so difficult. People like Dr. Joe and Gen Angelo welcomed me home with open arms and I was delighted to renew those friendships.

For some years, the Angelos had been interested in the research programs for cerebral palsy, and on many occasions had personally organized social events to raise money for the national fund. One fund-raising project to which I was invited was an afternoon of bridge, arranged in their home and attended by a group of more than 150 women. In a later interview, Gen recorded some of her impressions:

> Joe and I were worried most of all about Chris's ability to adjust to the storm of publicity. Before, we knew her as a terribly shy, inhibited person, but actually what we saw was a new woman coming into a world of her own. To us, she was a crusader, and the thing we admired most was her personal courage and the idea that she had never wanted to cheapen or pervert herself. Undoubtedly, that was the driving force behind her, in spite of the suffering it entailed.
>
> I watched her that day of the bridge party for the cerebral palsy fund. She was perfectly poised and outgoing, charming to everyone. We had a particularly large crowd, no doubt because she'd agreed to be there. I watched those women, the real smoothie, social types, and they'd get up out of their seats to get a closer look at her, not bothering to conceal their curiosity and bad manners. As a matter of fact, some of them didn't even bother to address me in my own home; they were too busy following Chris around.
>
> I can remember one of the few men present, who said, "The best-looking woman in the room is Christine!" That pleased Joe very much.
>
> I was bombarded with questions right and left, people wondering why she did it, asking if her hair was naturally blond and how she got her beautiful complexion. Oddly enough, several women came to Joe that day, asking for hormone treatments to give them the same smooth complexion.
>
> Joe was furious when one guest made a comment that Chris was still not a woman, but a freak. "She's as much

a woman as you are," he said. "She could marry, yes, and do anything you can do, and perhaps do it better."

Although most all of my old friends and family were as warmly supportive as the Angelos, it would be untrue to say that all of the reactions to my homecoming were enthusiastic. One or two of my relatives showed their deep distress, cause for a breach in the family that wasn't healed until ten years had passed.

However, with few exceptions, it was a time for happy reunions, and I remember it as a wonderful period when most everyone I love was a champion. One of Dad's much-quoted answers to a query from the press made it clear what he thought about it all. "She's ours and we love her," he snapped.

Having once overcome my initial shyness, or at least learned to hide it, I began to feel more freedom in my ability to make new friends. Outside of my own small circle, I met many people in the literary and theatrical world. Elaine Carrington, a radio-TV scriptwriter, was the first to invite me to her home, and for the first time among strangers, I felt nothing but friendliness and genuine interest in me as a person. Elsa Maxwell invited me to a luncheon at her suite in the Waldorf Hotel, and a few days later wrote in her *New York Journal-American* column:

> I reproached Bob Hope for saying on the air not long ago when he was asked if he were going to Copenhagen, that he wasn't because he didn't want to come back a new Elsa Maxwell. Bob roared and said, "That reminds me, you had a lunch the other day for Christine Jorgensen." "I did," I replied, "for I was full of curiosity because I couldn't believe that she was real." Russel Crouse, Howard Lindsay, and Leland Hayward said they would cut me dead if I didn't have them to meet

her, so that is just what I will do. Cole Porter was the only man who came to see her, and Cole was impressed, also Eleanor Loder and Margaret Case of *Vogue* magazine were the other two guests.

Christine is definitely on the level. Her voice is soft and low. She is quite beautiful, very intelligent, has poise and very good manners. When she left she thanked my maid, who had cooked lunch, which no one else has ever done that I can remember.

The excitement in the private entrance at the Waldorf Towers was something I have never seen before. Christine is certainly a celebrity and a nice one.

Columnist Leonard Lyons also gave a party for me to which he invited Sam Goldwyn, Dr. and Mrs. Ralph Bunche, Danny Kaye, and Milton Berle, and Truman Capote invited me to a delightful Sunday brunch.

Name-dropping by recounting some of those early meetings after my homecoming may seem to indicate shallow pride, but the fact of the matter was, at the time, I was flattered to think that I should be interesting and sought after, frankly charmed by the attention, and was guilty of some goggle-eyed celebrity-watching in return.

The poet Abraham Cowley wrote that "curiosity does, no less than devotion, pilgrims make," and there's no doubt that curiosity was the main reason why I was in demand socially, at that point. *New York Journal-American* columnist Louis Sobol commented: "Party-givers now plead with Christine Jorgensen to 'drop in.' It's a huge lift for the party—just like in other days the big feature was the huge 'pie' out of which would step unclad maidens." Now that I think of it, the simile seems questionable. Recently, one of my friends, who was an interested bystander of the period, has said, "At the time, everyone in the world wanted to meet Chris, and damned near everybody did!"

On the other hand, I knew that much of the curiosity and interest stemmed from the understandable fact that people were looking for answers. I had no reason to be concerned by that, for once having met personally, they showed their acceptance with kindness and warmth.

But most important to me at the time was the fact that those were the first steps in a difficult social adjustment for a person who had been shy and introverted for so long. It was my new ability to meet people and to be accepted by them in return that was deeply gratifying to me.

It's only fair to add, however, that not all columnists regarded me with as much favor as Elsa Maxwell. I found that I was frequently the subject of attack, invariably from people whom I'd never met. One writer in particular, in the *New York World-Telegram,* became so virulent that I began to wonder what his own personal problems might be.

If it was fashionable in some instances to meet me in person, it was fashionable in others to turn out a cleverly written phrase to prove the immense wit of the writer:

"The fellow who wanted to be his own girl—Christine Jorgensen."

"Sid Caesar thinks Ralph Edwards should glorify Christine Jorgensen on *These Are My Lives.*"

"Christine Jorgensen (a regular man-about-town) doing the swankier boîtes."

"Seeing pix of Christine (George) Jorgensen reminds locals of the collegiates in the Harvard Hasty Pudding show."

"Arthur Murray has a former teacher who has a new dance named after Christine Jorgensen—the Christine is a fast shuffle."

"Christine Jorgensen has treasury agents excitedly anticipating the surfacing of her income-tax report in the heap. Curious to know whether it was filed as male, female, or perhaps a joint return."

"With this year's Art Student League's ball using a Shake-speare theme, will Christine Jorgensen come as Romeo or Juliet?"

"Didjez see those photos of Christine arriving from Den-mark? Isn't she just George-jus?"

"I have friends who doubt the complete femininity of Christine Jorgensen, the ex-GI—but I'm one who believes she's all girl. For evidence I refer skeptics to her retort when a newspaper reporter, in a baiting mood, asked a too-obvious question about the fur piece Christine was carrying as she got off the plane. 'Don't you know mink when you see it?' Chris-tine meowed. You can't mistake that, kids. That's a female talking!"

There were many other samples, of course, equally tasteful.

It may seem like feigned innocence, but I had little idea of what effect the newspaper publicity was having on the rest of the community, though I soon learned what to expect. At that point, all sorts of new experiences were cropping up daily, one of which included an invitation to attend the opening of a Broadway show, *My Three Angels*. As I'd never been to a Broadway opening before, I looked forward to it eagerly, little realizing that I was going to cause a disturbance.

I was escorted to the theater by a friend of Irmy's, and once settled in our seats, we noticed a general lift in the usual pre-curtain buzz in the audience as men and women walked up and down the aisles, gaping with frank curiosity. I turned around to see what had caused the flurry, when my compan-ion gave me a sudden nudge and whispered, "Chris, it's you!" I read in the columns the next day that "Christine almost ruined the opening of *My Three Angels* just by going," and "the disturbance caused the management to darken the house for a few minutes before lifting the curtain for each act." Apparently, too, I'd incurred the wrath of the excellent cast of the play, headed by Walter Slezak, Jerome Cowan, and Darren McGavin, a reaction for which I couldn't blame them.

After the performance, we walked to a nearby restaurant for an after-theater snack, and were followed by a dozen or so onlookers, who frankly entered behind us. What I had expected to be an evening of enjoyment turned out to be one of discomfort and embarrassment, and I said as much to my escort.

"Face the music, Chris," he answered, "it can't last forever!"

I was by then beginning to get an inkling of what to expect, not only in public, but of the adjustments I would be making from then on. Apparently, I was going to have to get used to the idea of being stared at and inspected. People were going to be interested and inquisitive, I decided, and I would just have to accept it as logical, if I was going to function in the world at all.

———

ABOUT THREE weeks after my return from Denmark, I received a letter from the Scandinavian Societies of Greater New York, a charitable organization representing some seventy-five thousand Scandinavian-Americans, informing me that I had been selected as Woman of the Year — "because of your outstanding contribution to the advancement of medical science, and because of the dignified and courageous manner in which you have deported yourself through it all." To receive the citation, I was invited to attend a gathering of five thousand members on March 7, an annual event that included a concert and grand ball. Proceeds of the evening were to go to various Scandinavian charities. I must admit that I was surprised and very moved by that honor. To me, my accomplishments had seemed to be of such a highly personal nature, insignificant to anyone but me and the Danish medical men who had contributed so much to my existence. To receive a public award for something that was a transition to normalcy seemed an undue recognition, but I was grateful for their acknowledgment and accepted it with pleasure.

Accompanied by my family and friends, a citation scroll was presented to me. I made a brief speech of thanks, if somewhat timidly, for it was my first experience in front of such a large group of people.

That appearance, however, gave me sufficient courage to accept an invitation from Walter Winchell a week later, to appear at Madison Square Garden for a charity benefit. One of Winchell's pet projects, called "The Bravest and Finest," had been organized to help the families of New York policemen and firemen who had been killed in the line of duty. Entertainment was provided by a host of well-known theatrical stars, and although I had no way of entertaining, it seemed to me an opportunity to prove myself a useful member of the community. Having lived in Europe for several years, I felt a need for belonging and to satisfy that need by making some sort of contribution. I consented to appear, in spite of the fact that Winchell's personal barbs in his column had made him anything but endearing. Unsure of his reception, he offered the invitation through a friend, assuring me that my introduction would be simple and tasteful, and that I'd have little to do except to make an appearance with a brief speech.

On the performance night, I confess to being excited as I waited backstage at Madison Square Garden. There was certainly no doubt about my naïveté, when an ample gentleman named Gleason was introduced to me and I asked him if he was related to the Hollywood actor Jimmy Gleason. He said he wasn't and I asked him if he was in show business. "Well, in a way," he admitted. "I do a weekly thing on TV." I promised to look for his program the following week, and he was called onstage to do his stint for the show then in progress.

Hank Wall, who had accompanied me that evening, promptly set me straight, much to my chagrin. "Chris, Jackie Gleason is the biggest name in television!" I'd been away for almost three years where TV hadn't existed, and the entertainers who were then making their fame in America were unknown to me.

I was very big in the faux pas department that night. As the star-studded show progressed, I met a slim and smiling young man whose name I didn't hear when we were introduced. He was pleasant and congenial and I was enjoying our conversation, thinking perhaps that he was an observer backstage, when someone tapped him on the shoulder to indicate he was next to perform. In a moment, the Garden was ringing with his famous number, "Cry." His records were popular in Denmark and I knew them well, but as I'd never seen a picture of him, I didn't recognize Johnnie Ray.

At last, someone led me to the stage entrance, gave me a signal, and I walked out under the blinding spotlights to face the great darkened expanse of people. In a courteous gesture, Winchell removed his famous reporter's hat and said simply, "Ladies and gentlemen, meet Miss Christine Jorgensen." I know that I was nervous and frightened, but the brief speech I addressed to the audience was a simple expression of the honor accorded me at being invited, and the opportunity to be a useful citizen of New York City. Suddenly it was over and I walked offstage, followed by a deafening ovation, experiencing that peculiar excitement and stimulation that I would come to know better later on.

For some reason that evening, I thought of the last time I had been in Madison Square Garden. Seven years before, during my army service, I'd attended the circus there, and had I been asked then to do so much as get up and whisper "hello" from my seat high up under the roof, I'd have fled in terror. As a young army private, I'd had no idea I would someday make my debut as "Christine," in front of eighteen thousand people, on a stage under glittering lights, surrounded by showbusiness headliners.

A few weeks after the Garden benefit, Arthur and Kathryn Murray pledged five thousand dollars to the Damon Runyon Cancer Fund if I would appear on their telecast of *The Arthur Murray Party,* an invitation that conformed to my idea at the time to appear only for charitable purposes. However, I'd already been informed several times that although many TV personalities had wanted to invite me as their guest, the network executives had banned me from appearing. The Murrays succeeded in breaking that barrier, and I consented to appear and make a speech on behalf of the cancer fund.

On the day of the telecast, I sat in a corner of the studio, watching with fascination the preparations that went into thirty minutes of live television. Again, it was an alien atmosphere in which I felt out of place. Dancers were limbering up in corners, Kathryn Murray was rehearsing a skit with Charles Coburn, and Melvyn Douglas and Jane Pickens were listening to each other's speeches on behalf of the fund drive. Lights were set, microphones swung in from above, and cameras rolled into positions looking like uneasy squids, with masses of wires trailing behind.

As I watched all of these preparations, I was struck by the thought that I didn't really belong and I wondered what I was doing there, again in the company of successful stars. I had little or nothing to offer except a sincere desire to be helpful in the cancer drive.

————

THOUGH MY return to the United States had been in mid-February, a little less than two months earlier, my life in that brief span had been extraordinary in many ways. I'd renewed old friendships and met a great many new and exciting personalities. I had been both attacked and applauded in the press, and known the delight of being accepted by society, as well as the anguish of nonacceptance. An amazing thing in itself, I'd found the courage to make several public appearances in front of large crowds, and most satisfying of all, I was building a new home for myself and my parents.

There hadn't been much time to pause and reflect in those full and busy weeks, but when I finally stopped to consider it, I'd faced some extremely difficult adjustments. I'd been courted, derided, admired, made the subject of off-color jokes, and clothed in the light of half-truths and controversy. Apparently, there would be no attitudes in between complete hostility and total approval. I was going to be like eggplant—one either liked it very much, or not at all.

Miraculously, the past had led me to a life of fame and notoriety, with all of its attendant frustrations, pleasures, and responsibilities. By turns, I'd known delight, bewilderment, amusement, and resentment, but always supporting those personal reactions was a strong, underlying sense of happiness. In spite of all the perplexing events, in the deepest recesses of myself, I was a happy person.

Although I still had one more large medical step before total fulfillment, I had started on the new life I'd looked toward, prayed for, and knew was rightfully mine. In more ways than one, I had come home at last.

CONUNDRUM

Jan Morris

1974

*Jan Morris was born James Morris in Somerset,
England. An Oxford-educated journalist, she
covered the first ascent of Mount Everest for
the* Times *of London in 1953. She has written
over twenty-five books, most about travel.*

Chapter 1

I WAS three or perhaps four years old when I realized that I had been born into the wrong body, and should really be a girl. I remember the moment well, and it is the earliest memory of my life.

I was sitting beneath my mother's piano, and her music was falling around me like cataracts, enclosing me as in a cave. The round stumpy legs of the piano were like three black stalagmites, and the sound box was a high dark vault above my head. My mother was probably playing Sibelius, for she was enjoying a Finnish period then, and Sibelius from *underneath* a piano can be a very noisy composer; but I always liked it down there, sometimes drawing pictures on the piles of music stacked around me, or clutching my unfortunate cat for company.

What triggered so bizarre a thought I have long forgotten, but the conviction was unfaltering from the start. On the face of things it was pure nonsense. I seemed to most people a very straightforward child, enjoying a happy childhood. I was loved and I was loving, brought up kindly and sensibly, spoiled to a comfortable degree, weaned at an early age on Huck Finn and *Alice in Wonderland,* taught to cherish my animals, say grace, think well of myself, and wash my hands before tea. I was always sure of an audience. My security was absolute. Looking back at my infancy, as one might look back through a windswept avenue of trees, I see there only a cheerful glimpse of sunshine—for of course the weather was much better in those days, summers were really summers, and I seldom seem to remember it actually raining at all.

More to my point, by every standard of logic I was patently a boy. I was James Humphry Morris, male child. I had a boy's body. I wore a boy's clothes. It is true that my mother had wished me to be a daughter, but I was never treated as one. It is true that gushing visitors sometimes assembled me into their fox furs and lavender sachets to murmur that, with curly hair like mine, I should have been born a girl. As the youngest of three brothers, in a family very soon to be fatherless, I was doubtless indulged. I was not, however, generally thought effeminate. At kindergarten I was not derided. In the street I was not stared at. If I had announced my self-discovery beneath the piano, my family might not have been shocked (Virginia Woolf's androgynous *Orlando* was already in the house) but would certainly have been astonished.

————

NOT THAT I dreamed of revealing it. I cherished it as a secret, shared for twenty years with not a single soul. At first I did not regard it as an especially significant secret. I was as vague as the next child about the meaning of sex, and I assumed it to be simply another aspect of differentness. For different in some way I recognized myself to be. Nobody ever urged me to be like other children: conformity was not a quality coveted in our home. We sprang, we all knew, from a line of odd fore-bears and unusual unions, Welsh, Norman, Quaker, and I never supposed myself to be much like anyone else.

I was a solitary child in consequence, and I realize now that inner conflicts, only half-formulated, made me more solitary still. When my brothers were away at school I wandered lonely as a cloud over the hills, among the rocks, sloshing through the mud banks or prodding in the rock pools of the Bristol Channel, sometimes fishing for eels in the bleak dikes of the inland moors, or watching the ships sail up to Newport or Avonmouth through my telescope. If I looked to the east I could see the line of the Mendip Hills, in whose lee my mother's people, modest country squires, flourished in life and were brass-commemorated in death. If I looked to the west I could see the blue mass of the Welsh mountains, far more exciting to me, beneath whose flanks my father's people had always lived — "decent, proud people," as a cousin once defined them for me, some of whom still spoke Welsh within living memory, and all of whom were bound together, generation after generation, by a common love of music.

Both prospects, I used to feel, were mine, and this double possession sometimes gave me a heady sense of universality, as though wherever I looked I could see some aspect of myself — an unhealthy delusion, I have since discovered, for it later made me feel that no country or city was worth visiting unless I either owned a house there, or wrote a book about it. Like all Napoleonic fantasies, it was a lonely sensation too. If it all belonged to me, then I belonged to no particular part of it. The people I could see from my hilltop, farming their farms, tending their shops, flirting their way through seaside holidays, inhabited a different world from mine. They were all together; I was all alone. They were members; I was a stranger. They talked to each other in words they all understood about matters that interested them all. I spoke a tongue that was only mine, and thought things that would bore them. Sometimes they asked if they might look through my telescope, and this gave me great pleasure. The instrument played an important part in my fancies and conjectures, perhaps because it seemed to give me a private insight into distant worlds, and when at the age of eight or nine I wrote the first pages of a book, I called it *Travels with a Telescope,* not a bad title at that. So I was always gratified when after a few preliminary banterings — "That's a big telescope for a little boy! Who are you looking for — Gandhi?" — they wanted to try it for themselves.

For one thing I was a terrible swank, and loved to focus my lens for them deftly upon the English and Welsh Grounds lightship. For another, the brief contact of the request made me feel more *ordinary.*

I was intensely self-conscious, and often stood back, so to speak, to watch my own figure stumbling over the hills, or sprawled on the springy turf in the sunshine. The background was, at least in my memory, brilliant and sharp-edged, like a pre-Raphaelite painting. The sky may not always have been as blue as I recall it, but it was certainly clear as crystal, the only smoke the smudge from a collier laboring up-channel, or the blurred miasma of grime that hung always over the Swansea valleys. Hawks and skylarks abounded, rabbits were everywhere, weasels haunted the bracken, and sometimes there came trundling over the hill, heavily buzzing, the daily de Havilland biplane on its way to Cardiff.

My emotions, though, were far less distinct or definable. My conviction of mistaken sex was still no more than a blur, tucked away at the back of my mind, but if I was not unhappy, I was habitually puzzled. Even then that silent fresh childhood above the sea seemed to me strangely incomplete. I felt a yearning for I knew not what, as though there were a piece missing from my pattern, or some element in me that should be hard and permanent, but was instead soluble and diffuse. Everything seemed more determinate for those people down the hill. *Their* lives looked preordained, as though like the old de Havilland they simply stuck dogged and content to their daily routes, comfortably throbbing. Mine was more like a glider's movements, airy and delightful perhaps, but lacking direction.

This was a bewilderment that would never leave me, and I see it now as the developing core of my life's dilemma. If my landscapes were Millais or Holman Hunt, my introspections were pure Turner, as though my inner uncertainty could be represented in swirls and clouds of color, a haze inside me. I did not know exactly where it was—in my head, in my heart, in my loins, in my dreams. Nor did I know whether to be ashamed of it, proud of it, grateful for it, or resentful of it. Sometimes I thought I would be happier without it; sometimes I felt it must be essential to my being. Perhaps one day, when I grew up, I would be as solid as other people appeared to be; but perhaps I was meant always to be a creature of wisp or spindrift, loitering in this inconsequential way almost as though I were intangible.

———

I PRESENT my uncertainty in cryptic terms, and I see it still as a mystery. Nobody really knows why some children, boys and girls, discover in themselves the inexpungeable belief that, despite all the physical evidence, they are really of the opposite sex. It happens at a very early age. Often there are signs of it when the child is still a baby, and it is generally profoundly ingrained, as it was with me, by the fourth or fifth year. Some theorists suppose the child to be born with it: perhaps there are undiscovered constitutional or genetic factors, or perhaps, as American scientists have lately suggested, the fetus has been affected by misdirected hormones during pregnancy. Many more believe it to be solely the result of early environment: too close an identification with one or the other parent, a dominant mother or father, an infancy too effeminate or too tomboyish. Others again think the cause to be partly constitutional, partly environmental—nobody is born entirely male or entirely female, and some children may be more susceptible than others to what the psychologists call the "imprint" of circumstance.

Whatever the cause, there are thousands of people, perhaps hundreds of thousands, suffering from the condition today. It has recently been given the name "transsexualism," and in its classic form is as distinct from transvestism as it is from homosexuality. Both transvestites and homosexuals sometimes suppose they would be happier if they could change their sex, but they are generally mistaken. The transvestite gains his gratification specifically from wearing the clothes of the opposite sex, and would sacrifice his pleasures by *joining* that sex; the homosexual, by definition, prefers to make love with others of his own sort, and would only alienate himself and them by changing. Transsexualism is something different in kind. It is not a sexual mode or preference. It is not an act of sex at all. It is a passionate, lifelong, ineradicable conviction, and no true transsexual has ever been disabused of it.

I have tried to analyze my own childish emotions, and to discover what I meant, when I declared myself to be a girl in a boy's body. What was my reasoning? Where was my evidence? Did I simply think that I should behave like a girl? Did I think people should treat me as one? Had I decided that I would rather grow up to be a woman than a man? Did some fearful legacy of the Great War, which ravaged and eventually killed my father, make the passions and instincts of men repugnant to me? Or was it just that something had gone wrong during my months in the womb, so that the hormones were wrongly shuffled, and my conviction was based upon no reasoning at all?

Freudians and anti-Freudians, sociologists and environmentalists, family and friends, intimates and acquaintances, publishers and agents, men of God and men of science, cynics and compassionates, lewds and prudes—all have asked me these questions since then, and very often provided answers too, but for me it remains a riddle. So be it. If I have evoked my childhood impressionistically, like a ballet seen through a gauze curtain, it is partly because I remember it only as in a dream, but partly because I do not want to blame it for my dilemma. It was in all other ways a lovely childhood, and I am grateful for it still.

————

IN ANY CASE, I myself see the conundrum in another perspective, for I believe it to have some higher origin or meaning. I equate it with the idea of soul, or self, and I think of it not just as a sexual enigma, but as a quest for unity. For me every aspect of my life is relevant to that quest—not only the sexual impulses, but all the sights, sounds, and smells of memory, the influences of buildings, landscapes, comradeships, the power of love and of sorrow, the satisfactions of the senses as of the body. In my mind it is a subject far wider than sex: I recognize no pruriency to it, and I see it above all as a dilemma neither of the body nor of the brain, but of the spirit.

Still, for forty years after that rendezvous with Sibelius a sexual purpose dominated, distracted, and tormented my life: the tragic and irrational ambition, instinctively formulated but deliberately pursued, to escape from maleness into womanhood.

Chapter 3

I WONDERED occasionally if others might be in the same predicament, and once, choosing a particular friend at school, I tentatively began to explore the subject. It had occurred to me that perhaps mine was a perfectly normal condition, and that *every* boy wished to become a girl. It seemed a logical enough aspiration, if Woman was so elevated and admirable a being as history, religion, and good manners combined to assure us. I was soon disillusioned, though, for my friend deftly diverted the conversation into a dirty joke, and I withdrew hastily, giggling and askew.

That my conundrum actually emanated from my sexual organs did not cross my mind then, and seems unlikely to me even now. Almost as soon as I reached my public school, Lancing, I learned very accurately the facts of human reproduction, and they seemed to me essentially prosaic. They still do. I was not in the least surprised that Mary had been invested with the beauty of virgin birth, for nothing could seem to me more matter-of-fact than the mechanics of copulation, which every living creature manages without difficulty, and which can easily be reproduced artificially too. That my inchoate yearnings, born from wind and sunshine, music and imagination—that my conundrum might simply be a matter of penis or vagina, testicle or womb, seems to me still a contradiction in terms, for it concerned not my apparatus, but my *self*.

––––––

IF ANY institution could have persuaded me that maleness was preferable to femaleness, it was not Lancing College. The Second World War had begun now, and the school had been removed from its magnificent Sussex home to a congeries of country houses in Shropshire. I expect it had lost much of its confidence and cohesion in the process: certainly after the glories of Oxford and the volatile generosity of home it was disappointingly unstylish, and nothing about the school excited me, or ever renewed my sense of sacrament.

I was not really unhappy there, but I was habitually *frightened*. The masters were invariably kind, but the iniquitive prefectorial system could be very cruel. I was constantly in trouble, usually for squalid faults of my own, and was beaten more often than any other boy in my house. A silly and wicked ritual surrounded a beating by the house captain. The basement room was shrouded in blankets or curtains, giving it a true ambiance of torture chamber, and all the house prefects attended. I used to be sick with fear, and feel a little queasy even now, thinking about it thirty years on. Nor was any discipline I was later to experience in the British army, no bawling of sergeants or sarcasms of adjutants, anything like as terrifying as the regimen of the Lancing College Officers Training Corps, whose compulsory parades were held every Thursday afternoon. We wore uniforms from the First World War, and drilled with nineteenth-century rifles lately captured from the Italians in North Africa, and the slightest tarnish of a button, or the crooked wrap of a puttee, could bring savagery upon us. For twenty years or more I dreamed about the horror of those parades, and of the burning pale blue eyes of the cadet sergeant, approaching me expectant and mocking down the ranks (for if I was actually present, having failed to convince the authorities that I had sprained my ankle or developed a feverish cold, I was exceedingly unlikely to be correct).

I wanted no share in this establishment. I left Lancing as soon as I could, volunteering for the army when I was seventeen, and contemplating my years there I remember only two positive pleasures. One was the pleasure of roaming the Welsh border country on my bicycle; the other was the pleasure of sex. When I wandered off among the brackeny hills, or explored the castles that guarded that long-embattled frontier, I was retreating into a truer and more private role than anything Lancing permitted; and when I thrilled to the touch of a prefect's strong hand surreptitiously under the teashop table, I was able to forget that he had flogged me the week before, and could be my true self with him, not the poor hangdog boy crying over the packing case, but somebody much more adult, confident, and self-controlled.

I hope I will not be thought narcissist if I claim that I was rather an attractive boy, not beautiful perhaps, but healthy and slim. Inevitably, the English school system being what it is, I was the object of advances, and thus my inner convictions were thrown into an altogether new relief. It seemed perfectly natural to me to play the girl's role in these transient and gen-erally lighthearted romances, and in their platonic aspects I greatly enjoyed them. It was fun to be pursued, gratifying to be admired, and useful to have protectors in the sixth form. I enjoyed being kissed on the back stairs, and was distinctly flattered when the best-looking senior boy in the house made elaborate arrangements to meet me in the holidays.

When it came, nevertheless, to more elemental pursuits of pederasty, then I found myself not exactly repelled, but embarrassed. Aesthetically it seemed wrong to me. Nothing fitted. Our bodies did not cleave, and moreover I felt that, though promiscuity in flirtation was harmlessly entertaining, this intimacy of the body with mere acquaintances was inele-gant. It was not what the fan vaulting expected of me. It was not what my girlfriends had in mind, when they spoke in breathless undertones of their wedding night. It was a very far cry from virgin birth. It was also worrying for me, for though my body often yearned to give, to yield, to open itself, the machine was wrong. It was made for another function, and I felt myself to be wrongly equipped.

I fear my suitors thought me frigid, even the ones I liked best, but I did not mean to be ungrateful. I was not in the least shocked by their intentions, but I simply could not respond in kind. We indulged our illicit pleasures generally in the haylofts of farms, or the loose field ricks they still built in those days, and I think it a telling fact that of those first sexual experiences I remember most vividly, and most voluptuously, not the clumsy embraces of Bolsover Major, not the heavy breathing of his passion or his sinuous techniques of trouser removal, but the warm, slightly rotted sensation of the hay beneath my body, and the smell of fermenting apples from the barns below.

———

SO THIS was sex! I knew it at once to be a different thing from gender—or rather, a different thing from that inner factor which I identified in myself as femaleness. This seemed to me, while germane indeed to human relationships, almost incidental to Bolsover's cavortings in the hayrick—I was right too, for if Bolsover could not at that moment have cavorted with some nubile junior, he would undoubtedly have gone up there to cavort with himself.

To me gender is not physical at all, but is altogether insubstantial. It is soul, perhaps, it is talent, it is taste, it is environment, it is how one feels, it is light and shade, it is inner music, it is a spring in one's step or an exchange of glances, it is more truly life and love than any combination of genitals, ovaries, and hormones. It is the essentialness of oneself, the psyche, the fragment of unity. Male and female are sex, masculine and feminine are gender, and though the conceptions obviously overlap, they are far from synonymous. As C. S. Lewis once wrote, gender is not a mere imaginative extension of sex. "Gender is a reality, and a more fundamental reality than sex. Sex is, in fact, merely the adaptation to organic life of a fundamental polarity which divides all created beings. Female sex is simply one of the things that have feminine gender; there are many others, and Masculine and Feminine meet us on planes of reality where male and female would be simply meaningless."

Lewis likened the difference between masculine and feminine to the difference between rhythm and melody, or between the clasped hand and the open palm. Certainly it was a melody that I heard within myself, not a drumbeat or a fanfare, and if my mind was sometimes clenched, my heart was all too open. It became fashionable later to talk of my condition as "gender confusion," but I think it a philistine misnomer: I have had no doubt about my gender since that moment of self-realization beneath the piano. Nothing in the world would make me abandon my gender, concealed from everyone though it remained; but my body, my organs, my paraphernalia, seemed to me much less sacrosanct, and far less interesting too.

Yet I was not indifferent to magnetisms of the body. Some of the nameless craving that haunted me still was a desire for an earthier involvement in life. I felt that the grand constants of the human cycle, birth to death, were somehow shut off from me, so that I had no part in them, and could look at them only from a distance, or through glass. The lives of other people seemed more real because they were closer to those great fundamentals, and formed a homely entity with them. In short, I see now, I wished very much that I could one day be a mother, and perhaps my preoccupation with virgin birth was only a recognition that I could never be one. I have loved babies always, with the sort of involuntary covetousness, I suppose, that drives unhappy spinsters of a certain age to kidnap; and when later in life I reached the putative age of maternity, finding myself still incapable of the role, I did the next best thing and became a father instead.

What would Bolsover have said if, extracting myself from his loins, I had excused myself with these sophistries? But it all seemed plain enough to me. I was born with the wrong body, being feminine by gender but male by sex, and I could achieve completeness only when the one was adjusted to the other. I have thought about it for four decades since then, and though I know that such an absolute fulfillment can never be achieved—for no man ever became a mother, even miraculously—still I have reached no other conclusion.

Chapter 18

"IF A man can so inoculate himself with the idea that he is not a man, but a woman, as to be to all intents and purposes a woman, that idea may in turn be made to give way to a higher ideal—that there is neither man nor woman."

This quotation was sent to me by Henry from India, and it greatly comforted me, for of the problems that remained to me after Casablanca, much the most serious concerned my children. I would not know how these unusual events would affect them—nor shall I know, I suppose, for years to come. But at least I had not antagonized them. All four had been my staunchest allies throughout the change, screening me, supporting me, reassuring me, and nobody could be more punctiliously reproving than Susan, when some old acquaintance used the wrong personal pronoun of me. They knew how infinitely I cherished them in return, and the older two at least, now men themselves, were strong and wise enough, I knew, to look beyond sex for truth—"Ponder deeply," as another of Henry's quotations said, "and thou shalt know that there is no such thing as I." It was not such a terrible thing, after all. They had not witnessed the collapse of love, the betrayal of parentage, desertion or dislike. What they had watched was a troubled soul achieving serenity, and I hoped that in time they would come to see in my strange life, as I have seen it, some unexpected flicker of *baraka*.

Mark, the eldest, has read every word of this book in its successive drafts, and besides powerfully influencing its shape and character, has illuminated my task with cheerful perspectives of his own. It so happened that in the course of the work King Gustav of Sweden died. It was he, you may remember, who was reported to me in chapter twelve as plotting my sex change by secret rays, and in the margin of my typescript Mark added his own comment on the news: "Clearly the success of Gustav's machinations was too much for the old boy."

AS FOR myself, my difficulties now seemed petty. I had reached Identity. To my family and closest friends, I knew, the physical change would make no difference, imperceptibly gradual as it had been, and most other people too seemed predisposed to accept me for myself. Even the press was indulgent. When news agencies or American magazines rang up, I told them what I reasonably could and asked them, since the time to reveal everything was inopportune, and since after all I did have the happiest memories of that lunch we shared while covering Churchill's illness in the south of France, if they would mind spiking the story. Most of them obligingly did, perhaps on the principle that sensible dogs don't bite dogs, and being fairly jaded with sex-change stories anyway. From time to time wan local journalists, having heard the bizarre tale through the grapevine of country gossip, nervously drove up to Trefan to ask for interviews; but I persuaded them always that it was dead news, and not very sensational either, and they generally drove away with a perceptible sigh of relief, as though they had stood on the brink of the unknown, but had been snatched back just in time. The only interviewer who did throw me off my balance was an exceedingly clever and delightful girl from London, who besides being a detective's daughter, and thus adept at the unnerving silence, knew far more about transsexualism than I did myself, and capped my every speculation with a proven statistic or, still worse, a fact.

So I was able to change my public identity in my own time. Presently I took to signing articles and reviews as Jan; also letters to the *Times*, whose letters editor imperturbably printed them, through the sequence of male to female, without comment. By the end of 1973, I discovered, most people who would have heard of me anyway knew of my change of sex, both in England and in America, and those who were not sure whether to address me as Mrs., Miss, or just Jan were fortunately able to fall back upon a prefix recently and usefully devised, Ms.—just the thing, so everybody thought, for the likes of me.

The response to this cautious self-revelation was encouraging. People I had not seen for years wrote to wish me well. Editors politely asked me in which persona I now wished to be published, and a courteous functionary from the ministry, coming to Trefan to give me my new insurance card, apologetically explained that the question of my retirement pension would have to be settled nearer the time (women get theirs earlier than men, and I suppose he thought I might change back again). As my confidence grew, I devised new techniques for dealing with the complex social demands now made upon me—when to reveal all, when to let things go, how to discover what people already knew, when best to tackle an old acquaintance who, glimpsed through a sea of heads at a literary reception, was evidently unsure whether it was really I, or some martini hallucination. My new name, though just right for me, I thought, was sometimes itself confusing. "I thought Jan Morris was a man," said a jolly Australian at a *Spectator* lunch one day. "What happened, d'you change your sex or something?" Just that, I replied. Ask a silly question and you get a footling answer.

Gradually, on these terms, the range of my ease widened. Among all the hundreds of our acquaintances, only one true-blue Yorkshireman made me feel that my presence in his house would be an embarrassment, or vice versa. I was received with curiosity by most people, with amusement by some, with nonchalance by dons and aristocrats, with kindly incomprehension by soldiers and old ladies, with earnestness by those

who wanted to demonstrate their enlightenment, with a flourish by those who relished a nine-day wonder at their dinner
tables, with bold kisses by extroverts, with shy circumspection
by people who wanted to confide in me, over coffee, their
own little problems of personality. Finally, to cap this social
reincarnation, I was taken to dinner at the ladies' end of the
Travellers' Club dining room, one of my favorite rooms in
London, which lies chandeliered and portraited paralled with
Pall Mall, illuminated on days of state ceremonial by the six
gas flambeaux which blaze and flurry outside. This was a curious occasion by any standards, and unique, I would dare to
claim, in the long history of London clubs.

It was a happy evening for me. My host was an old friend,
the wine was better than I ever ordered for myself, and the
staff of the club, who had known me for so long in one guise,
welcomed me without a flicker in the other—only the wine
waiter betraying, in a faint gleam of his hooded eye as he
poured me another glass, a hint of amused collusion. I had
always admired the London clubman who boasted of himself
that he had experienced all the pleasures mankind was heir to,
except only the joys of childbirth; but I could not help feeling,
as we moved on to the green figs with cream, my favorite in
that room during so many years of manhood, that I had
beaten him at his own game.

———

FEW PEOPLE understood it. I did not expect them to understand the cause, since it was a mystery even to me, but I had
supposed more people might understand the compulsion. I had
once surmised that it might be an impulse common to all male
persons, and though friends of both sexes vehemently deny it, it
still seems to me only common sense to wish to be a woman
rather than a man—or if not common sense, at least good taste.

Those who easily accepted the proposition were mostly women themselves. Sometimes, perhaps, this was paradoxically because they had once themselves wished to be men—in a dilettante sort of way, a common enough inclination. More often it was because, being happy themselves, well balanced in their gender, unconfused, they well appreciated why I would wish to be the same. It would seem odious to them to be condemned to manhood, and they saw that it was odious for me. Among such people, whose company I have come to enjoy more than any other, I have found myself not merely understood, but positively welcomed to womankind.

Many men, on the other hand, and less well integrated women professed themselves stupefied. "This is very strange," was a typical observation on the first draft of this manuscript—"one is baffled"—"how *could* it be?" It was generally because they read my tale always as a parable of sex, looking in it for reflections or explanations of their own sexual preferences, and finding, when they hoped for sperm, orgasms, or erections, only frogs in an Oxford meadow, or Egyptian jasmine. They looked for lust; but though my life has been a life of lust, lust of the loins has been a lesser part of it, and has not been the thread of this story.

Occasionally, especially among the cruder kind of men, I have sensed an element of resentment in this blockage. It is almost as though I have let them down. More often, though, among women as well as men, I have detected envy. They wrongly suppose that I have chosen my own path. They think I have been doubly free. They quote to me W. E. Henley:

> *I am the master of my fate:*
> *I am the captain of my soul.*

when they should be quoting Cecil Day Lewis:

Tell them in England, if they ask
What brought us to these wars,
To this plateau beneath the night's
Grave manifold of stars—

It was not fraud or foolishness,
Glory, revenge, or pay:
We came because our open eyes
Could see no other way.

I am often asked if I have any regrets, and I answer frivo-
lously no, except that I seem to have lost some of the pleasures
of wine drinking, and wish I could still consult the railway
timetables at the Travellers'. But of course I have regrets. I
regret the shock I have given to others. I regret lost time.
Occasionally I regret my manhood, when it comes to getting a
job done properly, or having my opinion listened to. I regret
the necessity of it all, just as I regret the stolen years of completeness, as man or as woman, that might have been mine.

But I do not for a moment regret the act of change. I could
see no other way, and it has made me happy. In this I am one
of the lucky few. There are people of many kinds who have set
out on the same path, and by and large they are among the
unhappiest people on the face of the earth. Since I went to
Casablanca I have met some, and corresponded with many
more. Some have achieved surgery, some merely pine for it,
and every complication of the sexual urge, every tangle of
social neurosis, is to be found somewhere in their anxieties.
I know a university lecturer, born male, who underwent
surgery without any hormonal preliminaries because he
wished to live as a lesbian. I know a distinguished and exquis-
itely cultured civil servant, now in his late fifties, whose life
has been wrecked by his bitter jealousy of womanhood—his

confidence shattered by terrible aversion treatment, his powerful physique transformed by hormones, his marriage broken, his career abandoned. I know of an educated woman, converted to malehood, so terrified of her new role that she has forsaken home, family, and all, and shut herself up in loneliness in a distant country town. And these are clever, articulate people; I do not speak of all the poor castaways of intersex, the misguided homosexuals, the transvestites, the psychotic exhibitionists, who tumble through this half-world like painted clowns, pitiful to others and often horrible to themselves.

Sex has its reasons too, but I suspect the only transsexuals who can really achieve happiness are those of the classic kind, the lifelong puzzlers, to whom it is not primarily a sexual dilemma at all—who offer no rational purpose to their compulsions, even to themselves, but are simply driven blindly and helplessly towards the operating table. Of all our fellows, we are the most resolute. Nothing will stop us, no fear of ridicule or poverty, no threat of isolation, not even the prospect of death itself. During my years of torment I generally found it safer (for I did not wish to risk my sanity more than I could help) to approach my problem existentially, and to assume that it was altogether of itself, sans cause, sans meaning. It is only in writing this book that I have delved so deeply into my own emotions. Yet nothing I have discovered there has shaken my conviction, and if I were trapped in that cage again nothing would keep me from my goal, however fearful its prospect, however hopeless the odds. I would search the earth for surgeons, I would bribe barbers or abortionists, I would take a knife and do it myself, without fear, without qualms, without a second thought.

EMERGENCE

Mario Martino with harriett

1978

Mario Martino studied in childhood to become a nun. His is one of the first accounts of the female-to-male transsexual experience.

SOON AFTER my bilateral mastectomy, Becky and I joined group sessions with other transsexuals. But too much information disseminated there on gender identity could not be verified or was found to be inaccurate. There were too many half-truths. Doctors gave too much hope, which could not be substantiated: Rosy promises of cleared pathways seldom materialized—instead, the directions were thorny and often led to frustration and despair. Not from intent, but because the whole thing was so new to all of us. It seemed to me that we needed facts and figures from driver's license bureaus, departments of vital statistics, universities, research teams, medical centers. We needed it firsthand, not as hearsay.

Dissatisfied with the little that was accomplished in these meetings, I mentioned to Becky that we should start something of our own.

Becky and I discussed the idea of our own counseling service with Dr. Lake and he was all for it, going so far as to allow us to use his own office address for mailings. We asked a small fee from each patient—if he could afford it. If not, he was to be placed on the free list. We thought of this service as a child of sorts: a brainchild, one that would help compensate for the children we knew now we'd never have.

Contacting the newspapers, we met with refusal. They would not accept our ads. It was still too early in the sexual revolution. We appealed for financial assistance to a foundation already active in this area, but their reply was that they did not dispense money to private individuals. Yet, sometime later, we were to learn of such a service actually sponsored by this same institution. Their service, however, was for the male-to-female transsexual. Ours was designed for the female-to-male. It seemed evident to us that interest in transsexualism was predominantly in male-to-female.

BEFORE MY legal papers could be changed, I was required by law to have a pan hysterectomy, or removal of the uterus, and a salpingo-oophorectomy, the excision of tubes and ovaries. There was no area in our state where I could find a surgeon to perform this operation. Desperate, I wrote to Janet, asking her to contact her own physician, Dr. Jonas, for recommendations.

My insurance was under the name "Marie," and I kept it that way until after this second surgical procedure in sex change. (And who ever heard of having male insurance to cover a hysterectomy?)

Any skilled surgeon could do the operation. And aside from the legal requirements, every female-to-male transsexual requested these surgeries for reasons identical to my own: 1) to remove the unwanted organs, 2) to eliminate the hormone-interacting process of menstruation, 3) to remove an organ high in cancer susceptibility, 4) to enhance testosterone utilization in producing secondary sex characteristics, such as the deepened voice, hair growth—in short, increased masculinity.

Surgeons usually made the incision in the abdomen, but the transsexual usually wanted it done vaginally, thus leaving the abdomen unscarred for an eventual phalloplasty.

We waited impatiently for Janet's Dr. Jonas to make a recommendation. He had taken time to contact the surgeon, Dr. Adam Brown, before giving us the name and was pleased to say Dr. Brown would do my hysterectomy. I was to send a detailed background, listing goals already realized and goals yet to meet, directly to the surgeon. After reviewing this data, Dr. Brown asked that I come to his state, his hospital, for a personal interview and examination, with a tentative date set for surgery during the Thanksgiving holidays. Becky would have some time off then and could stay with Jan and Jim.

In the interim we bought a car, a luxury on our tight budget. The change of name on my driver's license was handled without incident. And now we left for Janet's home with the realization that we were taking still another step toward my sexual reassignment. I was to be in the same hospital where my father had died. I would be the first transsexual (but not the last) to have this procedure in this hospital.

———

THE WOMAN in admissions checked my name against the operating schedule and became flustered. Looking at me, at my full-face beard, she couldn't understand my feminine name. Regaining her composure, she registered me and sent me off for a chest X-ray.

Dr. Brown had informed the professionals on the unit but felt no need to brief the auxiliary staff as to the nature of my surgery. Becky was to be my nurse, and I would be a patient in a private room. Nor did Dr. Brown inform other departments with which I'd be involved, and some of the incidents there were not without their chuckles.

The X-ray technician became unsettled to the point of tearing the request in half, after which I helped her tape it together. Though I tried to maintain my calm, it came close to shattering when I noticed everyone outside the department lined up to take a look at this new specimen: *me*. In the laboratory for blood tests, the young woman dropped all her test tubes.

"Don't be nervous," I said to her. "I know exactly what you're going through because I used to draw blood."

Reassured, she had no further problems. In spite of the curiosity, everyone in this hospital treated me with professionalism.

Mrs. Thompson, the head nurse, came in almost as soon as we'd reached my room. She said my genital area must be shaved and I must have a vaginal suppository (as a safeguard against infection) and an enema. She agreed to Becky's helping me with these preparations.

Mrs. Thompson advised us as to hospital procedure, when we could expect Dr. Brown to visit that evening, and the time set for surgery tomorrow. Both my history and final examinations would be by Dr. Brown himself, not by one of the residents, to avoid any embarrassment on my part. His sensitivity endeared this man to both Becky and me.

I wakened in the early hours and was happy to see Becky, Jan, and Jim before going too far under from the preoperative sedation. More than anything else I was vaguely aware of the orderly standing at the door, squawking in a voice approaching terror: "I ain't never taken no man for a hysterectomy!"

"Get him out of here," I croaked. "God! This man is going to mess me up."

Janet ran to the orderly and asked him to see the head nurse—she'd explain. Within minutes, the man, sobered and wordless, returned and helped me onto the waiting stretcher.

Dr. Brown had been told that I'd gone into shock the first time I had surgery, so he was prepared for such an eventuality the second time. I remembered nothing about the operating table. On waking, I was happy this second procedure was over and that I was apparently doing well.

By the second day I was asking to get out of bed and on a regular diet. I was feeling great, anxious to get back to normal. And I was hungry. A liquid diet was simply not for me.

It was something of a surprise that Dr. Brown had not put a large dressing over the classical cut he had made in my abdomen. (He preferred the abdominal procedure, not the vaginal.) The incision ran from the navel to the hairline of the pubis and Dr. Brown had covered it with a Band-Aid and dispensed with the old-fashioned binder we'd always used after this type of surgery.

No incisional pain, but great discomfort from gas. Abdominal cramps were so severe I couldn't laugh. The cramps were to stay with me for about a week.

[. . .]

On a lark I called Becky at school.

"Becky, will you marry me?"

"Well," she teased, "do you think we've known each other long enough?"

We'd marry in January, we decided. We'd waited a lifetime, it seemed to us, and we hoped we'd be happy ever after.

Could we measure up to the fairy tales?

Well, since ours was a world of reality we'd have to work at happiness.

Becky could no longer postpone the letter to her mother.

Dear Mom,

I have been wanting to write for a long time, but haven't had a chance to sit down and really say the things I've wanted to say. We don't want to upset or hurt you in any way—guess that's the reason I've put off writing.

All the papers have been changed legally to the masculine name "Mario," male sex. We know how you feel about this and we both understand that we can't ask you to accept it just now. But we both pray that in time you will understand and accept us as a part of our family.

Please don't hate me for what I'm about to say. I love all of you very much and, as you already know, Mario thinks you are the greatest people in the world! *I say this because it is true.*

Mom, Mario and I love each other very much and are completely happy together. To have someone who really cares for me is one of the best things in my life. There is nothing Mario wouldn't do for me. I don't know where I could find a better man, one who would treat me as wonderfully as he does—and always be true.

I really don't know what it is that you don't like about him, but you say he might take advantage of me. Mom, that just couldn't be. Mario would give me the world if I asked for it. He is concerned enough about my welfare that, before surgery, he drew up his will. He did this to protect me should anything happen to him.

I would never be as far in school if he had not kept his word about my getting an education. Yes, you said if I married someone other than Mario I wouldn't need all this schooling because we'd have a houseful of kids. Well, you don't have to worry about that because we've decided against having children of our own. Not that we wouldn't love having them—it's just that we feel that there might be too many problems later on for them to understand all that Mario and I have faced together.

All these changes are difficult for parents to understand, let alone children. It was difficult for me to understand at first and, you may remember, only last summer I told you I was planning to come home. And then, finally, I saw it all clearly: My love for Mario was too great for me to leave him. I've been with him for so long and, loving him as much as I do, I made the only possible choice. Every day since then I realize more and more that my decision was the wise one.

I see no reason why anyone there needs to know about this. We understand, of course, that you don't want Mario to come home, and he won't. However, no one would recognize him, for he looks quite different now—and even better than he did as Marie.

Please try to understand, Mom, all of you. Just remember that we are very happy. I feel that nobody will ever love me as much as Mario does. This is the life I've chosen and we are to be married in January when I am on vacation from school.

We both love you.

Love,
Becky

We said a prayer together, asking God to help Mom understand. We posted the letter and went off to work.

———

NEEDLING BY the staff was often hellish, but I tried to underplay it for Becky's sake. To Becky, my hurts were her hurts too.

One thing was in my favor: rapport with the men on my unit. I learned firsthand how male patients react under stress, what they expected of themselves, of their peers, and of me. They needed to verbalize their fears: banteringly, if they were seriously ill—thinking of last rites, if mildly ill. They respected honesty. I was their brother, father, confidant—and, yes, sometimes their confessor.

The day people were softening toward me, but those on my own night shift still spat out their words when speaking to me. Well, things would eventually work out.

Nothing could down me for long. I was legally a male, free to marry my Rebecca. In January we'd marry and have a honeymoon. In February I'd get back to work on my bachelor's degree.

Life was opening to full blossom.

from Chapter 13

I WAS to wait another four years to find the surgeon I'd trust for my second—and successful!—phalloplasty. Dr. Robertson was truly interested in what he was creating, he cared about me as a patient, he inspired my confidence and respect. The work was done in a fine Midwestern hospital, staffed with friendly and sympathetic personnel. Doctors and nurses and new acquaintances went to extremes in making my long stay there a happy one.

My surgeon is proud of his work. And I am proud of it. His techniques are the conventional ones that are withstanding the test of time. After having made two incisions about three inches apart, he quite literally turned my skin *inside out* to make the "suitcase handle" (with seam side up) on my abdomen (rather than on my thigh as the first surgeon had done), just below the navel to the middle of the mons.

He took the additional skin graft from the hip and thigh and covered the entire "suitcase handle" so that a neophallus was formed with natural skin both on the outside and surrounding an interior duct which would accommodate the stiffener for intercourse. This stiffener is a pencil-sized tube filled with silicone which is inserted into what would be the urethra in a real penis.

As a skin graft is applied, it lays down cells which generate new skin, and the top layer gradually sloughs away. The small irregular pieces of graft leave the neophallus with the appearance of having both small and large veins in it, exactly like an erect penis.

Like all skin grafts, mine was excruciatingly painful. The pain and sensations of burning were dulled by medication the first three days and, within fourteen days, the area from which skin was taken had healed.

Four weeks later, the surgeon cut the top of the tube away from under the navel and let it fall into position at the mons. And now he formed the glans, or head of the penis, by cutting a half-moon incision under the umbilicus as the tube was cut away from the body. Then the two edges were folded in to make the head. No skin graft was necessary for this procedure of creating the glans.

At the time of my second phalloplasty, I was one of eight patients. None of the others had postoperative problems. I was the exception. Driving home from the hospital, a new friend and I took a circuitous side trip to visit a former instructor of mine. Because of its swelling during these days, the only inconspicuous and less painful way I could wear my new penis was positioned against my abdomen. Apparently, the blood supply was not sufficient to reach the tip of the penis, for within the week after the trip that area turned dark, signifying death of the tissue.

Did this mean I might lose the entire penis? All that money and time—and pain—for naught?

I telephoned Dr. Robertson on an every-other-day average. He agreed that warm baths would stimulate circulation to the tube, but that it would not save most of the head from turning black and foul-smelling. So, nightly, I sat in the tub and, very slowly, cut away the dead tissue.

Talk about castration complex!

Psychologically, this cutting was almost impossible for me, yet it had to be done. And now newly formed skin of the graft on the undersurface broke through, leaving the tube with a large flattened effect from the middle of the penis to the top of the head. Eventually, I lost three-fourths of the head—and the exposed area was too large to cover over without another graft.

Becky could not bring herself to help me through the cutting-away period, and I felt quite alone and upset. Even though I really didn't want her to see it in that condition.

Three months passed, and then I returned to my surgeon for another skin graft of the entire tube plus repairs on the head. By the end of the second week (a week before I was to leave there), the doctor said the earlier graft had not taken because the swelling had persisted longer than expected before the latest surgery and worsened afterward. Apparently, in my own case, when skin is removed, that raw area of my body swells and breaks the graft before it has time to heal.

With this news I hit bottom, so to speak. I felt down as I never had before. My happiness seemed to dim out.

That night I called Becky. And my mood did an abrupt upward swing. How comforting her words: "Mario, I've been looking at your body for almost twenty years now. I'm happy with it. I know you want perfection: a perfect phallus. But be happy with what you have. I will be."

Of course I wanted to give her a perfect phallus. But her attitude helped me accept the fact that, while little in life is perfect, she was happy with me as I was and am.

I saw Dr. Robertson again the following morning, and his report was better than I'd expected: "Mr. Martino, we had been afraid you'd lose the whole thing—but now, we're sure everything will be all right."

———

THERE WILL be no more grafts. Not ever. We'll simply wait until the tube is completely flaccid, or relaxed—then, again, the undersurface of the graft (which did not "take") will be sewn together. I ask for nothing better.

So today I'm happy with what I have: a respectable phallus—three-fourths perfect. . . .

Now, I can tell myself, there is a new part of me—a part I

have always conceived of myself possessing. It completes outwardly a picture of myself which I have always carried in my head. By day, whether working, driving, gardening, or relaxing, I sense always the presence of this outward acknowledgment of my maleness. And, by night, my new organ—for all its being less than perfect—is still deeply stimulating to both me and my mate, both psychologically and physically.

from Chapter 14

MANY FEMALE-TO-MALE transsexuals do not choose to have phalloplasty *at this time* because of the difficulties involved and because some find the results of phalloplasty inadequate. They find that, after about six months on male hormones, the clitoris has usually grown too large to be contained within the protective lips or labia and now it resembles a miniature penis. Resting on the outside of the labia, the clitoris is very quickly stimulated and even the feel of the dildo is sexually exciting: Any movement reminds the patient that he has a semblance of the male organ. So equipped and stimulated, the female-to-male transsexual realizes to some degree the satisfaction of being male and achieving climax. And even the artificial penetration of his mate adds to his heightened sexual drive.

Many patients are very nearly content with such an arrangement. Many have no plans for phalloplasty because of the cost, sometimes as much as $10,000. The procedure requires several periods of hospitalization and loss of work time, and often it is no more satisfactory than a strapped-on dildo. The combination of enlarged clitoris and dildo or phalloplasty seems to us an approximation of the normal male's response.

Because of their own insecurities and fear of the woman's rejection, many female-to-male transsexuals refuse to have a

sexual relationship before reassignment by surgery. Still, after
sex-change treatment the female-to-male may notice an increasing of the sex drive, the male-to-female a lessening. This reversal
in sexual desire is attributed to hormones given to bring about
the change from one sex to the other: estrogen for the male-to-
female, testosterone for female-to-male. Studies also indicate
that the male who turns to reassignment may have a lower sex
drive than the average male.

The reassigned male-to-female reports anything from
inability to experience orgasm to multiple orgasms. Postopera-
tively, the female-to-male reports ability to achieve climax and
perform as a male. Three factors contribute to the ability of the
reassigned, both male and female, to reach a satisfactory climax:
the skill of the surgeon, the effect of the hormone injections,
and the emotional/psychological makeup of the individual.

All transsexuals—female-to-male and male-to-female—must
maintain hormone treatment for the rest of their lives. Because
recent research indicates that with prolonged use of testosterone on genetic males for three conditions—eunuchism,
scanty sperm, and menopause—liver tumors may result, the
female-to-male is cautioned to have a liver function test at least
once each year.

I know of no female-to-male who has reported an unsatis-
factory sex life in the new gender. Even without phalloplasty,
each attributes his satisfactory orgasms to the psychological
change: Now he is at ease with himself—and having his mate
respond to him as a male is a dream fulfilled.

With phalloplasty, some females-to-males claim a wild new
urge to "sow oats," but, for the most part, they are content
with mild flirtations and remain faithful to their wives.

Infrequently, though, marriage will crumble after this type
of surgery:

Divorced, and the mother of two little girls, Dawn met Jerry
prior to his surgery. She married him after his legal reassign-

ment, in spite of the fact that she considered herself lesbian. But she had underestimated Jerry, believing she could dissuade him from phalloplasty. Jerry was not to be deterred. Dawn retaliated by divorcing him, declaring she really wanted to love a woman—not a man! In time, Jerry remarried and is now happy with Barbara. They plan to have babies by artificial insemination. Jerry does not consider his second marriage as a rebound romance—rather he thinks of it as God's way of compensation.

Among the many female-to-male transsexuals we know, all wish to go on with phalloplasty eventually, although fewer than fifteen have actually done so because of the almost prohibitive cost. With the exception of Jerry and Dawn, all husbands and wives seem happy with the results.

While it seems all-important to the husband to bring a phallic representation to the marital bed, the wife who loves him will learn—rather, husband and wife will learn together—how to adjust, and they will find mutual enjoyment.

Nothing is more vital to harmonious copulation than the woman's feelings about her man: To her, the absence of male genitalia need not make him less of a man. As we have reported, many transsexuals have good, stable marriages. And enduring ones.

———

TO LOOK backward is to be urged forward. Many of yesterday's children were thrown into the despair of gender dysphoria because doctors had to guess in assigning a sex at birth when the baby had "ambiguous genitalia."

Until very recently only the most casual inspection of the newborn was used to issue the birth certificate, which, in turn, decrees whether the infant shall be regarded as male or female. With today's new scientific tools, however, medical teams can now rationally determine the sex of a newborn within about thirty-six hours immediately following birth. Is the baby a chromosomal female with ovaries (indicative of fertility) or a chromosomal male without ovaries? *Yet chromosomes alone do not define gender.* Many doctors believe the determination of sex is far more complex than the results of a chromosome test. It becomes the responsibility of the team, therefore, to assign the sex in which it believes the baby can grow and mature most comfortably. Our general awareness of chromosomes began with the controversy over the East German women swimmers. The issue also surfaced with the emergence of Dr. Renée Richards in tennis competition. Perhaps athletic commissions will accept these tests as authoritative, but the debate, which is certain to take place, will raise the level of public understanding of this medical frontier.

———

HOW HAS sex reassignment changed me?

I have always had a strong sex drive, and with the rarest of exceptions have always been orgasmic. As everyone will recognize, attempting to describe or compare one's own orgasms is difficult. What I can say is that the pleasure I have had has always seemed to satisfy me, and that certainly remains true. I rather think that I have a higher intensity of sex pleasure now than ever before. What this may be attributable to is of course open to interpretation. No doubt the male hormone testosterone which I take produces a broad range of effects. Certainly the enlargement of the clitoris is arousing. The fact that I am no longer troubled by the use of a dildo, an instrument not of my own flesh, but can feel that an actual part of my own body is involved in the sex act is a source of immense satisfaction to me. There is of course also the absence of the tension induced by those feelings of being trapped in the wrong body. Before my change, there were parts of my body I did not want touched, my breasts and vulva. Now those feelings are gone.

Shift of weight has been my most noticeable physical difference. I have long since stopped worrying about a beard and body hair, having become hirsute. The natural curves of the female body have flattened into a strong semblance of the male. Trousers that had fit around my waist before hormones almost reached my chest afterward, even though there was no appreciable weight loss.

I credit hormones as well as surgery.

Prior to reassignment, I was much more emotional. I cried freely, with tears sliding down my cheeks—but, for years now, I haven't cried at all. I still talk from the soul, and one can go no deeper than that.

I'm more gutsy now. I call a spade exactly what it is. If necessary, I am brutally frank. A completely masculine trait, according to the dictates of my Italian American upbringing—unladylike before sex surgery, acceptable as part of a man's expressing himself. Some outbursts I attribute to my Italian temper: It may take hours to reach white heat, or mere seconds for the verbal response to blue the air. Usually I hold my temper in check, consider myself emotionally stable.

I'm more realistic today. More than thirty years have passed since Jimmy Stewart was my idol. I cannot say I've used him as a role model, at least what we see on the surface. About the only time I can match his calm is during an emergency. I don't walk slowly into things; I plunge. I like the good-guy image, but not at the expense of what I believe. Idols are to be admired and learned from, but not at the expense of losing one's own identity.

With maturity, one mellows or grows more inflexible. I like to think my views have mellowed.

[. . .]

Ten years ago I took a certain pride in being a male chauvinist, and this I attribute to my despair in having been born with a female body. *But brains, talents, and skills are not defined by sex.* Becky exemplifies the women who work shoulder-to-shoulder with their men. And I laud those women who support their families alone. And those women who excel in the professions, in administration, government, and industry, and in stamina and moral fortitude.

[...]

Certain social restrictions crystallized after my change. No longer can I jump over to visit a married woman two or three times a week without a neighbor raising an eyebrow—or the husband questioning my motives.

I have learned to play the games that go on forever between male and female. As a male, it is socially acceptable for me to casually flirt or tell an off-color joke—as a female, I wouldn't quite dare.

I am no longer a man searching for himself. My search ended in finding that man I always knew myself to be. And so it is that I presume to qualify the theory: "Anatomy is destiny." With talents from a power greater than mortal self, *Homo sapiens* is now radically changing the dictates of biology. We have advanced to an age in which anatomical alterations are not only a reality but scarcely a surprise.

Removing the procreative organs—and re-creating the genitalia—is often equated with living under false pretenses, living a lie. Patients report that occasional friendships (begun after sex change) terminate instantly with self-revelation.

I have yet to master my vulnerability. I have yet to reveal myself to friends we've met since my change, some as dear to us as family members—to explain to them there is a part of my life they know nothing about. Will they feel betrayed? Would this revelation affect the children we know and love even more intensely?

How do I explain my reticence?

All sorts of accusations are hurled at some transsexuals. "I can never trust you again!" "If you aren't true to yourself, you can never be true to anyone else." "And you call yourself a good Catholic?" "I refuse to talk about it." "You turn me off!"

These are not responses that encourage self-revelation.

Why, even today, are people shocked and frightened and angered by sex-change surgery? Or even the mention of it?

The degree and range of adverse reactions relate proportionately to an individual's failure to understand the problem. As society becomes more open and recognizes the scope of conventional sexuality, the more accepting individuals will become of transsexualism.

Not to typecast, generally, the greater one's own securities, the more receptive the individual is to opposing views in all controversies. Big or small.

To care, we must first be informed. Far too little information has been disseminated. All too hush-hush. Those persons afflicted with the gender-dysphoria syndrome are just beginning to come forward, most of them still too vulnerable to face the shock, the fright, the anger, the prurient curiosity of a scandalized public. Our puritanism is more ingrained than we might wish to acknowledge or even imagine.

For some, the thought of reversing the genitalia hits at the core of their own sexuality and shatters their faith in biological destiny.

Very often religious scruple is the excuse for nonacceptance. To some, the thought of sex amputation is repugnant: Re-creation of the opposite genitalia is beyond any vestige of human dignity.

Sex reassignment was not accepted by the Catholic Church in the early sixties, nor is it accepted wholeheartedly today. But their doors are opening to dialogue on the complex implications. As controversy about organ transplants and blood transfusions, even choice of sex at conception, leads to reevaluation, it seems logical to assume that one day transsexualism will be generally recognized by medicine and church as a medical-psychological problem, not a religious-ethical one.

Will society ever accept, without equivocation, the sex-changed person? Will the medical profession ever totally solve the problems of this syndrome? Will the laws of our respective countries protect us?

Surely the answer to all three must be an unequivocal *yes*.

Transsexualism is not what I would have wished for myself, but, since I am what I am, I strive to turn this liability into an asset, to establish a bridge of understanding between our segment and society in the main.

Taking a last backward glance, I realize that in envying the boy's rich maturation period I also denied myself many of the riches the girl experiences in the same period. On the brighter side, I have experienced some of the best of both. I've been doubly blessed.

As the calendar years mark time, I more fully appreciate that good things can come of miscarried plans. No experience is lost: It fits into our individual pattern. Out of trauma comes reinforcement in the relationships with family and friends.

Getting my own life in order was the first requisite in what I am doing today. This has been my major accomplishment. Being able to say *I have achieved* is the ultimate reward.

By nature I am a positivist.

On occasion I am asked how I've succeeded in the light of transsexualism. My code is simple and one I've followed all my life: *I will not fail because of my problems. I will succeed in spite of them.*

SECOND SERVE

Renée Richards, M.D.

1983

Renée Richards, M.D. (b. 1934), was Richard Raskind, a Yale-educated ophthalmologist and amateur tennis champion. Shortly after her 1975 surgery, she began to compete on the professional women's tennis circuit. Barred from the 1976 U.S. Open after her past was "discovered," she sued and won the right to keep playing.

SHORTLY AFTER my abrupt leavetaking, Meriam met a man with whom she developed a continuing relationship; eventually, they married. I continued as a heterosexual man and dated a tall woman artist for several months; she loved tennis and came to all my matches. I continued to win, spurred on by her support. My private practice was flourishing. I maintained my close relationship with Andy. The whole situation had a familiar ring to it; once again, I was in an enviable position. I was still young; I was divorced and freewheeling. I had a beautiful girlfriend, a delightful child, and yet . . .

Renée was beginning to tug at me again. It was probably because I was alone in my apartment for long periods of time. During my marriage I had seldom been alone. I think that Renée had, as in those days long ago in college and many times since, shrunk from emerging when I lived with someone. Dick was strong when he had the continuing presence and support of another; but when I was alone for long periods of time I could always feel Renée's strength. Then again, there was the breakup of my marriage and the specter of my advancing years. If Renée was going to make a serious bid for existence, it would have to be soon. As she had after other periods of suppression, she came back stronger than ever. I fought it. I even went to a psychiatrist though I had vowed never to do so again; his insulting suggestion was that I go out and get laid. Instead, I began to think about suicide. It would be easy; as a doctor I had access to all sorts of painless yet lethal substances. The force of my feeling for Andy was the most compelling reason why I didn't kill myself. The sense of betrayal that he would have felt made suicide an impossibility.

The only alternative was to allow Renée to emerge. It was not even an alternative; it was a necessity. She was coming out whether I liked it or not. In the evenings I began to dress again in women's clothes. Shortly after this development, I went again to see Dr. Benjamin. When I greeted Virginia, his secretary, she said, "You know, Dr. Benjamin has retired. His young associate, Dr. Allenfield, has taken over the practice." It was a poignant commentary on how long I had struggled with the step that now seemed inevitable. Dr. Allenfield was sympathetic. "Dr. Raskind," he said, "I think the medical profession has let you down. There is more than enough evidence that you are a genuine transsexual, and I'll give you my backing all the way." He started me on estrogens, and once again I felt that peculiar sense of well-being settle on me. The physical changes came faster this time. My recently flattened breasts began to plump out again. Because of the reduction surgery, however, they only reached about half their former size. The feminine adipose in my thighs and hips also came quickly. It was as if my body had been waiting patiently for the opportunity to be womanly again and then, given the chance, rushed toward it with unprecedented speed. Within three months I was fully feminine.

I gave up seeing my girlfriend and began to ready myself for the surgery that now seemed imminent. Every evening I would dress as Renée. I no longer cared about being seen; my only concerns were for Andy and my professional life. I continued practicing as a man during the day, though I looked more and more weird in men's clothes. Physicians who referred patients to me had to warn them with statements something like: "Dr. Raskind is an unusual-looking individual but he's the best in his field. Don't be alarmed by his appearance; he's a respected physician." Friends also came forward.

"Dick," one said, after a tennis match, "I want you to know that your good friends are aware of the changes that you are going through." "How long have you known?" I asked. "For a very long time." He stared at me for a moment. "And it doesn't make a damn bit of difference to us." The support of my colleagues and of my friends helped me to set my mind as much at ease as was possible under the circumstances.

During this period my father celebrated his seventy-fifth birthday. Responding to strong urging from the immediate family, my sister, Mike, traveled from her home in the north to Long Island for the occasion. I sat visiting with her after the party, and she asked me abruptly, "Are you sorry now that you never had that operation?" I could have told her then that I was soon going to have it, but I had learned my lesson ten years ago. I satisfied myself by saying only, "Yes, I *am* sorry I never had it."

I continued seeing Andy every day. He seemed to pay little attention to the changes in my body; as far as he was concerned I was the same person with whom he felt so very secure. In spite of the softening effect of the hormones, I remained fiercely protective. One evening Andy and I were riding in Central Park near Spanish Harlem; it was silly to be there in the early evening, what with night falling, but I had miscalculated the time. Suddenly three young toughs blocked the bikeway. By that time, I was hardly a ferocious-looking stud, and they probably anticipated an uncontested mugging. It infuriated me that they could stoop so low as to molest a biker with a child in tow. I accelerated, pedaling as fast as I could and aiming directly at the largest of them. I can remember baring my teeth as I leaned forward to get more leverage. Andy was laughing merrily as we flew toward them; it was like a game of chicken. At first, I don't think they believed that I'd actually ride right into them; however, when they got a good look at my snarling countenance and the ever-increasing speed of the bike, they leaped aside, and we sailed through untouched. Andy found it a delightful game, never once considering that there might have been danger. After all, Daddy was with him.

In the spring of 1975, I again consulted Dr. Laidlaw, the psychiatrist who years before had encouraged me to have faith in my own judgment. His advice had been instrumental in my decision to go to Europe. I knew that I would need a psychiatrist on my side when the time came to find a surgeon. I didn't want to go through another battery of psychological tests if I could help it; I told him what had happened to me since we last spoke. He was amazed and said, "Renée, you've been through more than you've deserved. I agree with Dr. Allenfield. Your medical colleagues have let you down. You've been frustrated and used as a guinea pig for too long. I promise that I'll do everything I can to help you find the right surgeon." He pulled out a copy of the interview I had had with him years before and said, "The answers you gave me today are the same as the ones you gave me in 1969. You've paid your dues."

Dr. Allenfield and Dr. Laidlaw began making inquiries in the ranks of those doctors who performed transsexual operations. Their highest priority was that the surgeon be competent and willing to do the operation based on my past testing. My nerves had been strained to the breaking point. I couldn't talk to any more psychiatrists, psychologists, or sociologists—the well was dry. My doctors understood this and humanely refused to accept any compromises. For a while it looked like the spot would be Stanford. I was acquainted with some of the physicians there, and it seemed possible to cut through the red tape. I was adjusting to the idea of traipsing across the country when I received a surprising phone call from Dr. Laidlaw. "Renée," he asked, "if I could schedule your surgery in New York with no red tape and under the medical standards that you require, how would you like it?" Of course, this was sim-

ply a rhetorical question. He knew that I'd like it fine. "Do it!"
I said.

The surgeon that my team had located was Dr. Roberto
Granato. Ironically, his office was only one mile from my
birthplace. He had already performed one hundred and fifty-
seven transsexual operations; obviously, his expertise was the
result of plenty of experience. I looked him up in the Blue
Book and saw that his credentials were good. He had been
trained initially in South America at an excellent school and
had completed his training in the United States. Furthermore,
I talked to physicians who had examined his postoperative
patients; their comments were complimentary. The fact that
he was on the faculty of the Columbia Presbyterian Medical
School was also a high recommendation.

In spite of my investigations I arrived for my interview
with a lot of suspicions. I was prepared to meet the same old
routine: a promising beginning followed by a flaccid retreat.
Dr. Granato's secretary showed me into his office, a bookish
room one wall of which was covered with his various degrees.
There I was greeted by the man himself. He was of medium
height, Latin American in appearance, and wore a thin mustache. His presentation was energetic and forthright. He
spoke with an accent but was perfectly fluent in English. After
the initial introductions, he sat down behind his desk and
leaned forward.

"How long have you had this problem?" He didn't go in
for small talk, nor did he want to discuss the obvious. After
all, I was sitting there in a dress.

"All my life," I answered.

"Silicone?" He pointed to my breasts.

"No, estrogens."

"How long have you wanted to be a woman?"

"All my life."

"Do you shave?"

"No, electrolysis."

"Did you want to be a woman when you were a child?"

"All my life." I realized that he was asking this same question over and over each time in slightly altered form.

"Do you live as a woman?"

"In my personal life, of course."

"And you've wanted to be a woman all your life?"

"All my life."

He stared at me intensely for about three minutes. His gaze swept over every part of my body. He held his eyes for short periods on my breasts, my face, my loop earrings, my lap, my legs, my feet, my hands. Finally, he reared back in his chair and locked his hands behind his head. "Look," he said, staring over my head, "I'm a surgeon. You come from a reputable psychiatrist who says you should have this operation. I agree with him, so I'll do it." I nearly fell off the chair. Was this man actually offering to do the deed? "You will?" I said lamely. He didn't bother to answer.

"Step into the examining room," he said brusquely, indicating a door at the rear of the office. I preceded him and was heading toward the examining table when he said, "Lift up that skirt." I stopped and turned around. Were there to be no formalities? He stood expectantly. I stepped out of my panties and, like a child playing doctor, raised the dress to display my privates. Dr. Granato grabbed my penis and pulled until I said, "Ouch!" "It is very small," he mused. "You are a tall girl and need a good-sized vagina. I will have to do a skin graft." He dropped it and grabbed my testicles. "Humph! These are shrunken. They are good for nothing." I agreed. Dr. Granato straightened up and motioned me back into the office. We talked for a few minutes more.

"I want it done in the next few days," I said. He looked amused.

"I have a waiting list that goes six months into the future."

"I've been waiting ten years," I said. "Besides, I've taken the month of August off to work on a medical text. It will be a perfect cover."

"I'll tell you what, Dr. Raskind, you call me tomorrow, Thursday, and meanwhile I'll see if I can arrange for hospital admission on Sunday and surgery on Monday." Without waiting for my thanks, he hopped up and escorted me to the door. "Yes, yes, yes, Renée. I know, I'm happy to do it. Call me tomorrow."

When I called, he had done as he said he would. The operation was on. I went to his office that afternoon for a more thorough checkup. He gave me antibiotics to start taking and instructions that included daily scrubbings in my genital area with a germicidal soap. He tried to convince me to use my Blue Cross–Blue Shield coverage to pay for the operation; I refused, insisting that I be as anonymous as possible. Actually, I wished that I could use the insurance, because the divorce, alimony, and child support payments had pretty much cleaned me out. I had to borrow thirty-five hundred dollars from friends to pay for the operation.

I signed only one document with my real name. This was the paper giving Dr. Granato consent to change my sex through surgery. Others I had seen used euphemisms like "sex reassignment." The one I signed said at the top: "Permission for sex change." I did like his style, no bullshit. I asked him if he considered it a big operation.

"Do you want me to describe the technique?"

"No, I just want a general idea."

"Generally, it's a hell of an operation. You'll be on the table four hours. Some patients cruise right through. Others have a rough time. You're a physician. You know that anything can happen. I'll get you a journal article reprint." He rummaged in a file cabinet and handed me a folder that I put in my purse. "I'll see you on Monday. By the way, you look terrific!" With this little stroke he dismissed me. Later that evening I took out the reprint and leafed through it. Strangely, I had never delved into the medical minutiae of the operation, though I was thoroughly familiar with the general procedure. When I came to the color-photograph plates showing the surgical steps, I couldn't retain my professional objectivity. The lurid pinks and reds jumped out of the page at me; it was all so wet and raw and bloody. I recoiled, put the article away, and have not looked at it since. I gave thanks that I was an ophthalmologist and worked in the clarity of the eye, where there was no such carnage.

I spent the couple of days before Sunday at a beach house I had rented. I couldn't believe that the monumental change would take place in seventy-two hours. This speed was a professional courtesy—doctor to doctor. Ironically, the feature of my life that had scared my colleagues off for so many years was now responsible for the incredible speed of the climax. During these two days I had a houseguest at the beach, my cousin Patrice. I had originally intended to go into the hospital without a word to any of my friends or relatives; however, as I passed time with Patrice and secretly anticipated the occasion to come, I felt drawn to her. In part, I suppose it was simply that she was there, and I clung to her for companionship. On the other hand, she had been close to me in the past and had a reputation in the family for sensitivity. I'd known her since childhood and had confided in her at times in the past, though I had never told her about my transsexualism. Finally, just before I left to spend Saturday night at my Manhattan apartment, I told her what I was about to do. She listened calmly and gave me no arguments; I swore her to secrecy and told her that, if she hadn't heard from me in three days, she should start calling the hospitals. I didn't tell her where I would be or the name of my surgeon. I didn't want to be vulnerable if she couldn't keep the news to herself. As it turned out, she was as good as her word, and I was unmolested.

On Sunday, I checked into the Physicians' Hospital in Queens. I used the name Renée Frick in tribute to Josh and listed my occupation as "writer." This step was doubly necessary since my father, who had practiced medicine in Queens for forty years, was a personal friend of the physicians who owned the hospital. If the unusual name "Raskind" had appeared on any admission documents, it would almost certainly have come to their attention. Ms. Frick was conveyed to a private room. In transsexual operations a private room and private-duty nurses are required for the first forty-eight hours, postoperative. Thereafter the patient may be moved to a semiprivate room under the care of the usual nursing staff. I had made arrangements for a private room all the way. After forty years of buildup I was not about to skimp on the trimmings.

[. . .]

While I was asleep Dr. Granato plied his trade. First he made an incision extending from the base of the penis down to about an inch above the anus. It was extended inward toward the area that was to become the vagina. Blood vessels were clamped, muscles dissected, and specialized structures like the urethra and erogenous tissue were prepared for future use. Extraneous structures like the vas deferens and seminal vesicles were excised. The vaginal cavity was formed by moving aside the structures occupying that space. Luckily, there is plenty of room in the body cavity for such relocation. My penis was denuded of skin and the useless leftover tissue discarded. The penile skin, along with a skin graft from my right thigh, was fashioned around a plastic mold. This form was placed in the vaginal cavity and sutured in place. My testicles were removed and the skin comprising the scrotum was used to create the vaginal labia. The urethra and nerve tissue were secured in their proper locations. The most sensitive erotic matter was located in precisely the same place as a woman's clitoris, so that my sexual sensations would parallel as much as possible a normal woman's. Packing was placed around the mold in the vagina and a catheter inserted in my urethra. During the operation I was given two units of whole blood.

The whole procedure, including the skin graft from the outer thigh of my right leg, took three and a half hours. I regained consciousness in the recovery room about twenty minutes after they had finished. The first thing I was aware of was that I could not stop shaking. It was as if my whole body had been seized by a racking chill; I was clattering like a box of marbles. It might have been simple shock or a by-product of my emergence from the anesthesia. I only knew that I was out of control; the nurse was alternately wiping my body with dry towels and checking my blood pressure, which—I found out later—was very low. My awareness of the shaking was almost immediately replaced by an overwhelming awareness of pain. My torso was afflicted with several different kinds. Sharp, shooting pains of searing intensity came from my now nonexistent penis and testicles. It was as if someone were repeatedly poking a firebrand into my groin. Mixed with this was a tearing sensation; it was as though someone were ripping at my organs with a pair of pliers. Underneath these sharp aspects was a dull, sickish ache such as you might have if someone had beaten you with a baseball bat in the area of your lower back. Beneath the ache was a pervasive sense of pressure, as if something inside me were enlarging, pushing outward.

It was a blessing that I was in shock; that helped to buffer my reaction to the crushingly intense flood of pain. Had I been more aware, I surely would have passed out. In spite of these incredible sensations, my mind did shift to the fact I was now a woman—and not once did I wish I hadn't done it. There was no remorse in spite of the suffering. In a way the pain seemed appropriate. It cast an intense atmosphere around a momentous occasion. Even the phantom pain in my penis was a consolation because I knew that it came from a thing that was gone from me. In a way this pain was Richard Henry Raskind's death throe. Even so, I would gladly have taken some Demerol to kill the pain, but this is not possible for anyone in shock because it might further lower an already low blood pressure. Added to this bath of suffering was my dawning realization that I might be having a transfusion reaction that could be fatal. I was afraid, and this fear fused with the pain. I wished that I didn't know so damn much medicine. It wasn't fair that I should be afflicted by this cruel understanding when I could only lie helplessly awaiting the outcome. Finally, they gave me an injection, and I passed out.

I don't mean to give myself airs about this pain. As a doctor I've attended people who were so racked with pain that they couldn't eat, sleep, or defecate. These are life's real sufferers, not Dick Raskind on the day his penis got knocked off. Still, this is my story and that was my pain, the worst I've ever felt. It was bad, but I asked for it, embraced it. I'm glad I felt it because it constitutes a personal testament: it showed me that I was right in becoming Renée. If ever there was an opportunity for regret it came when I was quaking in the recovery room, yet that opportunity was not seized. At that moment I realized that I would rather have died in the attempt than live any longer in a nightmare of duality.

Sometime later that day I awoke again and found that the pain had diminished somewhat. I had tubes sticking out of many of the natural orifices in my body; and out of one unnatural orifice. I had an IV bottle hooked up to each arm, a catheter in my bladder, an oxygen tube in my nose, and a plastic cylinder in my vagina. At least I had no nasogastric tube; that was a small consolation. I tried to move and received a shock of pain between my legs. It felt like someone had plunged a knife in to the hilt. I coughed in reaction to that sensation and felt the same pain again. I made a mental note: no moving and no coughing. This left me with a limited repertoire of amusements. Blessedly, my nurse was good. She sat beside me, constantly wiping my forehead and massaging my body. Her attentions made my immobility bearable; from time to time I'd risk moving my head to the right so that I could smile thankfully at her. The rest of the time I stared at the ceiling or closed my eyes and tried to guess which tube they'd take out first. Dr. Granato came by for a minute to say that everything had gone fine.

The next day was better. I could rotate a little from one side of my back to the other; and I could move my knees a little without the old knife in the groin. I still couldn't cough, though. They took the oxygen tube out of my nose, and that made me feel more human, leaving only four tubes still sticking out of me. I drank some juice and some tea. One sign that I was getting better was my irritation over the placement of the IV containing an antibiotic. They had stuck it in my left arm and it burned. Didn't they know that my left arm was my tennis arm, worth its weight in gold? On the fourth day the pain had diminished to the point where I was encouraged to get up. The philosophy after major surgery is to get the patient ambulating as quickly as possible. It seems to facilitate healing and prevents too much loss of strength from extended bed rest. Needless to say, I didn't look forward to it, but I went along with the doctor's recommendation. I stood up, passed out, and was caught by a strong nurse just before I hit the floor. When I woke up, I was back in bed. Later in the day Dr. Granato breezed in. "How do you feel?" he asked, flashing a cheerful smile.

"You must be crazy," I answered uncooperatively. I had no stomach at that point for a cheerful bedside manner. Dr. Granato pulled down the covers and lifted my hospital gown.

"Let's see what we've got here or, more accurately, what we don't got here." I wondered how often he'd made that joke. I guessed about one hundred and fifty-seven times. He removed the bandage, tinkered around down there for a few long moments, then glanced up at me. "Look here!" he waved his hand to present the area between my legs.

"I can't get into a position where I can see it," I said lamely.

"Nonsense. Don't you have a mirror?" He spotted a little stand-up mirror on a shelf over the basin. "There's one." He grabbed it and proudly lined up the reflection so that I could see it. What I saw was essentially what I had seen so many times between the legs of the women with whom I'd been intimate—a normal-looking introitus but incredibly distinctive because it was mine. I had the doctor hold the mirror at all angles so that I could see it from every possible perspective. My pubic area had been shaved for the operation, so I had a clear view of all the structures, the clearest I've ever had; there were not even any sutures visible. Dr. Granato stood by like a proud father, obviously relishing my delight. Finally, I laid my head back on the pillow.

"I was afraid to look."

"I know," he said, "that's why I made you." He smiled smugly and asked a needless question. "How do you like it?"

"Fine," I said. I'm sure he knew that it was an understatement.

On the fifth day I was lifted out of bed for a sitz bath and collapsed again in the bathroom. In a way this represented progress because it took me a lot longer to faint than it did the day before. Things started to get gray and continued until everything was gray. Not so much a blackout as a grayout. Otherwise I was doing pretty well. I was drinking more fluids, having worked my way up to diet soft drinks. The pain, though much decreased, was still substantial. One of the most distressing things about it was that it was no longer directly associated with any particular structure in my body. My phantom penis pain had had only a brief life on Monday following the operation. It had soon been replaced by an unlocalized burning and tearing sensation. It didn't emanate from the vaginal area; it was just down there somewhere. It was tremendously disconcerting to have big pain and not be able to pinpoint the source. After the fifth day, though, it rapidly diminished. As the major pain began to slack off, I started to feel pain in the portion of my thigh used for the skin graft. I wondered how I would explain the scar: Maybe I had slid into third base? No, that wouldn't do. A burn from a barbecue grill? It was a possibility. The one I liked best was that I had scraped it on a rusty tennis court fence while chasing a wide backhand return. As it turned out none of these fabrications was necessary. The scar is hardly visible.

With the lessening of the pain, I became a bit crankier. "Why don't you get that ten-inch plastic prick out of me?" I asked Dr. Granato irritably. "It's crushing my back and intestines." He explained that the offending object would come out about ten days after the operation. Meanwhile, it was sutured in to give the new tissue a mold to form itself around. Inside me, skin segments from my penis and my thigh were working together—knitting a vagina, as it were. And this cooperative effort was not the only miracle being wrought. This skin, which had been dry and a little leathery while in contact with the air, was adapting itself to internal life, taking on a mucous quality. This change would result in my vagina being moist, and would eliminate the possibility that any of the tissue might grow together. During the healing process, my body would generate connective tissue that would further strengthen this hardy, adaptable, and accommodating skin.

By Saturday I was off Demerol completely, and my head cleared noticeably. The discomfort, though still there, was easily bearable. I ate three hearty meals and walked in the hall for exercise. I read, wrote, and watched a tennis match on television. Most significantly, I put on a little eye makeup and some lip gloss. From my years in medicine, I know that this is a sure sign that a woman in the hospital is getting well. On Monday the doctor removed the packing around my vagina but left the tube in. This relieved some of the pressure and made me feel a lot better. On Tuesday I was released from the hospital. I spent a couple of days at my apartment in the city before I went to Dr. Granato's office for a checkup. He removed the tube and examined me; there were a few places where the skin had grown together. These adhesions had to be severed, so he gave me an injection of painkiller in my newly formed genitalia; it hurt like hell. Already, I was experiencing an increased sense of vulnerability in the vaginal area. I felt rather demure as I was examined and manipulated by the doctor. At length, he gave me a clean bill of health, and I drove out to the beach, where I planned to recuperate.

When I arrived there I called Andy, since I hadn't talked to him for over a week; he was chatty and full of life. I felt no strain as a result of my transformation. Naturally, he called me Daddy, as he had before and as he continues to do to this day. At the time of my operation he was only three and a half years old. My plan was to continue relating to him as a father until he was old enough to understand. The operation made no real difference in my appearance, and if he had accepted me up to then he could surely continue to do so. Even after he was told, I didn't expect that our relationship would change. I would always be his daddy; but, at the time of this first call from the beach, that particular problem was several years away. As I talked to him I felt happy in a way that I had not felt immediately following the operation. Since waking up after the operation I had been struggling with the problems of recovery and didn't have much of a chance to feel euphoric. Even when the realization had thoroughly pressed itself on me, I felt no particular elation. I just felt like Renée, the person I knew I had been all along; however, when I heard Andy's lyrical laughter I realized how complete my life now was. I had myself; I had my son. Things had finally turned out well, and I was happy. Thereafter, I called Andy every day.

The rest of the time I spent recuperating. I slept a lot and rarely left the house for more than an hour at a time. I continued to take antibiotics for a few days after being released from the hospital, but then I required no more medication. It was just a short while, three days or so, before I dispensed with the bandage between my legs. Actually, my instructions from Dr. Granato were quite simple. I had to do two things to promote healing. First, I periodically sat in a tub of hot water laced with salt. I wasn't allowed to use soap in my genital area for a couple of weeks. The second instruction resulted in an amusing activity. I had been told that the sun's rays would be beneficial, so every day I lay in my secluded backyard presenting my newly formed anatomy to the sun. Somehow this seemed right; it smacked of some ancient ritual, as if this were Renée's introduction to the cosmos.

Another of Dr. Granato's instructions did not deal with healing so much as it did maintenance. He had supplied me with what he referred to as a dilator. This looked like nothing so much as a crudely made dildo; it is a cylindrical piece of white, rubberlike material about ten inches long. The business end tapers like a sharpened pencil but has no point; it's just lopped off bluntly. The other end sports a squarish knob that looks like it has been whittled. I guess this texturized effect is supposed to give the user a good surface to grip. The doctor told me to use this thing frequently to keep the channel open and to discourage it from shrinking. By "using it," he meant that I was supposed to insert the device and slide it in and out. Before you get a picture of me ecstatically working away with this thing, let me say that I never got a second's sexual pleasure out of it. First of all, it's too hard and, even though it's only a bit over an inch in diameter, it always feels uncomfortably big. During the first couple of months that I used the dilator, it would often come out stained with pinkish blood. Nonetheless, I faithfully continued and often slept with it inside me as I was instructed. Even now if I go through a period of extended sexual inactivity, I use my dilator.

During my first few days on the beach, my cousin Patrice came and stayed with me. I had called her from the hospital once I was coherent, to let her know that I was all right. As my only confidante, she felt rather protective and played nurse through the early period of my convalescence. Actually, aside from Dr. Granato, she was the first of my friends or relatives to see me dressed as a woman after I had finally made the grade—from an anatomical standpoint. She even went with me on a shopping expedition to a secondhand store, where I bought a pair of tight jeans. I remember feeling elated at the unbroken curve of my pubic area; nothing remained to be tied down or jammed up. Patrice agreed that I looked good.

By the end of my month's leave I was pretty well healed. Naturally, there were residual effects; it was a long time before I was as strong as I was before the operation. I had also been forbidden to have sex for at least six weeks. Just to be on the safe side I waited three months, resigning myself to a lengthy virginity.

Meanwhile, the doctor's warning did not keep me from doing a little sexual experimenting without a partner. I could tell right away that there was one big sexual difference between Dick and Renée. Dick had been very inhibited about his body, one might even say a bit prudish. He didn't enjoy touching his sexual parts, and he didn't enjoy having them touched. I conclude that this was a symptom of his ambivalence toward them. Renée, however, had no such ambivalence. She couldn't keep her hands off herself. I don't mean to give the impression that I was embarrassing people in public or anything like that, but finding out whether I was in good erotic working order was a high-priority item. In the first couple of weeks after the operation I was too knocked out generally and too tender specifically to do much investigating. Then again, my erogenous areas had just been sewn in, and I didn't want to risk disturbing the relocation process. I tried to remain businesslike as I looked after myself, but I discovered that erectile tissue is extremely hardy stuff. It took to its new home in a most wholehearted way. My overall contentment probably helped a lot, too. A satisfied patient is a fast-healing patient.

Whatever the reason, it wasn't long before I began to get interesting tingling sensations from my clitoral area as I went about my daily routine of self-care. Once I got past the salty sitz bath stage, for example, I could gently wash myself in the pubic area. To my delight, this excited me; little stabs of sensation originated in the area. Whatever I'd gotten in the past from down there had been associated with a penis. This was different though recognizably sexual. It wasn't as pointed; it seemed generalized yet definitely was associated with my new clitoris. I thought that this confusing vagueness might simply be the result of my unfamiliarity with the new ground rules. After all, stuff had been moved around down there. On the other hand there was less tissue than before and maybe that meant a vaguer sensation. In those early stages, though, I was not inclined to overanalyze, much less to quibble. It was a relief to know that I could feel something and that it was pleasurable.

Those first nudges were indirect, the result of nonsexual activities. Gradually, as the days went by, these little flares kept bursting with greater intensity and soon demanded concentrated attention. I proceeded carefully, avoiding direct contact with the point of sensation but massaging the soft areas around my clitoris. It was indirect, but compared to the random washing movements that had excited me before, was highly focused. It was slightly higher than where my penis had been located; the one big difference was that there was no sense of projection. The sexy feelings (and by now they were intense) were more associated with the main flesh of my body. The tendency to thrust was lessened. I felt more inclined than ever to receive, to be moved toward rather than to aggress. As I continued to rub myself, the intensity of sensation grew higher. The buildup was slow, and the sensation remained more general, though it definitely strengthened and took shape as if working toward a peak of some kind. I grew more vigorous and occasionally my hand or one of my fingers would slip into direct contact with my clitoris. There was no pain or discomfort when this took place, so I felt less tentative and let it happen more often. As I went higher, I began to perceive a climax. The peculiar awareness of a finish, a final push, a barrier to be broken, loomed ahead. There is no way to adequately describe that moment when I knew for certain that I would make it.

For most people it's a given, but for Renée it was a magic place; it was almost as important as the orgasm itself—that came quickly on the heels of that instant of comprehension. It was not as well defined as a man's orgasm. The moment of ejaculation, the clear-cut pumping of semen that is so entwined with the male orgasm, was missing. This climax was more rounded, less intense but longer-lasting, and especially gratifying in the warm sensations that flooded me and that continued to do so for some time. More than anything else it reminded me of those peculiar dreams I had experienced during my trip to Europe. I would awaken at a moment of sexual climax and find my ineffectual man's genitals responding as if with a long-

lasting, low-key vibration. This sensation, though not cli-
mactic, had been intensely pleasurable. My first orgasm as a
woman took me beyond this rudimentary response, but there
was definitely an echo of it. As I lay there regaining my composure, I noticed that my vagina was wet, and I marveled
that in this regard too, I was a woman. Over the next few weeks
my ability to become excited and to give myself orgasms
improved. I went through a period of shameless preoccupation
with autoeroticism. This was as much a testimony to my relief
at having my sexuality intact as it was to lasciviousness, though
there was plenty of the latter.

[...]

About three months after my operation I attended a medical conference in Dallas, Texas. Even though I'd have to dress
as a male, I looked forward to this trip because I knew that I'd
be meeting an important friend there. He was an ear, nose, and
throat man whose interest in me was not professional. We'd
had a little ongoing affair since before my operation. It had
been difficult because he was not only married and a father,
but a homosexual as well. His advances to me before the operation had been as a gay man, but I had seen him as a masculine
counterpoint to my femininity. Frankly, I think he enjoyed me
in spite of my female qualities rather than because of them. He
had said several times, "Renée, you don't have to get this operation on my account." I had assured him that his account had
nothing to do with my reasons for getting it.

I always insisted that he relate to me as if I were a woman.
When we made love it was in the missionary position even
though that is not the most effective arrangement for two
men. I had not had a homosexual encounter since that time
long before when Jimmy, the manager of the Satin Slipper,
had taken me to bed. I had made the same proviso then with

regard to our lovemaking position. The one big change was that this time I was able to enjoy the experience. Being entered anally was still no real fun, though I got so that I could grin and bear it. No, the enjoyable part was having a sizable man on top of me. I liked the weight of him and the feeling of his strength when he thrust against me. Most of all, I loved his open expression of pleasure. I got a real sense of satisfaction out of being the object of his desire and knowing that my qualities were the source of his stimulation. I didn't care that it was partly my masculinity that turned him on. All I cared about was that he enjoyed me, whatever the terms.

I looked forward to the time when we could make love in a way that was even more fulfilling—when I would be a woman. So, in Dallas, we climbed the stairs to my hotel room, where I made that dream come true. It was a peculiar moment; this dear friend was gay, and I had fixed it so that he had to go straight. I know his emotions were mixed. He did really like me, and it wasn't as if he couldn't make it with a woman. On the other hand, I had heretofore been a refreshing change of pace. Now I was more like what he was getting at home. Outwardly, he remained unchanged; in fact, he was very kind. If he felt ambivalent he kept it to himself out of deference to me, since, in a way, he was deflowering Renée.

If I'm a little vague on his attitude, it's because this moment was something that I had looked forward to with a mixture of anticipation and dread. I knew from my experiments in self-stimulation that I could respond sexually, but putting the new equipment to work under field conditions was another matter. Suppose I found out that it didn't respond or, worse yet, that I didn't like it as much as I thought I would? Suppose I was a flop as a lover?

I was positively demure as I unveiled my new body; I even asked for the lights to be out. Daryl came over to me and helped me take off my clothes. He was taller than I and heavier too. I felt comfortable in his arms, and as he kissed me I could feel the raspy texture of his five-o'clock shadow. These masculine features were strangely comforting, and I relaxed as he guided me to the bed. He was in good shape himself, an athlete, too, of course. I could feel the various muscles of his back when he covered me with his body. There wasn't too much in the way of preliminaries that first time; both of us were nervous. He came into me, and it felt right. There was no pain, no discomfort of any kind. I had a sensation of fullness, and when he began to move in and out I knew it was going to be fine. There was no weakness or sense of artificiality about my genitals—they were sound. The firm fleshiness of Daryl's penis was in wonderful contrast to the inhuman qualities of the dilator and, though the motions were similar, the sexual response lacking in my therapy came flooding through my body when that warm extension of Daryl entered me. Tremendously exciting also were his encompassing size, the smell of him, his hairiness, and his weight pressing down on me. I had experienced all these before but never in combination with a woman's sexual response. That first time he finished quickly, and I loved that as well. I was warmed by his sense of urgency and the forceful thrusts that accompanied his climax. I didn't have an orgasm myself; in fact, I didn't come near one that time or any other time for several months. Nonetheless, I loved it. I was at last fully capable of the woman's role. I could have been content for the rest of my life with that satisfaction alone.

MY STORY

Caroline Cossey

1991

Caroline Cossey, a.k.a. Tula, was born Barry Cossey in England. A successful model and dancer, she was one of the James Bond girls in For Your Eyes Only *and posed nude for Play-boy in 1982.*

Chapter 14

THE SHOOT was in Corfu, and we were given a great press send-off. There were eight "Bond girls" of all nationalities, colors, shapes and sizes. I knew several of them from previous modeling assignments, so it was not as if I were joining a group of complete strangers. Despite the fact that we were really nothing more than glorified extras employed to decorate the set, we were given star treatment on the plane and were put up in a comfortable family hotel.

We were there for two weeks only, and much of that time was spent waiting for the right light. Filming is a slow, laborious process, and each shot takes forever to set up. But the sun shone and the company was good.

I was in two scenes, but my performance was hardly memorable. It was a case of "don't blink or you'll miss me!" I remember being asked to walk around a swimming pool, dressed in a bikini, and then scream. So I walked and I screamed and everyone seemed more than happy.

I got on well with Roger Moore. Three other girls, the producer, the director and I all had dinner with him one evening. We ate great Greek food, drank retsina and ouzo, and even tried a little ethnic dancing. He is a very easy man to like— unaffected, humorous and friendly.

While I was in Corfu, I was introduced to a representative of *Playboy,* who asked me if I would be interested in doing some shots. I told her that it would very much depend on what sort of shots.

"I want to get away from nude modeling. But I'd happily do swimwear or even topless, if it's tastefully done."

She assured me that that would be possible, and I instructed her to get in touch with my agent to negotiate a fee.

When I returned to London, Yvonne told me that *Playboy* had rung. They were doing a fashion spread in Guadaloupe, and were short of a model. They thought that if they used me for the spread, they could combine that with the publicity shots for the Bond picture. It was a smart idea, and I agreed.

Guadaloupe was everyone's idea of the perfect West Indian island. With its white beaches, palm trees and blue, blue ocean, it seemed like paradise on earth. Unfortunately the shoot was nowhere near as idyllic. The photographer wanted to shock the eye with contrast, so he positioned me dressed in finely sculpted, elegant clothes against the backdrop of a stinking, tumbledown market. I stood staring enigmatically into the lens whilst chickens struggled in hessian sacks and fish flapped around in buckets of filthy water. A group of locals gathered around us and stared openmouthed in disbelief.

Two days later we traveled up into the forest for the Bond pictures. There, surrounded by huge green plants, I was photographed perched on a rock in the middle of a fast-flowing and icy river. Up above in the sunlight flocks of exotic birds were calling to each other as they flew from tree to tree. It could have been the Garden of Eden were it not for the mosquitoes. When I returned to the hotel that night I counted a total of eighty-seven bites on my body.

I arrived back in London full of travelers' tales and longing to speak to my parents. But when I phoned home I got a nasty shock. Dad came on the line: "You won't believe what I'm going to tell you," he said.

I guessed it could only be bad news. Things had been going so well, and I had had the feeling my luck couldn't last.

"What is it?" I asked.

"That bastard Rankine from the *News of the World* has been snooping around the village again, asking questions."

I listened in silence while he told me what had happened. This time they hadn't stopped at my family, but had been questioning neighbors, my old schoolteachers, and even the boys I'd been at school with.

"They've got some photos of you, shots with the hair touched out, and they've been showing them to all sorts of people, asking them if they recognize you."

"Has anyone said anything?" I asked, feeling my heart pounding with terror.

"I don't think so," he said. "One bloke told him that you were effeminate as a kid, but most have kept quiet."

"Have they been asking you and Mum what all the fuss is about?"

"We've had a few letters from neighbors saying that they're sorry we're being given such a hard time. But most people don't know what to think. I suppose they feel awkward about it."

"Oh, Dad," I said, beginning to cry. "I'm sorry to have caused you all this trouble."

"Don't you worry about it," he reassured me. "All that matters to me is your happiness."

Later Mum told me that Rankine had been back to the garage, asking to talk to Mr. Cossey, but his boss had told him that Dad wasn't there. "But then he thought that Rankine might come to the house and question me," she said. "Your dad didn't want that, so he went out and caught him just as he was getting into his car. He gave him a piece of his mind, and now he's worried that he's done the wrong thing and shouldn't have got angry."

"Tell him he did what was right, and he's not to give it another moment's thought."

I felt terrible for my family. These journalists were placing them in an impossible position. Terry rang. He had been approached again and had been offered money for "an inside story."

"I feel like killing the bastards," he told me.

"Try to forget all about it," I said.

It was good advice I gave, but I couldn't follow it myself. I had been looking forward to going to the premiere of *For Your Eyes Only* at Leicester Square, but with the *News of the World* back on the trail, I knew I couldn't risk it. I accepted a job in Rome, and told the publicity people that I would be out of the country.

The Rome job shifted to Sardinia. The photographer chose some fantastic locations and I should have enjoyed the work. But I was sick with worry, and rang Pam every day to see if the story had been printed. Everything stayed quiet. It seemed that once again they had lost interest.

Two months passed, and I returned to Rome on another assignment. Late one afternoon, walking back to my hotel and enjoying the warm sunshine, I felt more relaxed than I had in a long time. *Perhaps things really will work out for me,* I thought.

As I walked through the foyer, the receptionist called: "There's an urgent message for you. You must call home immediately."

"The news isn't good, I'm afraid," Pam said when I rang.

"What's happened?"

"Yvonne has had a call from the *News of the World.* They say that they are going to print a story on you, and they asked her if she would like to comment."

Pam said that Yvonne had denied everything, told them I was out of the country, and then disappeared for the weekend.

I caught the next available flight to London, arriving at Heathrow on Sunday morning, the day the article was due to appear. I rushed to the first newsstand I saw and bought a copy of the paper. There was nothing in it about me.

I spent the rest of that week in a state of nervous terror. On Friday the *News of the World* contacted Yvonne again. They sent her a copy of the article with an accompanying letter asking for her comments. She rang them straight back: "If it's taken you three years to come up with something as ludicrous as this, you're in the wrong job. That article is laughable."

She was convinced they were bluffing, and when another Sunday came and went and there was still nothing in print, I began to hope that she was right. Then, in the middle of the third week, Rankine himself called and asked to speak to Caroline Cossey. As I took the phone I was shaking from head to toe, but I was determined to keep any tremor out of my voice.

"Have you read the draft of the article?" he asked.

I told him I had and found it utterly ridiculous.

"Caroline," he said. "Be sensible. The piece *will* appear. If you give us an exclusive, or even just a quote or two, you'll be able to exert some control over how your story is told."

I fought to keep my temper. "You go right ahead and print. Your story is garbage and so are you. I have nothing whatsoever to say to you. But if that article appears you'll be hearing from my solicitor first thing on Monday morning. I hope you can afford it." I put the phone down.

On the next two Saturday nights I took a taxi down to Leicester Square to pick up the early editions of the tabloids. I sat in the back of the taxi leafing through the papers, my heart in my mouth, searching for the headline. It was over a month since the first threat of publication, and still nothing had appeared.

"They haven't got enough evidence to go to print," my friends reassured me. "The story isn't coming from you, and without you there isn't a story."

I began to relax. And then, the next Sunday, it happened.

JAMES BOND GIRL WAS A BOY

The headline hit me like a slap across the face. There beside the article was a picture of me wearing a £1,500 chinchilla bikini that I had modeled three years previously. They had done it. Despite what they must have known it would do to me and my family, they had printed their article. And in the name of what? Surely not news. How could my very personal and private struggle merit coverage in a national paper? "The people have a right to know," one journalist told me. *What right?* I thought as I stared at that paper. *What right does anyone have to hound another human being, to harass their family, to ruin their career, to take away a dignity that was so hard-won?* That story wasn't news. It didn't help people to live better lives; it didn't enable them to understand current affairs, or make sense of British politics. I wasn't even a criminal whose misdemeanors should be held up for all to see. I had hurt no one, and now felt that my life was in tatters. Everywhere I went I would be known as "Tula—the transsexual." How could I hope to establish a relationship with any man?

I needed to talk to my mum. As soon as I heard her voice I began to sob. All I could say was, "Mum, it's in." I didn't need to elaborate. She began to cry as well, and I heard her calling, "Bob!" My dad came to the phone and, speaking calmly and slowly, asked me to tell him what had happened. Between sobs I explained. "They've done it, Dad. They've printed the article."

"Where's Pam?" he asked. "Is she with you?"

But Pam was still asleep. "Go and wake her up," said Dad. "I need to speak to her."

By now I was incoherent with grief. I could say no more and I put the phone down. Stumbling into the bathroom, I locked the door behind me and then sank down onto the floor, my head in my hands. At that moment I felt I couldn't possibly go on. The thought of having to face all those people, of having to answer questions, of being laughed at, despised, misunderstood, made me frantic with grief. An overdose seemed the only answer. In the distance I heard the phone ringing and

Pam answering. I knew she would be talking to Dad. I looked at the bottle of sleeping pills on the shelf above me. It would be an easy solution. But it was a solution that would cause my mum and dad untold suffering. They had stood by me through all this, and I couldn't let them down now.

No one who hasn't been in that situation can imagine how ashamed and frightened I felt sitting on the bathroom floor that Sunday morning. As time has gone by and I have become accustomed to interviews, articles and public curiosity, I have grown to accept the idea that my transsexuality does fascinate people. But at that time I was in no way prepared for exposure. It should have been my choice to discuss my sexuality when and if I felt ready to do so. The *News of the World* had taken that choice away from me. I felt raped, and was overwhelmed by fears and feelings I hadn't experienced in years — an awareness that I was different, a freak, someone who could never hope to lead any kind of normal life. My long struggle to achieve normality and acceptability seemed to have been for nothing. The *News of the World* had sent me right back to the nightmare of my teenage years.

The sound of Pam tapping at the door pulled me from my thoughts.

"Caroline, are you OK? Come out, sweetheart. Dad's on the phone and he wants to speak to you."

I got up slowly, went to the sink and threw some cold water on my face. Then I unlocked the door and walked to the phone.

"Now listen to me," said Dad. "I want you to come home."

"I can't, Dad. I have to sort this out for myself."

There was a silence before he spoke. "Well, OK. But I've told Pam that she and her boyfriend are to stay with you. We'll face this out together. As a family. Don't crumble. You have to fight. Remember, you're not a criminal and you've done nothing wrong. Find your anger. That'll help you through."

As time went by and the hurt turned to fury, I was better able to follow his advice. But on that Sunday I felt too devastated.

In the afternoon Pam persuaded me to go out with her. "You can't stay inside forever," she said. "There's a heat wave, so grab your bikini. We're going to Regent's Park to soak up some sun."

I remember walking to the park in a haze of tears. I couldn't stop crying. Pam and her boyfriend struggled to keep me distracted, but every time a passerby looked at me my eyes would fill.

"They're all staring at me," I muttered to Pam.

"Don't be paranoid," she said. "People always look at you. You're beautiful and that's reason enough."

In the park we lay on the grass. My head had begun to throb and I closed my eyes for a moment, trying to relax. When I opened them again there was a man standing a few feet away. He was focusing a camera on Pam and me, and was about to snap.

"They're after me," I hissed.

Pam sat up. "Don't be daft. He's not a journalist. Look at his camera. He's just a tourist taking shots of London."

"I want to go home," I said.

She could see that I was in a bad way, and we walked back to the flat. I had a small supply of Valium, and as soon as I got in I took two and fell into an uneasy sleep. The following day all the other tabloid journalists would be on my case, and I expected to be under siege. I was booked for a calendar job at the end of the week—a press launch in Leeds. Would they still want me to do the job? And, more important, would I feel able to face the cameras?

Yvonne called me first thing on Monday morning.

"The agency wants to know if you're still prepared to do the assignment. I've told them that the *News of the World* article was untrue, and they don't seem at all worried about it. What do you want to do?"

I paused for a moment, then, remembering my dad's advice, I answered: "Tell them of course I'll do it."

"Good girl. How are you feeling?"

"Not too great. I'm going to see my doctor later today."

The doctor prescribed more tranquilizers and complete rest. "Go on holiday for a week or so," she advised.

That seemed like a good suggestion, and Mum and I arranged to go to Italy for a week as soon as I returned from the Leeds job.

By Thursday I still hadn't left the flat, even though I needed to buy things for my holiday. Finally I plucked up enough courage to wander down to the local supermarket. The place was crowded and I didn't notice any reactions. My confidence began to return—until I made the mistake of calling in at the local greengrocer's.

The shop was run by a couple of London lads who had gotten to know me, and would smile and wolf-whistle whenever I walked by. This morning I was met by a cold silence. Neither of them would look me in the eye, and the one who served me asked abruptly, "What do you want?"

Not a word was said as he went through my list, but as I was leaving he made a strange remark: "Try to have a nice day." And then he laughed.

He wasn't the only one to treat me like a social leper. A neighbor of mine, a man called Gregor, had always made a point of looking up at my flat whenever he passed. It was obvious that he fancied me—both our flats had balconies, and if I went out to water the plants or sit in the sun, Gregor would always find some excuse to wander out onto his balcony. But it was also apparent that he was very shy, and I had doubted if he would ever summon up the courage to talk to me. In the end we met over a taxi—we both hailed the same cab, discovered that we were heading in the same direction, and shared the journey. I learned that he was in show business too, and we found we knew some of the same people. When he dropped me off he asked me if I'd like to have a drink with him one evening. I said I'd love to, and he promised to phone me. That had been a few days before the *News of the World* article appeared. The Thursday morning when I had returned despondent from my shopping expedition, I looked out of the window and saw Gregor walking by, his shoulders hunched and his eyes firmly fixed on the ground. It was obvious that he had read the exposé and would never phone. It wasn't a major blow, but it was yet another disappointment. *Oh, God,* I thought. *Is this how life is going to be from now on?*

I was dreading the Leeds job. What if there were journalists there? How would I cope if anyone was abusive? I traveled up on the train with a man from the agency. We had a couple of drinks together, and then I broached the subject of the press. I told him that the matter was in the hands of my solicitors, and that I didn't want to discuss it at the launch. He was very understanding and promised me that I would not be given any trouble.

But I was so nervous when I got to the hotel that my hands shook as I tried to apply a fresh coat of lipstick. I decided to phone Mum—she would give me the moral courage I needed.

"You've got nothing to be ashamed of, darling. You're a beautiful girl and a successful model, so hold your head up high. And if you start to panic, just think of me. Do it for me. I love you very much." I went down to the reception with a new resolve. No one mentioned the *News of the World,* and I calmed my nerves with alcohol. Nonetheless, I was relieved when the whole thing was over and I was sitting on the plane bound for Italy.

That week I spent in Rome with my mum gave me a chance to think about the future. It was only a matter of time before newspapers all over the world picked up on my story. It was obvious that my life would never be the same again. The exposure would have an immediate effect on my modeling career. The catalog assignments, corsetry, swimwear, which provide the staple of a model's income, were likely to dry up. I had had regular work modeling things like maternity bras and pregnancy fashion; those companies would not want to use me again. Any big campaign that brought too much publicity would also be out of the question. The moment my face was recognized, the journalists were bound to come sniffing around. Besides, the fashion world is a very gossipy one—it wouldn't take long for the story of my past to circulate.

But if I didn't stay in modeling, how was I to earn my living? I had a mortgage to pay and no other qualifications. I talked it over with Mum and she agreed that it would be best if I restricted myself to low-key work in the future.

"Perhaps if you told your side of the story," she said, "it would stop all the speculation. Then at least the agencies wouldn't feel that they had been deceived in any way."

Her suggestion made a lot of sense to me. The inaccuracies that had been printed about my life were adding to my growing sense of outrage. One magazine in Italy claimed that a boyfriend had paid for my operation; another had printed a photograph of me beside a shot of a group of schoolboys, one of whom was supposed to be Barry Cossey. In fact, the boy they'd picked out had been at the school five years before I had gone there. Most damaging of all was the constant misuse of the terms "transsexual" and "transvestite." Journalists genuinely didn't know the difference, and they seemed to feel that my transsexuality was some vast joke made at the expense of an unsuspecting public. As the days went by I felt a growing need to set the record straight. It might be too late for me, but an honest account of what it means to be born transsexual might be of tremendous value to all those people who were going through a similar experience.

I put the idea to Yvonne when I returned to England. She was very much in favor.

"I've already been approached by a number of journalists," she said. "But instead of writing a newspaper exclusive, why don't you write a book?" She told me that she had spoken to several publishers and a great deal of interest had been shown.

And so I wrote my paperback, *Tula—I am a Woman*. It was written with the help of John Goldsmith, who provided invaluable advice, and was tireless in his efforts. The book was put together at great speed, and was fueled by my sense of anger and hurt. I felt that I needed to make a statement, to help right some of the wrong that Rankine and his kind had caused. I had never wanted to stand up and be counted as a transsexual, but now that everyone knew the truth, I felt I had to put in my own plea for tolerance and understanding. *Perhaps when people read my story and look at the photographs of me, they will see that transsexual women are not freaks with stubbly faces and hairy chests,* I thought. And I do think that that book and my subsequent interviews did go some way to changing public opinion.

The book went a long way to putting me back on my feet; I was ready to speak out. But I was in no way prepared for the publicity and the promotional tour that accompanied publication. I was still remarkably naïve about the kind of rough questioning the media can come up with in pursuit of a good interview or story. The idea that everyone knew about my past had not had time to sink in. Now, when I do television shows or radio phone-ins, I can take whatever insults anyone likes to throw at me—I'm a seasoned campaigner. But at that stage I felt as though I were being fed to the lions. They were ready to make money out of me, and all I wanted to do was hide away. I decided I couldn't take it anymore and told Yvonne that I wouldn't do any more promotional work for the book. My behavior put everyone in an awkward position. But I did what I felt I had to.

I left the country and went to Italy by myself for a week, spending the days wandering along the beach. I needed time alone to do some serious thinking. I decided that now that I had made a public statement, in the shape of a book, I wasn't prepared to talk any more about my transsexuality. I had done my bit and I was ready to return to anonymity. I would accept only those assignments that would safeguard my privacy.

I resolved to change agents. Yvonne had been as kind, as lovely and as helpful as she possibly could have been. She was excellent at her job. But I felt that by turning down so many offers of work, I was proving to be a real disappointment. I wanted to make a complete break with the past. When I returned to England I explained how I felt. She was very understanding: "I wish you all the luck in the world, Caroline. If you ever want to come back, I'd be more than happy to represent you again."

I found myself a new agency, Take Two. I established with them from the very beginning that I wanted to pick and choose: no glamour, nothing with major publicity, and as much high fashion as possible. It is possible for models to work in very low-profile jobs and still make a living, and Take Two was prepared to find me the right assignments.

There was only one thing left that I had to do, and that was to return to Brooke and face the neighbors. Brooke was still my home, and I was determined that the *News of the World* wouldn't rob me of that security. Mum and Dad had already broken the news of my operation to the rest of the family. When the press harassment was at its worst, they had decided that they must protect the relatives from any determined journalists.

"Don't worry about what they think," Dad had said. "They're all a hundred percent behind you."

It wasn't easy going back, and I did feel apprehensive. But I had my family's support, and with that I felt I could face anything. In the end everybody was incredibly nice. I was never made to feel awkward, but was welcomed back as though nothing had changed. Even the lads who had teased me as a boy would stop to say hello!

I went around to my nan's house to see her and Uncle Brian. It was a difficult reunion, and I think they felt as tense as I did. Nanny made a cup of tea, and we all sat around the table making polite conversation. She wanted to know about my life as a model, the places I had been, the people I had seen. As I talked I sensed that they weren't really taking it in; they were so busy accustoming themselves to my new appearance. It must have been a real shock. But it didn't take them long to relax, and soon I found myself cracking jokes about my situation. Even Uncle Brian, who had worried about my effeminacy when I was a child, behaved brilliantly.

"I expect you're every bit as nervous as me," he said when he saw me as a woman for the first time. He was very complimentary about my looks, and it was great to see him again.

Tolerance and understanding came from the unlikeliest of places. The men at Dad's garage were magnificently supportive. One of his mates came up to him and congratulated him on having such a lovely daughter.

"I think she's been given a really tough time," he said. "And I'd like you to know that I admire her bravery and determination. She's a stunning girl." Dad had always feared the reactions his workmates might have, and nothing could have made him happier than hearing that heartfelt and unrehearsed speech.

As I walked across the fields that weekend, and enjoyed the peace and tranquillity of the Norfolk countryside, I felt clearheaded and resolute. I had faced the worst and survived. I would continue to earn my money as a model, and try to live a life of some dignity. I wished to be left alone, untroubled by media interest. *I've taken enough from them,* I thought. My greatest hope at that moment was to find a man who would love and accept me for what I was. Little did I know it, but that dream was to cost me dear.

Chapter 20

MY WEDDING. A day I had so often dreamed about in those distant times when Pam and I had watched the brides all in white being showered with a storm of confetti outside our local church before climbing into their chauffeur-driven cars and heading off to a life of romance and luxury. They seemed then like princesses from a fairy tale. Time and experience had taught me that reality did not consist entirely of long pale dresses and a happily-ever-after. But I had never stopped believing in romance. Nor in the dream of marriage. My parents had loved each other all their married lives, and, to me, marriage seemed the right and proper destiny of love.

It was May 21, a hot day blessed with an incredibly blue sky. A car came to pick up my mum and me and take us to the Savoy, stopping off en route to pick up my wedding dress, which had had to be altered yet again. I was shaking with nerves, but I was also strangely excited. Seeing the cloudless sky and the beauty of the city in the early-morning light, I felt that nothing could harm me. *It's going to be all right,* I thought.

When we arrived at the hotel, Mum and I were shown to a double room where we could change and leave our belongings. Mrs. Fattal had booked the bridal suite for Elias and me, but that was to be left untouched until after we were married. I went downstairs and spoke to the florist and she showed me my bouquet and the flower arrangements for the reception. I was too distracted to absorb what she said.

Mum helped me change and wove my hair into a French plait. Then I climbed into my dress. It was fastened at the back by scores of tiny silk-covered buttons, and I stood waiting patiently for each one to be done up. Then I put my headdress on. I had two large and beautiful orchids at either side of my head, and a veil that covered my face. Even I had to admit that it looked stunning. I wore ballet shoes, as I didn't want to tower over Elias, and silk underwear bought by my mother. I had a necklace borrowed from Diana, and a blue garter from Pam over one of my stockings.

"You look like a dream, darling," said my mother.

The ceremony was to take place in the Upper Berkeley Street synagogue, and my brother, dressed in top hat and tails, came to pick me up in an old chauffeur-driven Rolls. As we passed through the streets of London I fell silent. I had never felt so nervous in my entire life. Terry gave my hand a squeeze.

"You look beautiful," he said.

Beautiful or not, I was dying for a cigarette. I fished one out of the little clutch purse I had with me.

"You're not allowed to smoke in here, madam," said the driver.

"We'll have to stop the car, Terry. I'm desperate for a ciggie."

"Don't be daft," he replied. "You can't get out of the car dressed like that and stand smoking a cigarette by the side of the road!"

I could see his point. But I had another plan. Concealed among the makeup in my purse was a tiny bottle of vodka. I took it out and swallowed a stiff measure.

"Caroline!" hissed Terry. "I don't want you staggering down the aisle!"

"Don't worry," I said. "I'm far too sober to get drunk!"

When we arrived at the synagogue, I was ushered into the bride's room. From that room double doors led into the main hall. There was a tiny window in the door that enabled the bride to look out without being seen by the congregation. I caught my breath. The synagogue was packed with hundreds of people. Diana and Pam helped me with my veil, straightening my train and arranging my bridesmaids and pageboys. By now I was stiff with fear.

A man peered around the door. "Ready to go?" he asked.

I couldn't speak.

"Are you OK, Caroline?" asked Terry, squeezing my arm.

"Yes," I whispered.

I heard the music start up, and the choir rose from their seats. The doors opened and I walked out holding on to Terry's arm. I had to proceed slowly up an aisle toward the chuppah, where Elias, my mum, Mr. and Mrs. Fattal and William were standing. The music rose to a crescendo as I reached the canopy. I could see Elias's face. *He looks anxious,* I thought. My mum had tears in her eyes, and I felt a lump in my throat. As the music died down and silence fell I offered up a prayer to God.

Let me marry this man in peace and happiness.

As Rabbi Goldberg began the service I was waiting for disaster to strike, for a voice in the crowd to cry out an objection to the marriage. But no one broke the solemn silence; no one interrupted the rabbi's beautiful words. We exchanged rings, we shared the wine and smashed the glass, and then we walked up the steps to sign the register. We were pronounced man and wife, and the choir, the organ and the trumpeters combined together in the most spectacular chorus.

It was the happiest moment of my life. I looked into Elias's eyes. He was smiling, his face lit up with love, and I was certain that our marriage would last a lifetime. At last, after years of struggle, pain and turmoil, I had found a partner who not only accepted me as I was but was prepared to make me a gift of total commitment. I was his woman and he was my man.

We drove back to the Savoy high on excitement and dizzy with relief. At the hotel the staff were waiting at the door to greet us.

"Congratulations, Mr. and Mrs. Fattal," said the banqueting manager. We were married at last! I could hardly believe it.

The ceremony may have been over but the celebrations had only just begun. The other Mrs. Fattal was hot on our heels, and she threw herself with near religious zeal into organizing the photographs.

For a full hour we posed in every conceivable permutation: aunts next to uncles, Cosseys shoulder-to-shoulder with Fattals, men with top hats and men without. Elias and I were snapped from all angles, and I dabbed powder on my nose in between shots. Diana ran into the room and threw her arms around me. "You looked *so* beautiful!" she exclaimed, showering me with kisses. Mrs. Fattal, in a fury of creative excitement, glowered. Diana gave me a grin and slipped out of the room. *This is tougher than any modeling assignment,* I thought to myself.

When the photographer had finished, we began to greet our guests. It took another hour to get everyone in. A master of ceremonies in top hat and tails announced every guest as they moved forward to the receiving line. It was the same man who had announced the guests at the Conservative Ball. Mrs. Fattal's eyes shone with delight; this was a social coup of sorts. Needless to say, it was she who stood at the head of the line. My mother stood at the end.

Once all the guests had been announced, dinner was served in the Lancaster Room. Decorated in blue with a dazzle of gilded mirrors, it was large enough to seat all the guests for dinner, and there was room for a dance floor. When everyone was seated, Elias and I entered amid applause. The band struck up and together we danced the horah. I was so anxious lest I trip on my train that I hardly had time to worry about the steps. At one point Elias and I were both lifted on chairs and carried around the room before being brought together above the heads of the crowd to kiss. The satin of my wedding gown made it difficult for me to stay seated, and as the dancers lurched and swung I struggled not to pitch forward onto the floor.

The dinner was lavish and the Savoy performed the great feat of serving all the guests simultaneously with hot soufflés. We ate poached salmon, ice-cream truffles, and a dessert served on trays of smoking ice. Between each course we danced, Elias and I opening the ball to the strains of "Sweet Caroline." Elias, not normally an enthusiastic dancer, was irrepressible. He moved around the floor, laughing and chatting. I looked at his happy, relaxed face as he asked Myra to dance. *He's really enjoying himself,* I thought. I was not the only one to notice. All our friends were delighted to see him so gleeful. He was like a little boy at a birthday party; he couldn't stop smiling.

During dinner, Elias and William made speeches. William was witty and self-assured, and he complimented me on the changes I had made to Elias's life. "We all thought he had taken up lifelong membership in the bachelor's club," he joked. I knew Elias was nervous about speaking, but in the end he gave a fine speech and thanked my mother for giving him such a beautiful wife. Mum was sitting next to me at the table and smiled with real pleasure.

The rest of the evening passed in a whirl of music, laughter and dance. Elias and I were in perpetual motion, talking to old friends, circulating around the room, drinking champagne. We were full of a kind of dizzy euphoria born of months of worrying and planning. Every so often I would catch his eye and find in his face a secret expression of deep content.

Just before midnight we retired to bed. I hugged Pam and Mum. "Be happy," Mum whispered to me. "It was a wonderful day."

It had been wonderful, a dream wedding. But I was glad it was over.

Elias took me up to the bridal suite. As soon as he shut the door, he threw his arms around me.

"Now you *are* my wife," he said, "and I want you to feel proud. You'll never be ashamed or insecure again. No more worrying—you can hold your head up high and enjoy the wonderful life we are going to have together."

We both breathed a sigh of relief. I felt exhausted, but the bridal suite was beautiful, with baskets of flowers, cards and bottles of champagne. We felt like naughty truants who'd just escaped from the classroom.

"Come here," said Elias. "Let's see what you've got on under that dress!"

He began chasing me around the room as I shrieked with laughter. When he caught hold of me, he was faced with the challenge of the buttons. "How on earth am I supposed to get all these undone?" he exclaimed. His large hands were not best suited to the task. We both began to giggle.

"Shall I just rip it off?" he asked.

By the time I was undressed we were nearly hysterical with mirth and exhaustion. We collapsed onto the bed and fell into a profound sleep wrapped in each other's arms.

Everything is going to be all right, I thought as I drifted toward unconsciousness. *I am going to live happily ever after, after all....*

from Chapter 21

SEX CHANGE
PAGE THREE GIRL WEDS

Pam handed me the paper. On the front page of the *News of the World* was a picture of me posing in a bikini. Mum began to cry.

"The bastards!" I exclaimed, feeling the blood drain from my face. "They've done it again."

Not content with having ruined my career and caused untold suffering to me and my family, now they were damaging my marriage. The final sentence stuck a knife in my heart. It read: *She's really landed on her back this time.* I threw the paper across the room in a rage.

"What are we going to do?" said Elias. He was pale with shock.

"Maybe there's a chance your parents haven't seen it," I replied. "Don't panic. Call them up and tell them we're back. That way we'll know what's going on."

He walked slowly to the phone and dialed the number. His mother answered.

"Hi, Mummy, we're back."

There was a silence. Then we heard him say: "No, Mamma. Yes, Mamma. OK, Mamma."

He put the phone down and turned to face me. "She knows and she wants to see me straightaway."

He collapsed into a chair. "What am I going to do? How can I possibly explain?"

We sat and talked for about half an hour. "Come with me, Caroline. You are better at explaining about your past than I am."

"The last person in the world your family wants to see is me. I'm sorry, Elias, but I can't sit and listen to the insults. It's going to take them a while to get used to the idea. It's better they have a chance to get rid of their prejudice privately."

He fell silent. He had broken out into a sweat and was tapping his foot nervously. "I could tell them that I didn't know," he suggested.

"Don't be ridiculous," I snapped. "How can you expect your family to have any respect for me if they think I've been dishonest with you?"

The phone rang.

"It's your brother-in-law," said Pam, holding the phone out for Elias.

"I'm leaving right now," he said, replacing the receiver.

"What did he say?" I asked.

"Mummy's very upset and wants me home now."

Elias paced the room while I called a taxi. When the car drew up I walked with him to the door. "Be strong and be honest," I said. "And please protect my dignity."

"I'll ring you," he said, and walked away.

BODY ALCHEMY

Loren Cameron

1996

*Loren Cameron is a San Francisco–based pho-
tographer and bodybuilder. In 1994, he opened
the landmark photo exhibition "Our Visions,
Our Voices: Transsexual Portraits and Nudes."*

MY AFFINITY for photography began as early as I can remember. My parents had lots of photo books with pictures of the war and pre–World War Two America. There, I first saw images by Walker Evans and Dorothea Lange, who greatly influenced my artistic and aesthetic sensibilities. My father had stories of his own about what it was like to grow up in Iowa near the end of the Great Depression: he and his siblings would scour the railroad tracks to find bits of coal that had fallen from the trains' coal cars, and he quit school at thirteen so he could work to feed his family. Through Lange's photographs, I gained a visual understanding of my father's stories about working-class survival. Her images touched me deeply and helped me understand his tough attitude about living and his generation's no-nonsense work ethic, as well as the universality of the human condition of pain, strife and the will to persevere.

I've looked to these images from the past to learn something of compassion and a sense of the heroic. In my own life, along with my father's words, they have taught me to honor labor and to keep putting one foot in front of the other. Being drawn to photography as a medium of expression seems only natural for me, given the emotional impact it has had on my life. It has been the most powerful teaching tool for me to date, and I feel the message in my work isn't very different from Lange's or Evans's: it is a vision about strength and will and everyday people.

———

A TOMBOY as a child, I shunned dresses and rolling down my socks. I loved playing army games, and my favorite doll was a G.I. Joe. When my mother died in 1968, I moved from

Pasadena, California, to rural Arkansas to live with my father, his wife and her two teenage children. I didn't see my three sisters again until I was nearly twenty.

My father's farm was just outside a small rural town of thirteen hundred people at the foot of the Ozark Mountains. He raised horses for the love of them and was employed at the nearby nuclear plant. A lot of my adolescence and early teens were spent working with my father, building fences and feeding the horses. In my spare time after school, I explored the lush and wild countryside with my small pack of canine companions. Many afternoons were lazed away on the bank of a pond while I fished for perch and daydreamed.

At the onset of puberty, that slightly insane time in all our lives, I grew very restless and became a regular fixture down at the local greasy spoon in town. I dressed in overalls and work boots and learned to swear like a trucker and smoke cigarettes and marijuana. I loved anything daring and adventurous. My friends and I rafted swollen rivers, drag-raced, rode crazy horses and ran from cops.

———

DURING MY teens and even before then, I had begun to feel terrifically uncomfortable as a female-bodied person. When I was twelve years old, I heard of people changing sex, and I even wrote away for information. But who could I tell? Who would understand what even I could barely verbalize? I could only wear baggy clothing to hide my ever-developing breasts and somehow learn to cope with the inconvenience of menstruation. At about seventeen, I had barely begun to experiment sexually with boys when one of my older female friends returned home on leave from the army. As we took a pleasant drive down a dirt road, she very carefully inquired about whether I had ever considered being a lesbian. The thought hadn't even occurred to me. I was elated at the suggestion!

Why not? If I couldn't be a boy, then I could be a dyke! Come to think of it, women were very attractive!

Unfortunately, my excitement wasn't shared by my heterosexual friends. Like greased lightning, the news of my new-found identity got around town. It took even less time for all of my friends to turn their backs on me. I was in my junior year of high school, where I had been unexpectedly elected class president and student council president. All of a sudden, I was outcast.

Finding no support or solace, I quit school and ran away from home. I spent the next couple of years struggling to survive and taking long bus rides across the States, trying to see the world beyond that small place. Working labor jobs—fruit picking and construction cleanup—I barely got by. I returned to Arkansas, not having found the place to call home, and worked until I felt the urge to buy the next bus ticket. I ran a truck-stop fuel station for a while; then I got a job on a youth conservation-corps crew. One day, while I was mixing cement for a rock wall we were building, these two very lesbian-looking women approached from a nearby campground. They were from San Francisco. Within a few hours of friendly conversation, these seemingly sophisticated dykes convinced me that my fame and fortune were to be found in a city by the ocean. Weeks later, I purchased my last bus ticket, grabbed my duffel bag and went out west.

———

I HAD lived in the San Francisco lesbian scene for nine years when, at twenty-six, I finally began to address my discomfort about my gender. I can only speculate about the timing. Maybe it was because I was finally living by myself and didn't have to contend with any negative peer pressure, or maybe I was finally old enough to deal with it. Other things had changed too. I had quit smoking pot and tobacco, which I suspect had, until then, suppressed my feelings. In addition, I was recovering from the failure of a very passionate relationship that had left me devastated. For the first time in my life, I wasn't numb.

The need to change became all-consuming: I started the step-by-step process of therapy, doctors and surgeons. Taking testosterone as hormone therapy and developing a body-building regimen, I ever so slowly and painfully began to reinvent myself. I photographed myself and sent amateur snapshots to friends and family in order to show them how happy I was; I wanted them to get used to the idea of my body being different. If they could see my new beard and chest sans breasts, perhaps it would be easier for them to accept my new identity. You know, so they would stop calling me "she." I was excited, too, much like when I had discovered my sexuality as a teenager. Only this time, I refused to feel any shame. I was creating a beautiful new body image, and I was proud of it.

———

WHAT WAS initially a crude documentation of my own personal journey gradually evolved into an impassioned mission. Impulsively, I began to photograph other transsexuals whom I knew, feeling compelled to make images of their emotional and physical triumphs. I was fueled by my need to be validated, and wanted, in turn, to validate them. I wanted the world to see us, I mean, really see us.

Since I'd had no formal training, I took a basic photography class and learned to print my images. My first work was done with a simple Pentax K1000. Within a year, I managed to have my first show, which earned critical attention. After several more exhibitions, I graduated from thirty-five-millimeter to medium format. Still preferring the simplicity of a manually operated camera, I bought a used Pentax six-by-seven body and a new one-thirty-five macro lens. Finding the rectangular negative more appealing than the shape of a two-and-one-quarter-inch square, I decided to continue using a field camera. Besides, this Pentax was as durable as a tank: I could drop it and still be in the running. Transitioning to a larger negative helped me regard myself more seriously as a professional photographer, and the crisp, beautiful quality of the photographs inspired new images.

———

DESPITE THE financial challenge, the work has taken on a life of its own, and I am pressed to keep producing. I use a shutter-release bulb in my self-portraits because I usually work alone; my camera doesn't have a shutter timer, so I have to press the shutter button myself. I actually prefer this method to ensure that the work is entirely of my own vision. People have asked me, however, why I don't try to conceal the bulb in the photographs. At times, given the composition of a photograph, concealing the bulb may not be possible. I also feel a certain pride in making a decent image without seeing through the lens, so I don't really mind that the bulb is visible. Its presence serves as a metaphor: I am creating my own image alone, an act that reflects the transsexual experience as well.

———

FOR THE longest time, transsexuals and especially transsexual men (female-to-males) have been virtually invisible to the dominant culture. Marginalized even within the gay and lesbian subculture, transsexuals have occupied no real space of our own. In the last decade or so, more and more transsexual people have been speaking out about our experiences. We are beginning to represent ourselves for the first time and to develop our own voice. *Body Alchemy* is the first photodocumentation of transsexual men from within our community.

———

AS I have observed another movement paralleling that of transsexuals, it is my intention to embrace and include in this work those people who may identify more comfortably as "transgender," or "gender transgressive." A growing number of people are and have been questioning the more usual representations of gender. Some have had chemical and surgical enhancement, and many have not. Inhabiting a less static gender identification than that of typical transsexuals, they are exploring and experiencing a fluid range of gender embodiment. My own intimate partner, Kayt, is one such individual. Ironically, it has been through knowing and loving her that I have gained an even deeper understanding of the mutable soul. Her flexible consciousness has encouraged me to be generous in my thinking and less rigid about the way others self-define, or, in fact, when they choose not to.

In an effort to address these issues, I have produced a very personal project with Kayt. Along with my photo essay and its symbolic representations of the two of us, I have invited Kayt to write about her experience of being transgendered and about our sometimes conventional, sometimes unconventional relationship. We hope that this inclusion will offer yet another perspective on what it means to be transgendered.

The Suit

———

I BOUGHT my first fine Italian suit at a shop for men five-eight and under. My good friend Terence told me about the store, where he had shopped himself. He assured me that I could find a variety of suits from which to choose, despite my slight stature, and that the salesmen would be very understanding since they were all short too. I was more than a little nervous about it. I knew next to nothing about men's fine clothing: I had never put on a tie or even owned a pair of dress shoes.

Fortunately, Terence agreed to come with me for moral support, and I set out on one of my first coming-of-age adventures. Upon arrival, we were graciously met by a well-groomed fellow who quickly summed me up. Obviously I was a working-class Joe who had never dressed a day in his life—not very far from the truth really. Relieved by his assumption, I was glad to avail myself of his expertise.

After what seemed like hours of deliberation about color, style and fabric, I finally made a selection. Marvin, the tailor, asked me to try on the suit so he could refine the fit of my manly new garment. While he measured and creased, he told me important things about being a man of taste: about the cut of a good tie, the difference between a Windsor and a full Windsor, that I should never lean back in a chair while wearing my coat, and to always pull up my socks. I remember panicking when Marvin asked which side I dressed on (I quickly thought about being right-handed). He speculated that women would find me irresistible in my lovely new suit and said that I must learn to slow dance. Marvin was adamant that I should never offer a rose on the first date: it should be a carnation instead. He also warned me that women who like ties can choke you in the heat of passion. Beware! Terence and I exchanged a quick glance at each other and laughed out loud. Boy, was I getting my money's worth—a tailored suit *and* free advice on dating etiquette!

After he showed me four different ways to fold my handkerchief, and I was out about six hundred clams, Marvin patted me on the back and expounded on how all the world respects a man in a good suit. I felt at least two inches taller when I walked out of there, and it wasn't because of the elevator shoes.

Testosterone

I INJECT myself with a dose of testosterone every two weeks, the standard maintenance schedule for men like me. Between injections, the oil-based drug absorbs slowly through the muscle tissue. I admit I've become very attached to taking the hormone, which is responsible for all my physical masculine attributes, like my facial and body hair and muscle development. I've also noticed that it affects my sex drive and emotional state too. During the peak part of my cycle, I turn into a randy, greasy kind of guy who is more than a little irritable.

Learning to manage the emotional and physical effects of testosterone hasn't been easy. There are moments when I don't do well at all. I've had many regrettable fights with my partner that could have been avoided had it not been for the rapid escalation of my temper. It's hard to describe the way it makes me compulsively react to situations. Once, I actually slugged a man on the street for verbally assaulting a woman. The anger I felt was swift and instinctual. My brain didn't have a second to consider the consequences before my fist was flying. Luckily, the man wasn't really hurt, and being a weenie, he just went away. What if he hadn't?

I have found that people in the bodybuilding community are the most familiar with this kind of chemically induced behavior. They call it "roid rage." Fortunately, my occasional meltdowns are mild in comparison to what competitive athletes experience. Learning to recognize when I feel unusually agitated helps me get a grip, and so does a good workout at the gym. Discontinuing the testosterone isn't really an option, since so much of my identity hinges on it. Maybe, over time, medical science will find a more efficient way to administer this drug for transsexuals. Until then, it's a great lesson in self-control.

So much about my coming to manhood has been about a quest for size. I mean, I really need to be a big man. All of the men I've looked to as role models have been bodybuilders and athletes. They seem like gods and great beasts to me in their huge and beautiful bodies. I envy them. I want to be like them. They look so virile and invincible.

I know deeply that being a man and having strength isn't at all about my maximum bench press, but it doesn't seem to matter. All I can say is that, as my muscles grow, being five-foot-three doesn't feel quite so small.

Sometimes I wonder if I'll ever feel big enough. I wonder if I'll ever feel safe in this body.

DEAR SIR OR MADAM

Mark Rees

1996

Mark Rees was born in England, where he con-
tinues to be an activist for transgender rights.

MY "BIRTH" as Mark was due to take place at the beginning of the autumn term in October. It was now March 1971. I was doubtful that it would be possible for me to pass as a man by then, but had to trust Dr. Randell's assurance that all would be well. I was changing roles but once, whereas he'd seen it many times. The results of the hormone therapy were more immediate than I'd expected. Menstruation ceased almost immediately, to my profound relief, and within a few weeks my voice was changing enough for people to ask what was wrong with my throat. Any inquiries I answered by explaining that it was a bad bout of catarrh, which was partially true. The friendly lady in the Students' Union cloakroom continued to inquire about my "bad throat" for some weeks. "I'm worried about your throat, dear. It's not getting any better at all. You should see someone about it."

"Don't worry, Elsie. I'm seeing a doctor!"

My already small breasts decreased in size, then, somewhat cautiously, I abandoned the hated bra that I'd first donned so reluctantly in the forces. It gave me a wonderful feeling of mental and physical liberation. Ingeniously, I thought, I made a binder from the now-redundant elastic suspender belt, wearing it to conceal what seemed to me nipples and breasts too large for a male. My sister, Jane, who in her very matter-of-fact way was giving me greatly appreciated support, said that looking bound-up would make me more conspicuous. Many men had larger breasts and nipples than I now had. With glee I dispensed with the binder but continued to wear a vest and thick sweaters until my mastectomy four years later. It was some months before facial hair appeared.

Although Wendy and John said it wasn't necessary, I decided to move out of my digs at the end of the summer term and into University House. I wanted to spare them any gossip, but we kept in touch. Their friendship meant much to me.

Fellow students, noticing changes, began to quiz my friends, but most of my colleagues took the matter very phlegmatically, which was a relief.

I passed my first BDS examinations. To spare my mother stress I considered staying in Birmingham for the vacation and getting a summer job. When I went to the Labor Exchange they directed me to the men's section. I wasn't ready for that and decided to bite the bullet and go home even though it would be difficult.

I returned to my former holiday jobs of laboratory work at Pembury Hospital and taxi driving in Tunbridge Wells, which brought their moments of confusion! Happily the lab staff didn't make any comments, and to my delight, most people who didn't know me treated me as male, even to the extent of issuing me with a male overall. One of my taxi passengers, an old lady, spent the whole journey repeating that she'd been told a lady driver was going to collect her. I feigned deafness.

At a garage, I forgot to collect my petrol receipt. The attendant called out.

"You've forgotten your receipt, mate!"

"I'm sorry, my mind wasn't on my work."

He laughed. "Got a piece of crumpet tucked away then?"

I smiled to myself as I drove away. He'd treated me as a man. It was wonderful.

At home I was still "Brenda" and had yet the daunting task of telling friends and more distant relatives of my change of role. It needed much thought. Would they all accept it, or should I just fade quietly out of their lives? I didn't discuss this very much with Mum, because it was too sensitive an issue, or with Jane, because she no longer lived at home but told me to call in when I felt like it, which I was glad to do. Obviously to some people, like my mother, it was very difficult. I'd left it to Mum to tell the family, but realized years later that I should have done it myself and not relied on a sort of osmosis for the news to filter through. One aunt, who had been rather antagonistic, confessed twenty years later that she'd been hurt because she'd not been told directly. It is very easy for those of us involved to assume that everyone knows as much as we do. They don't. In our pain it's also easy to underestimate the emotions that are stirred up in others, especially when there is such a lamentable ignorance of the matter.

For my mother, to whom the situation was so blatantly obvious, it was still extremely perplexing and threatening. Added to her own fears she had fears for me as I entered a new life. She also saw that she'd lost a daughter, although ultimately she was able to accept me as a much happier son. Because it was a loss, there was mourning and all the associated feelings of grief—anger, bewilderment and even perhaps a sense of guilt. She had also lost the possibility of my having children. It was made all the worse because I seemed to be blazing a path. There were few guidelines. No one told me or her how to cope with all this. My sister, Jane, was the first— and for a while the only—member of the family to support me. She wrote a letter "to cheer you up . . . You are entitled to be happy. I'm sure that everyone will get over it. . . . Lee [her husband] says that he's very happy for you and a little relieved, as he's always wanted to call you 'mate' anyhow." She said that she was glad to know at last what the problem was because she'd always known that something was wrong but knew that I wasn't a lesbian.

My sister's unsentimental encouragement was something that helped me immensely. It is a tragedy that in January 1984 she turned violently against me and cut herself off from most of the family, including her own mother.

One or two of the immediate neighbors (and probably others unbeknownst to me) knew of my plans and were not in the least surprised. One immediately called me "Mark" because she said that she and her husband had wondered about my sex for years. I wrote to most of my friends and was in for some surprises. Former WRNS colleagues (including Emma) did not accept the situation as expected. Her friend Meg totally ignored my letter, and another wrote politely but made it clear that it was the end of our friendship. Years later she admitted that her reaction had been due to the fact that at the time her parents' marriage was breaking up because her father had declared himself homosexual.

I decided to fade from the scene as far as some of my Christian friends were concerned, thinking this would be too much for them to accept, but they doggedly kept in touch with me! To my surprise their reactions were positive. "I had always been aware that there was a conflict inside you ... you had masculine tendencies ..." wrote one such friend, Carolyn. "First and foremost you need to be accepted. ..." "What a sense of relief you must have," wrote Pauline Spencer, another teacher friend from the grammar school. "I knew when I met you just after Easter how much more relaxed you were. ... I look forward to seeing you again." Ken, my former chaplain at Culdrose, said, "You must always regard us as your friends. ..."

Pam, now a sister at Malvern, said: "There is always something to thank God for ... the progress in the medical field that has made this treatment possible. ... You will keep in touch, won't you?"

Some letters were touched with gentle humor. My singing teacher, Phyllis, said that it was a major upheaval for her to have changed from soprano to contralto, so she had some idea of what I was going through! Another choral society friend hoped I'd be a tenor because they were rather short of them. Her hopes were not met—I became a second bass! An ex-nun friend declared that it was more dramatic than turning a nun into a lady!

Apart from Emma's letter, all those I received were understanding and compassionate. As with my father's death, two years earlier, I became very aware of love. Medical treatment alone would not have been sufficient.

The administrative side of my role change was the most tedious. Dr. Randell had written to various authorities to support my request for a change of documentation, and Professor Marsland saw to it that my way was smoothed through such problems as reregistration and issue of an LEA grant in my new name.

My name seemed to be stored in dozens of places: the LEA, the university, insurance companies, the bank, NHS, DSS, the Department of Employment, doctor, dentist and organizations to which I belonged and wished to remain a member of. Miss Rees left the Association of Wrens! I shall not forget the courteous and tactful way in which Miss Williamson of the Passport Office issued me with a new passport, or the understanding and discreet representative from the local office of the Department of Health and Social Security. Others were equally helpful, to my relief. Years after my role change I continued to find documents that had somehow been overlooked. Certainly, if I'd had any doubts about the wisdom of my action, this would have been the point at which to abandon the plan, but I had none.

My wardrobe had to be changed from "female ambiguous" to "male unambiguous." None of the assistants (usually at Marks & Spencer) took any notice as I handed them such items as male underwear for wrapping. (I regretted that the fly fronts would be useless.)

Some of my female clothes were sold but most were given to my mother, friends, the Oxfam shop and jumble sales. In later years I was to acquire most of my clothes from charity shops and jumble sales but at that time was either too snooty or stupid to think of buying my male clothes from these sources. It was therefore an expensive exercise.

Marks & Spencer posed no problems, but would I have the courage to go to a men's tailor? I decided that I wanted a man's suit and sports jacket. Cowardice made me go to Burtons in another town.

"Can I help you, sir?"

There was an eager young assistant at my side. This gave me confidence, and later I left the shop with a sports jacket and a suit on order.

It was a little daunting in the fitting room trying to behave as if I'd always lived as a man. What was expected? Worst of all, would my measurements arouse suspicion?

"I always have trouble getting things to fit, being a bit broad in the beam," I remarked casually to the tailor but feeling anxious. "It's a family thing; my uncle was just the same" (or so my mother had told me). The procedure was especially nerve-racking when the courteous tailor measured my chest and inside leg, but if he suspected anything odd it was not evident to me. I related the incident to my sister.

"Did they ask you which side you dressed?" Jane inquired.

"No, and I don't know what it means."

"Then you were very lucky and you ought to know for the future!"

Although I didn't have to change my behavior to fit the male role, knowing the "clan jargon" was, as Jane had shown me, another matter. In a matter of weeks I was attempting to do what normally takes years—to become an adult male member of society and know all about man talk, etiquette and expected behavior. Dr. Randell had emphasized that attention had to be paid to factors that were influenced by social conditioning and said that greater problems were experienced by male-to-female than the other way around. During an early visit he had asked me if I'd used the term "fibber" because it was more ladylike than "liar." He was right. Since then both speech and dress have become more casual for both sexes, and what is now considered normal for a woman would once have made a navvy blush, but it was a great relief for me to be able to say what I liked without having to pass it through the refining filter necessary for a young lady!

There were numerous pitfalls to be avoided. I had to remember to be careful not to let out such comments as, "When I was in the WRNS . . ."

It was quite difficult to conceal twenty-eight years of life, but with care and some evasion I succeeded. The WRNS was the only "female job" I'd done. As time went on and a male past was built up it became less difficult. These problems were totally removed when, fifteen years later, I "went public."

There were minor practicalities that would not occur to most people, like mounting my bicycle in a male fashion and pulling off my sweaters in a male way. It was no problem with buttoning coats because I'd been doing them up the male side since schooldays. Dr. Randell, my friends and Jane were a great help in all these matters.

One of the greatest moments of my transition was when I tried on my new suit. The reflection in the mirror was of a smart young man. The frump was no more! It was some time before my mother could bring herself to look at me in such definite male attire, but eventually she became proud to see me looking smart—something she'd been denied when I was in the female role. She especially liked to see me in my dinner jacket and would tell her friends that I was like my father, suited to formal dress, but her change of attitude took a long time. Lacking the courage to make my male debut in Rusthall,

I wore ambiguous dress at home but began to wear obviously male attire out of Tunbridge Wells. My first such venture was on a visit to see Dr. Randell. With my male clothes in a holdall I crossed the recreation ground next door to our house. Some children there sang out.

"We thought it was a man, now a woman . . ."

With the hope of things improving, I felt able to cope with what had previously been intolerable. On the train I went to the toilet and donned my jacket and tie. The nun who had been sitting opposite smiled as I resumed my seat. No one else took any notice; I might have been invisible. Was it possible that I looked so ordinary? My elation increased as I went about London and did some shopping. There were no turned heads, no sniggers and no comments. People are anonymous in London, but the indifference of the train passengers convinced me that I had merged into the background. On that occasion I found being ignored a very happy experience.

My big worry was using a public loo. What were they like? Did they have cubicles? Gingerly I ventured into the "gents" at the Charing Cross Hotel, where I was due to meet Mrs. Cordell for tea before seeing Dr. Randell. It was empty, clean and cubicled. Subsequent experience taught me to use toilets in museums, art galleries and department stores, if possible avoiding public loos. I decided that men weren't as clean as women, most not bothering to wash their hands. "They think they wee distilled water," Mum had caustically remarked.

Doreen Cordell greeted me warmly: "You look fine."

The waiter reinforced her opinion by handing me the bill! Mrs. Cordell spoke of the errors many transsexual people, usually male-to-female, make in dressing too extravagantly and behaving in a way that they perceive as feminine but that only draws attention to themselves. I have met one or two female-to-males who try too hard to be "macho." Thank goodness that this is now on the wane with society being less bothered about sexual stereotypes than formerly.

After my appointment with Dr. Randell I met my teacher friend, Pauline.

"You look super," she commented. "How long have you been dressing like this now?"

"This is the first day."

"That's tremendous. I can't think of you in any other way now."

Similar comments were to be made by countless people over the next few weeks and months.

I felt very relaxed and happy as we walked along the embankment, the lights twinkling on the dark river, but when reluctantly changing back into my "unisex" outfit on the homebound train I knew that my difficulties weren't all over. I was like Cinderella after the ball. Fortunately the train reached Tunbridge Wells without turning into a pumpkin!

I decided to make my new name as similar as possible to my old one so that if people did make mistakes it would not be so obvious to bystanders. It also made it easier when signing my name to retain my former initials. Thus Brenda Margaret became Brendan Mark. The solicitor recommended to me by Dr. Randell for drawing up the change-of-name deed thought this a wise plan, and so it seemed for a while. People called me "Bren," which was totally asexual. In quite a short time I felt that my name should be unmistakably male, so settled for Mark.

The solicitor told me that I'd be able to alter every document except my birth certificate, which meant, of course, that marriage to a woman would be impossible. It didn't worry me unduly at that point, but lack of legal recognition would eventually prompt me to take up a campaign that would change my life. Father Taylor and his assistant curate, David Dunn, witnessed my change-of-name deed. If I were, as Emma had said, "going against the God-given," then I had some unlikely supporters!

A few years later I had another change-of-name deed drawn up. "Brendan" was discarded and instead I became Mark Nicholas—the latter name because I was born on St. Nicholas's Day. Father Taylor thought that with saints' names I couldn't lose! On this occasion I went to a local solicitor who was unaware of my situation, a rather aristocratic man who thought it very strange that I should have reached my mid-thirties before deciding that I didn't like my name! However, he didn't refuse my business.

It was undoubtedly a strain living both as Mark and Brenda. If I had hoped to continue going home after my role change then sooner or later my debut as male would have to be made in Rusthall and Tunbridge Wells. I anticipated it like an execution. I was under too much pressure to realize that most people are caring and would endeavor to understand. Hadn't I coped with the local kids yelling at me? Surely the neighbors wouldn't be worse?

"You'll have to make the break," said Father Taylor. "It's no good living two conflicting roles."

One of my friend's mothers, a bluntly spoken Frenchwoman who'd taught at the grammar school where I'd worked, made a similar comment.

"But what about the neighbors, madam?" I had asked her.

"Bugger the neighbors," she said. "You have to live your own life." She was right. I had to end my ambiguity.

Father Taylor suggested that I go for a week or so to the Anglican Franciscan Friary at Hilfield in Dorset. It would give me a break and the chance to live as a man in an all-male establishment. He thought that once I'd lived in my new role for a while it would give me more confidence to face the people who knew me. It would also act as a preparation for my return to university as "Mark."

On September 20, 1971, I set off for the friary. For the first time ever I left home in proper male attire, praying that I'd not meet anyone I knew. (It had become quite a habit to gaze into a shop window if I saw a familiar face approaching.) It was the "birth" of Mark, and I was determined that whatever happened, "Mark" I was going to remain.

Chapter 18

I WAS terrified. It wasn't the actual surgery or the prospect of pain that frightened me, but the possibility of dying under the anesthetic. My slender faith had never been strong enough to remove the fear of death, yet this fear had positive results. It produced in me a heightened awareness of the wonder and greatness of human love and the beauty of the world around. I left Mum at Tunbridge Wells station, buoyed up by her love and the good wishes of many friends and neighbors. As the London-bound train sped through the Kentish scenery, resplendent in its May dress, I was held by its loveliness. It was as if I were seeing it for the very first time—the countless greens of the new leaves, the blossoms and the rolling downs. All was fresh and intense, illuminated by a bright but gentle sunlight that made every detail clear. Every moment of that journey was cherished.

My anxiety was considerably lessened by the cheery ward clerk at the hospital who told me that cases like mine were always allocated single rooms.

Visitors soon began to arrive, one of the first being my teacher friend, Pauline. I was overwhelmed by what seemed to me undeserved concern. I decided that as far as possible I'd enjoy my stay.

The staff seemed kind and my fellow patients friendly. I met several when helping with the tea next morning. In one of the other single rooms was a slight young man with a scarred chest. We had a chat and he confirmed what I'd suspected, that he was also a female-to-male transsexual. The scars were from a mastectomy, but he was just recovering from a hysterectomy. Ian was a friendly person and spent much of the morning with me, trying to allay my fears about the imminent operation. He said that he was able to go swimming. The scars were certainly faint. I'd always believed that life would improve after such surgery but was less certain about a hysterectomy. That, however, was not mentioned by the doctor, and I had no wish to rush into it, my view being that if I couldn't see my uterus, why undergo the risk of surgery? As far as I was concerned, with my breasts being the most visible reminder of my past, they were the most important things to remove.

Ian had had an unhappy home life and because of missed schooling was virtually illiterate. Not for the first, or last time, I thought how lucky I had been.

The patient role was an entirely new experience for me. I was now the one with the name tag around my wrist, not the white coat on my back. Although never achieving my ambition to become a doctor, as a dental student and lab technician the patient had always been someone else. Now it was me. It was my turn to show trust. I believe that my hospital stay was to prove of emotional and spiritual, as well as physical, benefit.

As I signed the operation consent form, my feelings were of apprehension and incredulity. After years of struggle I was about to undergo what had been thought impossible. I was afraid but knew that my fear and any discomfort would soon be forgotten when I enjoyed the benefits of a flat chest!

On the day of the operation I felt strangely calm. Was it because of the love that I knew was being directed at me? This serenity didn't last long. My experience with the preoperative procedures was unhappy, so by the time the kindly anesthetist arrived I wanted to go home, and struggled with her. Eventually, exhausted with anxiety, I succumbed and woke up in the recovery room with a bound chest and drainage tubes protruding from the crepe bandages.

In a short time I was wheeled back to the ward and was conscious enough to ask the attractive blond nurse accompanying me if she was Scandinavian. She was, but to my dismay, belonged to the theater, not my ward.

Later that day the surgeon visited me and expressed satisfaction with my general condition. Unlike women who had similar surgery I was healthy. There were to be no problems.

Although feeling a bit light-headed, I was able to ring Mum, who was relieved to know that all had gone well. It must have been a very strange experience for her, first seeing her daughter become more masculine, then watching her undergo surgery which some would deem a mutilation. It was the removal of a very visible sign of womanhood. In addition to her natural concern for my well-being, she must have had very mixed feelings that day.

Gwen had always been scathing about agency nurses. She must have had in mind the one who attended me, who, after showing an appalling carelessness in basic procedures, as a final insult brought me a urinal bottle instead of a bedpan. She was an exception. The regular nurses, both male and female, were kind, friendly and efficient. Ian said that he felt embarrassed when the nurses washed him but it didn't bother me at all; in fact I enjoyed it! He, like many people, believed that in the hospital he'd lost his dignity, but what do we mean by dignity? Perhaps we lose our pretenses. I never found having a kind and gentle nurse of either sex doing personal things for me humiliating. Dignity means "worth." They treated me as if I were of worth. I thanked God for people with such vocations and gratefully accepted their loving care, and of course fell in love with several of them as well!

Mum visited the day after surgery, laden with bits and pieces, including some lilies of the valley from our garden and a small vase in which to put them. Their fragrance delighted me as I awoke the next morning. In spite of the journey she visited me many times during my ten-day stay. My mother and I had undoubtedly become much closer once the initial upheaval and shock of my role change had worn off. I sensed that my relationships with others had also deepened. Was it because my inner conflict had been resolved? Freed to be myself, I was now able to be more honest. The acting and hiding were over.

Several friends, including Father Taylor, also made the journey from Tunbridge Wells to see me. Some people called two or three times. I'd not seen some friends for a long time, so I enjoyed the opportunity to "hold court" like royalty. The nurses teased me about the large number of cards that arrived. I really did feel enfolded in love.

However, I was greatly saddened and perplexed by the fact that my sister neither visited nor wrote. Mum, obviously equally upset, said that Jane didn't approve of my treatment. "But Mum, she was the first person to back me!"

Was she jealous because I was getting so much attention and remembering that while my parents had given her all their support when she became pregnant, she was not admired but regarded as "a naughty girl"? Would she have continued to support me if the rest of the family had turned me away?

Of the many cards I received there was only one that proved disappointing. It was a very formal one from Gwen. She was still very much on my mind, although it had been over a year since we last met. When I telephoned to thank her the conversation was stilted, although I did make her laugh once. It was to be our last communication.

I wrote later to congratulate her on the fact that she'd won a gold medal for nursing, but she did not reply, and later I heard from the people at the church we both attended that Gwen had met a man she was going to marry and had left St. Peter's. I wrote to congratulate her—which was sincerely meant—but for my pains received a very unpleasant telephone call from her fiancé, a belligerent Welshman. He asked me what sex I was and said that Gwen didn't want to hear from me again. Furious, I said that it was a pity Gwen hadn't the courage to tell me herself instead of getting someone else to do her dirty work. For some reason I was perceived as a threat, but the threat was in her mind, not mine. I was certainly no longer in love with her, but genuinely wished her well. It was sad that she could not realize that. With such a man I doubted her future happiness, but she had made her choice. I hope Mother approved.

At the Eucharist on the day of my discharge the chaplain spoke of God's love being shown through others and told of a patient who had said that had she not been in the hospital she would not have known the depth of people's love. That was exactly how I felt, not just about my hospital stay, but about the whole process of changing roles. There had been much pain, but out of this had come the joy of experiencing love. Would I have been so aware of this had my life been "normal"?

Yet, on reflection, perhaps I was too grateful, somehow feeling exceedingly obliged to anyone who treated me as normal, as a person. It took some years to realize that it was wrong to feel amazement and fawning gratitude because someone was being accepting and caring to me, a transsexual. It demeaned myself and others to imply that it was out of the ordinary to show love to a fellow human. Why shouldn't I be as worthy of love as the next person? I am certain that my friends would not have wanted me to feel " 'umbly grateful." I had to learn not to debase myself.

I was surprised (and relieved) by the speed of my recovery and relative lack of discomfort. The worst bother were the vacuum bottles that drained my chest. They sat neatly in my dressing gown pockets and I labeled them BILL and BEN. The only real pain experienced was when the drainage tubes were removed. Although very sharp, the pain was short. With the dressings removed I was able to see my "new" chest for the first time.

My breasts were gone and the only scars were about three or four inches long that were almost under my arms. I was very pleased. In the years before this surgery I had wondered how I might react at this moment. Would I be shouting for joy that I'd lost a despised part of my body? In the event it wasn't like that at all.

Immediately after the surgery I'd been bound up; then, by the time the dressings were shed I had become accustomed to having a flat chest. In a way it was as if my breasts had never existed. They had been a bad dream and I'd woken up. Yet even though there was no sense of euphoria, I did feel that something alien had gone from me and I was becoming more normal. The only strangeness was when I suddenly realized that a bit of me had been removed. I wanted it gone but it still felt odd to think that it was somewhere else. But was it "me" any more than my hair cuttings? I wondered if this was a common feeling for people who had had surgery.

I was sorry to leave the hospital. It had been a wonderful opportunity to see many friends, make new ones, to reflect and learn. The fact of my mastectomy seemed almost incidental, especially as I was still swathed in bandages and not yet fully able to appreciate its benefits.

My few days' convalescence was spent at the Retreat House in St. Albans, which was staffed by the Sisters of the Holy Name from Malvern. Sister Pamela, a former nurse, was there, so I was in good hands. Mum insisted on paying for a taxi to bring her to London then take me on to St. Albans. I appreciated it, not just for the convenience but for what it symbolized—her acceptance. I wondered too if she was attempting to atone for her earlier lack of understanding, for which I never blamed her anyhow. Perhaps it helped her to do this for me.

My first week as Mark had been spent in a religious house, the friary. Now, after another step in my role change I was again with the religious.

Over the years a few people have accused me of going against God in what I did, but not the religious. They showed only acceptance, understanding and love. As Pamela remarked, if the treatment made me more of a whole person, how could it be wrong? It could only bring me nearer to God.

Exactly three weeks after my operation I was back at work in the laboratory. I was stiff and sore (perhaps my GP's partner had been just a little too enthusiastic to sign me off), but it was not long before all was forgotten. With it now behind me I had to turn my thoughts to a future career.

Chapter 22

WAS CELIBACY the answer? After all, I'd not had much success with my sexual relationships so far.

Just after my role change, Sister Pamela had remarked that by choosing to live as a man I had, in effect, opted for celibacy. It was unfair to expect a woman to enter into a permanent relationship knowing that her own sexual fulfillment would be denied. (What about *my* fulfillment? I asked myself.)

It was interesting that female friends who were married took an opposing view. Without exception they said that they would have married their partners had they been transsexuals (if the law had permitted it, that is) because they loved them as people and there was more to a relationship than sex. (One friend commented that there were many ways of killing a cat!) Sue felt it was important to get to know the person first; it is the person one loves, not the body.

As for denial of sexual fulfillment, the Canadian research, and latterly my experience of talking with female-to-male transsexuals and their partners, clearly shows that far from being denied, women find transsexuals good lovers.

Sister Pamela may have been thinking of the problem of not being able to father children, but that is no longer an insurmountable obstacle. Children have been born to partners of female-to-males following artificial insemination by a donor. The particular family I know is one of the happiest and most loving it has been my pleasure to meet.

My reply to Sister Pamela was that I had not chosen celibacy. It was only in my former role that I had been truly celibate, because it would have been psychologically, and probably therefore physically, impossible to have had sexual liaison with either a man or a woman. After my role change it became possible, even taking into account my physical limitations.

As for choosing to change roles, what is choice? There's a difference between the kind of choice that involves deciding whether to wear a red or green tie and one such as taking the opportunity to jump into the firemen's blanket because the flames are licking under the door or staying put to be roasted alive. A role change is the latter type of choice.

Sister Pam conceded to my view of myself as a forced celibate, a state that could change with circumstances. If someone loved me and I her, assuming that she was not already in a sexual relationship, would it be right of me to deny her myself? What good would come of it?

My Canterbury GP thought I should not exclude the possibility of a liaison with a woman. He believed that people with problems of this nature often formed better relationships than "normal" people (he called them "gray") because they are accepted in spite of their problems and loved for who they are.

A priest adviser said it was wrong to impose celibacy upon myself, as it was a negative decision. He was certain that many of his colleagues would conduct a religious ceremony in place of the standard marriage. God would recognize what the law would not.

Sex, my friends told me, was overrated, and love could overcome such difficulties. I am ambivalent about a physical relationship, but my misgivings are not for moral reasons. They are perhaps peculiar to me; I do not know if others share them.

First, I am afraid of rejection. This has been my main experience so far. Since I do not believe that women judge men by their genitals and I am aware that they can have satisfactory sexual relations with female-to-males, then my transsexual state is not necessarily a reason for rejection. My conclusion is that my lack of success must be due to my lack of acceptability as a person. One flaw has been my appalling lack of judgment—I should have heeded warnings about Debbie's moods. My feelings of being rejected for who, not what, I am, are reinforced by the fact that amongst female-to-males I am unusual in not having a partner.

Second, I didn't find the sexual experience with Debbie as wonderful as one might expect. For me it had been frustrating and uncomfortable and had given very little relief. There has been research into the feelings of the partners of transsexuals and they seem to be positive. One woman who had been sexu-

ally active for years with several partners said that her transsexual lover was the first man (she used that word) to induce
an orgasm in her. To my knowledge there have not been questions asked of the female-to-male transsexuals themselves, so I
do not know if my discomfort and frustration is limited to me
or common amongst us.

For these reasons I believe that life would be better were I
totally asexual, but I am not. It lurks in the background, and
when I've reached a stage of smug detachment, it leaps in for
the attack. It might be provoked by a particular woman, perhaps an erotic picture or a sex scene on the television. I recall
being aroused in my teens by *Lady Chatterley's Lover* when it
was first published. There's a conflict between my feeling of
wanting to be vicariously involved and the knowledge that it
will leave me frustrated. Sometimes the television gets
switched off, sometimes not.

Certain women have left me in a state of arousal for weeks
or more. (This was the case before any hormone treatment, so
it cannot be due only to that.) This is far more difficult to cope
with than with a book or film. It would therefore be sensible
to aim for detachment, but that's difficult if the sources of
arousal are unexpected. At the same time I yearn to have a satisfactory and loving physical relationship. Neither total
detachment nor the relationship seems a possibility.

One day perhaps I shall meet someone whose love will
enable me to overcome my fears and frustrations, but it seems
unlikely, since I am now over fifty. For now I have to live
with the tension of being outwardly asexual but inwardly a
Don Juan!

CROSSING

Deirdre McCloskey

1999

Deirdre McCloskey is best known for her numerous books and articles about economic theory and history. Her 1985 book The Rhetoric of Economics *is widely considered a classic in its field. She is currently Distinguished Professor of the Liberal Arts and Sciences at the University of Illinois at Chicago.*

From the Preface

I WANT to tell you the story of a crossing from fifty-two-year-old man to fifty-five-year-old woman, Donald to Deirdre.

"A strange story," you say.

Yes, it's strange, statistically. All the instruments agree that what's usually called "transsexuality," permanently crossing the gender boundary, is rare. (The Latin in "transsexuality" makes it sound sexual, which is mistaken; or medical, which is misleading; or scientific, which is silly. I'll use plain English, "crossing.") Only three in ten thousand want to cross the boundary of gender, a few of them in your own city neighborhood or small town. Gender crossing is no threat to male/female sex ratios or the role of women or the stability of the dollar. Most people are content with their birth gender.

But people do, after all, cross various boundaries. I've been a foreigner a little, in England and Holland and on shorter visits elsewhere. If you've been a foreigner you can understand somewhat, because gender crossing is a good deal like foreign travel. Most people would like to go to Venice on vacation. Most people, if they could magically do it, would like to try out the other gender for a day or a week or a month. The Venice visitors as a group can be thought of as all the "cross-gendered," from stone-butch dykes to postoperative male-to-female gender crossers, all the traversers, permanent or temporary, somber or ironic. A few people go to Venice regularly, and you can think of them as the cross-dressers among these, wearing the clothing of the opposite gender once in a while. But only a tiny fraction of the cross-gendered are permanent gender crossers, wanting to *become* Venetians. Most people are content to stay mainly at home. A tiny minority are not. They want to cross and stay.

On a trip to New York to see a friend after my own crossing I stood in the hall of photographs at Ellis Island and wept at the courage. Crossing cultures from male to female is big; it highlights some of the differences between men and women, and some of the similarities too. That's interesting. My crossing was costly and opposed, which is too bad. But my crossing has been dull, easy, comfortable compared with Suyuan's or Giuseppi's outer migrations.

Or compared with some people's inner migrations. Some people cross this or that inner boundary so radically that it would look bizarre, a slippage in the normal order of the universe, Stephen King material, if it were not so common. The most radical one is the crossing from child to adult, a crossing similar to mine that we all experience. I once saw a spoof scientific paper titled "Short Stature Syndrome: A Nationwide Problem." The strange little people, whose thoughts and actions were so different from normal, requiring the compulsory intervention of psychiatrists, and lots more money for the National Institute of Mental Health, were . . . children.

The word "education" means just "leading out." People are always leading themselves out of one life and into another, such as out of childhood and into each new version of adulthood. Not everyone likes to keep doing it, but the women I most admire have. My mother educated herself to earning her income and writing poetry after my father died. My roomer for a year in Iowa educated herself as a hospital chaplain after a third of a century teaching elementary school. My sister got a second degree in psychology; my former wife made herself into a distinguished professor. May Sarton, so glad to become by forced crossing an American rather than a Belgian woman, an English rather than a French poet and novelist and memoirist, kept crossing, crossing, and looked forward at age seventy to "what is ahead—to clear my desk, sow the annuals, plant perennials, get back to the novel . . . like a game of solitaire that is coming out."

It's strange to have been a man and now to be a woman. But it's no stranger perhaps than having once been a West African and now being an American, or once a priest and now a businessman. Free people keep deciding to make strange crossings, from storekeeper to monk or from civilian to soldier or from man to woman. Crossing boundaries is a minority interest, but human.

———

MY CROSSING—change, migration, growing up, self-discovery—took place from 1994 to 1997, beginning in my home in Iowa, then a year in Holland, then back in Iowa, with travels in between. As Donald and then as Deirdre I was and am a professor of economics and of history at the University of Iowa. From age eleven I had been a secret cross-dresser, a few times a week. Otherwise I was normal, just a guy. My wife had known about the cross-dressing since the first year of our marriage, when we were twenty-two. No big deal, we decided. Lots of men have this or that sexual peculiarity. Relax, we said. By 1994, at age fifty-two, I had been married those three decades, had two grown children, and thought I might cross-dress a little more. Visit Venice more too.

I visited womanhood and stayed. It was not for the pleasures, though I discovered many I had not imagined, and many pains too. But calculating pleasures and pains was not the point. The point was who I am. Here the analogy with migration breaks down. One moves permanently from Sicily to New York because one imagines the streets of New York are paved with gold, or at least better paved than the streets at home, not mainly because back in Catania since age eleven one had dreamed of being an American. Migration can be modeled as a matter of cost and benefit, and it has been by economic historians. But I did not change gender because I liked colorful clothing (Donald did not) or womanly grace (Donald viewed it as sentimentality). The "decision" was not utilitarian. In our culture the rhetoric of the very word "decision" suggests cost and benefit. My gender crossing was motivated by identity, not by a balance sheet of utility.

Of course, you can ask what psychological reasons explain my desire to cross and reply with, say, a version of Freud. Some researchers think there is a biological explanation for gender crossing, because parts of the brains of formerly male gender crossers in postmortems are notably female. But a demand for an answer to why carries with it in our medicalized culture an agenda of treatment. If a gender crosser is "just" a guy who gets pleasure from it, that's one thing (laugh at him, jail him, murder him). If it's brain chemistry, that's another (commit him to a madhouse and try to "cure" him).

I say in response to your question, Why? "Can't I just be?" You, dear reader, are. No one gets indignant if you have no answer to why you are an optimist or why you like peach ice cream. These days most people will grant you an exemption from the why question if you are gay: in 1960 they would not and were therefore eager to do things to you, many of them nasty. I want the courtesy and the safety of a whyless treatment extended to gender crossers. I want the medical models of gender crossing (and of twenty other things) to fall. That's the politics. I am ashamed that from the 1960s to the 1990s, in the political movements for black civil rights, women's liberation, gay rights, and opposition to the war in Vietnam, I had sound opinions but never really took a chance on them. Telling you my story is my last chance to be counted.

And incidentally, Why *do* you think you are the gender you were officially assigned to at birth? Prove it. How odd.

Ah. I think you need some treatment.

Chapter 8

ALL THROUGH the summer Donald and his wife quarreled about Jane. "Learn about it," he would say, angry or pleading. His cure for everything was book learning. He would press books and articles on her. She wouldn't read them.

"I can't handle it," she would say. "I'm tired. No, no, *no.*"

"I'm just a heterosexual cross-dresser," he would reply, convinced and argumentative, guy-style, professor-style. "No problem. We can work it out. Let's talk."

"No, no. I don't want to talk now."

"Call up the women I met at Cincinnati, the wives who have adjusted. Mrs. Realtor, Mrs. Chair of the National Cross-dressing Group, Mrs. Endocrinologist."

"I can't handle it." Donald realized she was ashamed to face another woman. What kind of woman am I, she would think, that my husband dresses in women's clothes? Ugh.

"Come on, dear, call them up. Come on."

After weeks of hectoring she called up Mrs. Endocrinologist, who at the convention had been kind to Jane. It turned out to be a consultation with an anti-cross-dresser. According to Donald's wife's report, Mrs. Endocrinologist sneered at the silly little cross-dressers buying "Melanie's Tape" and trying to achieve a female voice. Hopeless. They would never be women. Ha! Donald imagined that the sneers reflected her negotiated relationship with her own husband, in which he was "permitted" to come to such conventions and dress, so long as it was understood that gender crossing all the way was out. Donald was reminded of a little man at a Tri Ess meeting in Chicago dressed in a skirt and blouse, the visit a birthday present from his wife, who accompanied him, the first time he had been allowed to dress in five years.

The conversation with Mrs. Endocrinologist hardened his wife's attitude. In June, while Donald was away at the convention in Cincinnati, his wife had gone to the medical library and did her only reading about cross-gender, some psychoanalytic papers redolent of the 1950s and its homophobia. Then Mrs. Endocrinologist, then no more Mrs. Nice Gal, until a brief softening, and back.

———

HE AND his wife went on a cruise up the Inner Passage from Seattle to Juneau. He still believed himself to be a heterosexual cross-dresser. For a few days they forgot and wondered at seals and glaciers and a bear slaughtering salmon on the beach. His wife believed this was typical: that he could be distracted; that he didn't really cross-dress very much. In Juneau they shopped and Donald bought Jane a cheap hematite necklace. His wife was angry, disappointed that Jane was back. That night in the motel she said, "You've got to stop this."

"No, leave me alone." And they quarreled loudly in the thin-walled room.

———

ABOUT NOON on August 20, 1995, Donald had started the drive back from Aurora, Illinois, to Iowa City. He had spent the night at a pajama party at dear Robin's apartment, then a few hours of sleep after greeting the dawn in Aurora. Robin had just decided to go full-time as a woman. They had come home from partying through lesbian bars with Nikki from Milwaukee, Nikki the computer programmer, four years on hormones, Nikki with the lovely long, brown hair. Nikki had taught him how to hold a bottle of beer as a woman: "Not by the neck, dear. Delicately, around the body."

As the car pulled out of the parking lot Donald thought,

I am a fifty-three-year-old heterosexual cross-dresser, mar-ried thirty years, two grown children, a professor of economics and history. I don't want to be a woman.

Of course not. Just a hobby. Relax.

Let's see: East-West Tollway. He thought he knew the road well.

What a night. The last dance at Temptations at four A.M. The staff at the grocery store spotting us in drag. It's so easy to tell: the smiles, the startled looks. Getting read was my fault, mainly, since Robin is passable and Nikki even more so. Then the chatter until dawn at Robin's apartment. Crazy, harmless fun.

Just try it on, he said, as the car carried him west toward the Mississippi. *How would it feel to actually be a woman?*

A mental exercise. I'm in male drag now, of course, no women's clothes. Appropriate: heterosexual cross-dresser. Not *a transsexual! Not me.*

Go ahead: think about it. I've spent eight months January to August dealing intensely with this stuff. A convention, a few crazy, fun nights at Temptations, coming out to clubs of cross-dressers after forty-one years entirely in the closet. Oh, yeah: and that mall in the northern suburbs. And the trip to Des Moines and the angry janitor at the rest stop.

Just a guy who gets off dressing occasionally as a woman. No one knows in Iowa City. No problem.

Maybe one guy in a hundred does cross-dressing, otherwise straight and married. Or gay. Women, too—though they can cross-dress without anyone caring, like that wife of a colleague who wears men's shoes. None of them want to be in the other gender for real. Out of a hundred cross-dressers maybe three do want to change. Three in a hundred out of one in a hun-dred. Hey, a different thing, very rare. Not me. It makes cross-dressing look conventional.

I'm not transsexual. I don't want to cross permanently, be a woman. I don't want to become a Venetian. In the past eight months I've spoken to lots of transsexuals, though. Just out of interest.

Wife, grown kids. Me still Tarzan, not Jane. We can work it out. If my wife will be reasonable. Just reasonable.

But let's see.

Try it on. A mental experiment.

Just thinking.

Near De Kalb, the only town between the outskirts of Chicago and the Mississippi, after twenty miles of just thinking, he said,

Wait.

Good Lord.

I can become a woman.

I have always wanted to. I have learned by accident that I can.

I am not a heterosexual cross-dresser. All this time. I am a transsexual.

I can be a woman, he said. And he wept in relief, as the car drove itself. *I am a woman,* she said. *Yes!*

She said again, *I am a woman,* and wept.

————

THAT'S WHAT the cross-dressing since age eleven had been about, closeted over four decades, confined within marriage. And the open dressing in clubs and at home during the eight months past, more and more. The womanhood was there beneath the surface and yearned to take form.

Later in an interview with the student newspaper he described the feeling on the toll road as an "epiphany," which was a dangerous choice of words. It is a religious word, evoking Saul on the road to Damascus. "And suddenly there shined 'round about him a light from heaven, and he fell to the

earth, and heard a voice." Donald was not then religious.
Deirdre later was noncharismatically so, and the experience
was not spiritual. No light, no presence of God, no voice. The
danger is that newspapers and psychiatrists treat religious
experiences as madness. Donald's epiphany was merely a
moment of personal insight, a realization on the toll road near
De Kalb. This "epiphany": people have moments like that,
Deirdre would say, moments when self-knowledge becomes
more than a swirl of facts. A singular truth of character stands
in front of you, as clear as a crucifix. *Watch it: more religious
talk in an irreligious world.* Secularly speaking, understand, it
is knowing yourself instead of knowing about yourself. He
knew the dam. On the twentieth day of August 1995, a little
after noon, the dam broke and the water of his life swirled out
onto the plain. He knew himself. Herself.

That's it, she said: *I am a woman.*

And later in the crossing from man to woman, Donald/
Deirdre never doubted. He and then she didn't "decide,"
though an economist would like to think this way, in terms of
cost and benefit and a decision. Donald's son's letters of
protest later in the year were that way: How can you want to
be a woman? It's stupid. Let's see: adding up the convenience
for career of being a man, the inconvenience of hair and panty
hose, the cost of clothing—but its benefit in prettiness and
variety . . .

A few months before, Donald had actually done such a calculation. A man's way of thinking and an economist's:

THE COSTS AND BENEFITS OF WOMANHOOD

At the limits of my fantasies is transsexuality—but I
believe it's only a fantasy, stimulating in the mind but
not something I want. As a literal woman, gender reassignment surgery and all that:

My wife would leave me. This would be the loss of my best friend.

My daughter would reject me, though my son, I think, would continue to love me.

My birth family would be appalled. My mother in particular would be unable to handle it. Though my sister would be fine. Cousins — no way. Granny likewise.

I'd lose all my more casual friends, essentially — think of Dick! Or many, many of my professional friends, whom I really do value highly: Joel, Dick S., Bob H. Jesus! None of these people could handle it.

The transition is impossible in my occupation.

A woman would not be allowed to have the intellectual style I have.

I couldn't possibly just drop out and go get a job as a clerk. At fifty-five I would not be a hot property for development in the business world.

The hormones do nothing like the job in your fifties that they do in your twenties.

On the positive side, I get to be pretty — ho, ho. I would make a not very attractive woman, certainly *very* tall and *very* broad shouldered, things that nothing whatever can be done about. A plain face, though not hideous.

I could — here's a wild one — get the love of a man, maybe. But it's not anything I want now. I am determinedly heterosexual. Maybe I would fall for a man, as a woman. I'm not repulsed by the idea. Just uninterested.

Silly, he said to himself as he recalled the calculation. (And later Deirdre learned that the judgments about almost every person mentioned were wrong, the opposite of what happened.) *It's identity, stupid. Not cost and benefit.* She merely was.

As he crossed the Mississippi into Iowa the old uneasiness

dropped away. The question since age eleven was answered. He knew: another life.

An hour later he pulled into the driveway at home in Iowa City and smiled.

"You're home," said his wife, who was watering flowers by the driveway.

"Yeah. I had fun."

Angry. " 'Fun.' I'll bet." He didn't tell her.

———

DONALD AND his wife went briefly to a square dance in a small town Saturday night but came away early because they didn't like the caller. They crept through the parking lot giggling to get to the car without offending the hosts. Donald played the manly role but daydreamed at the dance about what it would feel like to be a woman. He watched a woman across the school gym talking animatedly to other women, with the self-deprecating style women use when charming others of their tribe. *Unlike the boasting of my tribe,* he thought. As they drove home he could feel himself resist telling his wife about his new conviction. *It would only upset her. Without medical backing she will scorn it. She feels that scorn is her only protection, her only hope. I've got to talk to the psychologist.* Donald practiced feminine ways of holding the steering wheel. For the past two months he had never sat down without crossing his legs. The unaccustomed pressure on the nerves around his knees made his feet partly numb. *Or maybe it's walking in heels that don't fit very well.*

———

A FEW days later he told his wife about his epiphany, and she cried and raged.

Who wouldn't? She couldn't talk to Donald about her feelings, but Deirdre later speculated: *Women tell a story of connection, and my wife's was a connection to Donald, not Deirdre. The story of her life was being shredded. Who am I, she would ask, a woman who lived thirty years with . . . a woman?*

Is that right? Is that how she feels? Oh, God, I could help. I could show her that she is mistaken about our past. I wish she would talk. Talking cures do sometimes work. She wants to be strong. Oh, dear one, please, please.

DONALD WENT to the year's first faculty meeting in the department of history and found himself playing his usual role as smart aleck, pushily male, presuming to take up emotional space the way men do. He found he still liked doing it, or maybe by now it was automatic. He was angry at himself: *Jesus, what a stupid performance. I don't deserve to be a woman. Could I absorb the "dose of humility" for a woman's role?*

Yes, by recovering the character I had as a child. He did not mean being childish, but being as he had been before putting on manhood like a football uniform. Deirdre was later something like the boy Donald, less stupidly assertive or smart-mouthed than Donald the man, less joking—though still it was there, the trick practiced since high school of searching for double meanings and topical references to set off laughter. The lessening desire to practice the trick came from his new aversion toward the "*io, io,*" the "me, me" of men's conversation, as he began to think of it. In a marketplace in Italy Donald had once seen a little boy, three years old, furious at not being allowed to have an ice cream. The boy filled the market with his cry of egotism thwarted: "*Io, io, io.*" Me, me, me. The *io,* the me, became less important to Deirdre. She would say to herself of some potential story or remark, after the moment had passed: *Let it go.*

———

HE WOKE at three A.M. and called JCPenney's catalog number and ordered a set of underwear for his new, weight-reduced body. First time buying lingerie from a regular store. He had spent some time the day before preparing the order, reflecting on bra sizes. On the phone to Penney's the woman was not contemptuous and acted as though it were natural for someone with the name Donald McCloskey on the credit card to specify a post-office-box address for "Jane Austen" for receiving four half-slips, three bras, and so forth. Actually, it is not rare. Men order for women and women for men. Maybe not to a post office box. Maybe not in the name of the first big female voice in English literature. They were good pieces of clothing, and Deirdre wore them out.

———

HE WONDERED: *Is it significant that this crisis has come near the anniversary of my father's fatal coronary, at age fifty-three, which I become next month?* His wife later told a psychiatrist, according to notes in a legal record, that "Donald did not expect to live beyond age fifty-three," and the psychiatrist, in the tendentious style of his profession, wove it into the story of "a danger to himself" that he wanted to tell.

No. It was the end of a summer free for tacit and then explicit deliberation.

———

A CERTAIN amount of underdressing now seemed appropriate, trying on his gender crossing, a token of sincerity. After a while he gave it up. It was not presenting as a woman. It was continuing forty-one years as a male with a secret vice.

———————

AFTER HE had told her about the epiphany he and his wife visited their psychologist, Frank, whom they had seen a few times to try to save their dissolving marriage, first about crossdressing. His wife seemed comforted by the visit that morning, and when she got home she hugged Donald and said she loved him. He wept, as he hardly ever did. He wanted to stay married to this woman, or to stay close.

Donald, though, was still going to electrolysis, two hours that same day, and his own hour with the psychologist.

About the gender crossing, Frank said, "You get to decide."

"What do you mean?"

"I mean that you are a free, sane, adult person. You get to decide about whether to transition or not." Frank did not like to make his patients into children.

"I agree, Frank. I think it's political."

"Political or not, you get to decide. It's not to be forbidden by the fears of outsiders." Grow up: take responsibility for yourself.

Frank suggested Donald make an appointment with a psychiatrist in town, to check for major mental illness. Donald's wife and sister were demanding that he be "treated" for "mania." Their notion was that he had gone crazy, and that if treated for the craziness he would drop the silliness about becoming a woman. *Maybe it would satisfy them.* The appointment was made for Donald's fifty-third birthday.

He told his wife what Frank had said and about the appointment with the psychiatrist; she wept in turn, and he held her.

Chapter 39

NINETY THOUSAND dollars. That was the money cost, far above the $20,000 or so for electrolysis and the operation that constitutes the minimum for crossing male to female all the way. An economist would predict that if the monopoly restrictions arising from the Benjamin Standards and the Johns Hopkins–influenced psychiatrists disappear, and if laser hair removal becomes cheaper as it becomes more common, the cost could fall a good deal: perhaps to $10,000 in total someday. That's a debt paid off in five years at about $53 a week, if your credit is poor, ten hours a week at the minimum wage. People finance cars at that level.

The $90,000 for Deirdre was grotesquely higher than the minimum because she had cosmetic surgery and voice surgery from the best, with a lot of surgery to fix their surgery, and because her sister had so courageously opposed it, adding some $25,000 to the bill, and because Deirdre wanted it all to be over quickly. Had she paid every extortionate bill generated by her sister's intervention or by the insurance fraud of hospitals there would have been an additional $22,000. As it was, she battled the hospitals for years. It was like purchasing a top-end Mercedes rather than a Ford, and not bargaining, and then being sued in the middle about one's right to make the purchase, and then being cheated by the car dealer.

But economics correctly teaches that "cost" is not these money costs. It is what you sacrifice by taking the path. Two roads diverged in a yellow wood, and you chose one at the sacrifice of the other. Well, then, Deirdre sacrificed the $90,000 worth of things that could have been bought. A little earlier retirement. A much better car.

But the biggest cost to Deirdre, not to be measured, was the sacrifice of wife and son and daughter.

And cost to whom? Economics also teaches that question: Cui bono, to whose benefit? It was certainly not a benefit to Deirdre's marriage family, in their reckoning. As they accounted it, they paid the cost.

However accounted, they *were* the sacrifice.

———

DONALD'S WIFE was angry and ashamed that Donald had become Deirdre. When Deirdre came back to Iowa after the Dutch year and asked to meet, Donald's wife promised, then could not, then would not. Every few months Deirdre would appeal by e-mail across campus: Please, please, just a mild, normalizing chat. Thirty years of marriage. A good marriage. What did I do wrong in all that good time? Please. So we don't meet in the ladies' room. Please.

No. You have hurt me. You did wrong. It's weird. I don't do weird. You should be ashamed. I am ashamed. I can't handle it. No, no, no.

The way she thought of it, she had lost what Deirdre had gained. It was zero-sum, and as Donald/Deirdre became happier the other became more miserable, until she had to break contact. She divorced, she would not meet, she moved to another town, she never shopped in Iowa City. No other contact. It was embarrassing. Mortifying. Wounding. Donald's wife thought of the loss as a death—except that there across campus sat the murderess, alive and happy and unpunished. It was worse than a death. Had Donald died of a heart attack at age fifty-three, as his father had, the wife would have acted the widow for a while, sad to see her life's companion leave, dignified in her grief. But, for God's sake, he became a woman. Deirdre tried to imagine her feelings. Donald's wife would not speak or write, and Deirdre was inexperienced at a woman's imagination. *She feels that her marriage was meaningless. "Was I married all those years," she asks, "to a woman? What does that make me?"* A woman raised in a small town in the 1950s was not relaxed about homosexuality. She felt the crossing made thirty years of her life meaningless. Yes, worse than a death.

For months Deirdre was circumspect when attending committees of the university or passing the Nursing Building on her way to work or shopping for groceries at the Hy-Vee. Would she encounter Donald's wife? Couldn't they just acknowledge each other and then go about their lives unrestricted? Deirdre would check the aisles in the grocery store quickly before shopping. At length she realized that her former wife had shifted everything out of Iowa City and only worked there. Deirdre was startled once to see their old car at a distance, with Donald's wife driving to her new home.

————

THEIR SON, a businessman in Chicago, late twenties, was also angry and ashamed. After several months of e-mails in the turbulent fall of 1995, arguing that becoming a woman was irrational, he wrote by e-mail that he would not open letters, would not read anything, not anything at all. Deirdre tried postcards for a while, probably unread; e-mails, probably unread; finally the titles of e-mails, saying "I love you" in a place he could not fail to read.

Silence. Deirdre thought, *Men feel no duty of love, except to those assigned to them by some exchange of favors, and toss love away lightly.* Her friend in Australia, Kate, had one out of three who continued loving. *No, no; not my son.*

A year's silence, and then she returned from Holland hopeful. *Surely now I am home I can heal my broken family. Surely they will love me as they did.* On a night a few weeks after Deirdre's return to Iowa that winter an e-mail appeared in the list from her son.

Wonderful! He's writing! Praise the Lord, she thought as she scrolled through the list and highlighted the title and pressed Return.

No, said the message. I was married last week. Full ceremony. You were not, of course, invited. This is all I will say.

Married. Not invited. To the wedding. Later she would remember, waking at night with his words, or catching sight of his photo in the upstairs hallway, age three, the little blond boy smiling up at the camera.

That summer in the dining room of the Iowa house during a fit of womanly cleaning Deirdre found his baby cup inscribed with his initials. She knelt a long time in front of the open cabinet, rocking. She would write to her son's new wife. She got up clutching the cup. Surely another woman will understand.

No answer.

Six months later her son returned a final letter from Deirdre unopened, unable to endure Deirdre's plaint, and wrote passionately, this one and last time. You have betrayed me, he said. Love is an exchange.

Men's talk, Deirdre said to herself as she read. *Yet even in such manly terms,* the economist thought, *I stand ready to exchange. No takers.* Deirdre's mother comforted her in the stoic way: "You must expect this in a divorce. The children go with the mother."

———

DEIRDRE BELIEVED her daughter, early twenties, was more hopeful. People said, It will be easier on a daughter. She lived in Lawrence, Kansas, a college student. Deirdre supposed that she did open the monthly letters, with the little presents and the accounts of Deirdre's travels, cheerful invitations to visit at their old home in Iowa City, or to come along on Deirdre's business trips to Europe, a communication every month for a year in each epistolary form. Deirdre remembered a trip to England the two of them had taken when her daughter was twelve, lining up for the Hard Rock Café in London, walking the haunted stones at Avebury, punting on the Isis, father and daughter.

She did not answer. She had learned about the gender crossing two months after her brother did, late in the fall just before Deirdre went to San Francisco and then in the new year to Holland. She had sent one letter, pleading with her father not to do what he intended. She viewed it then as a failure of duty. *How far does duty extend?* Deirdre would wonder. *To avoid their self-defined hurt from embarrassment am I to refuse my life? They could be proud and loving, as my mother is, as many friends are. Instead they are ashamed, making everything worse.* After her one letter the college student wrote nothing, though taking $10,000 a year in support. At one point Deirdre looked into the law of child support and contemplated cutting her off. Once she did, and the bank made it worse by not restarting the transfers when she thought better of it, but then she paid in full with interest, ashamed of the unstoical act. *I'm as confused as my son: love, Deirdre, is not an exchange. No parent with sense expects to be paid back in any coin.* During the two phone calls Deirdre made when back to Iowa she ended by crying, which her daughter did not like. Silence.

Yet Deirdre was hoping, hoping. *Children are that way. I was,* she thought, though the truth did not relieve the throbbing. A woman friend said, "There is nothing more focused on itself than a twenty-something child. It's genetic, not moral. Believe me: I've known a half dozen of them well." Deirdre thought, *I said in effect to my mother at my daughter's age, "See you around, Mom." It's the same.*

Six months back in the United States after the Dutch year, twenty-one months into womanhood and twenty-one months of silence from her daughter, Deirdre wrote again.

My dearest daughter,

I'm awake at 3:30, unable to sleep. It doesn't happen much. I got back from Mexico and the conference there with a cold and a case of traveler's diarrhea. What really got me up was the ache about you.

You are my only spot of warmth, I hope.

I will be in Kansas later in July for a couple of days, visiting my friend Patty's family in Topeka. I could visit you in Lawrence. A brief meeting, on neutral ground if you want, would be healthy. It would show you that I am presentable and that I love you.

I wonder how you are doing, how I might help. I worry that in turning away from me you may leave yourself regretting later a lost chance to help your parent in need. I regretted not more vigorously trying to help my mother when she was left with two bratty teenagers to raise after my dad died. And in a smaller matter I regretted not visiting my dad in the hospital years before when he was sick with appendicitis—it was in a Boston suburb, when I was in college in Cambridge six miles away, and though I didn't have a car I could have gone often. I only went once, with my mother. In both cases (and others: how much cause for regret a human life contains) I hurt myself, by not assuming an adult role for my mother and by not getting closer to my father in his illness. It was intrinsically bad, bad for my soul; and it was imprudent, too. It gave me less of a life.

But all this aside, I love you and want to meet. Can't we?

Love,

Deirdre and Dad

No answer.

———

A FEW weeks later Deirdre and Patty approached Lawrence in the car on the way from the Kansas City airport to Topeka.

"We've got to stop," said Deirdre.

Patty looked at her. "I don't think it's a good idea. Are you sure?"

"Yes. I'll go in for just a few minutes."

"If she's home. She might be in class."

"It's summer, Patty."

"Yes. But she might not be there."

They found her daughter's address, a worn frame house with a big porch on Kentucky Avenue, divided into three student apartments, and Deirdre ached. *Please, please, dear God.* Deirdre was by this time attending church, and her prayer was more than a figure of speech. She knocked. No answer. She could feel her heart pounding, the weakness. *Oh, wrong door. Hers must be the side apartment.* She went around the porch and knocked. *Wait; no rush; polite.* The cicadas twanged and the air-conditioning roared. Kansas hot. She knocked again. *Not so loud; this isn't a police raid.* Then she tried the door. *Careless; it's open.* She stepped in and called in her new, soft voice from the operation two months before.

"Hello! It's me!"

No answer. The air-conditioning, the disordered student apartment. One room far at the end had the door closed. Deirdre stood in her sundress. *These three,* she thought sardonically, out of tune with her anxiety, *must be the only people in the world who haven't seen me. These I love more than anyone. Is my hair all right? Oh, I wish, I wish she would love me.* Tears. She called again, standing tentatively. *Please. My little girl.*

The door of the far bedroom opened slowly and her daughter shuffled out, wrapped in a blanket as when she was a toddler in the Chicago house coming out of her room at the head of the stair dragging the cozy.

"Oh, no!" she said when she saw Deirdre. "No! I can't handle this!"

"Please, just a few minutes of talk."

"I can't handle this! *Please* go away!"

"Oh, please. It would be so much better if we could talk."

Her daughter seemed weary, not hostile. "No, no. I can't handle it. I can't."

"All right. All right." *It's not going to work,* and Deirdre's hope deflated. *Why should she handle it? It's my life, not hers. Patty was right.* "I'll go. But please, please give me a hug." Her daughter didn't like it. "Please." Deirdre was crying. "My little girl." Her daughter was reluctant, but accepted the hug. Not in the repulsed way. *Not eagerly, exactly,* Deirdre said to herself, *but not repulsed. At least not repulsed.*

"Good-bye, dear. I love you." *She needs to separate as adult children anyway do. Maybe when she has her own children. My God, my God.*

"Good-bye, Dad."

Her daughter changed her phone number and moved to a new address. *Maybe it's just the college student's usual change of apartment with every new year, one step ahead of the rent collector. Maybe it's not repulsed shame.* Donald's wife would not give their daughter's new address. Her daughter didn't want to give it. The phone number was listed under her roommate's name. Embarrassment. *Remember: it's not hatred, and cannot be called that in fairness. Oh, God.* Her son moved too, with his wife by now perhaps pregnant with Deirdre's grandchild. *That would feel more like hatred, to be kept from my grandchild.* Later her son's wife was in fact pregnant, and they tried to keep the knowledge from Deirdre. "I am not authorized by him to tell you," said the ex-wife. *My grandchild. Have you no mercy?* On Saint Patrick's Day of 1998 a grandson was born. Deirdre learned of him nine months later.

But try to feel it as they do, she would tell herself. *Would you do better? Did you?* Donald's wife would not give either child's address. She was stern in forwarding two last pleading notes to the children: All right, "*but*—I will not do this again. If you send me notes to them, I will discard them." *No, no, please, no. I understand your belief that it's best to walk away without loving remembrance from three decades of life. For yourself, you think. But how am I to speak to my children? My grandchild?*

————

DEIRDRE TALKED to an elderly neighbor about her mother's disapproving of her marriage to a non-Lutheran.

"She wouldn't speak to me for years after."

"Not speak to you? That's terrible. How many years?"

She reckoned it up. "Thirty."

————

MUCH LATER Deirdre talked to Carol about it.

"Your son deserves a more heroic role in your story," said Carol as they finished eating the luncheon salad she had assembled out of leftovers. Deirdre admired Carol's swift efficiency in the kitchen and tried to help by closing cabinets and wiping counters and filling the dishwasher, the unskilled assistant.

"What, for abandoning his father?"

"No, for *not* abandoning his mother and his sister— assuming the role of the man of the family. After all, you had given it up."

Deirdre slumped on the high stool at the counter.

She's right. At my son's age I walked away from my father in the hospital and then from my widowed mother with her teenage children. These are my own stories to my daughter.

"Good Lord, Carol, you're right." *It's only fair that my son and daughter support their mother: she has lost in this. True, she left me, and the children left with her, as much as I wished them to stay.*

But I left her.

Yes, she would think when turning it over again and again, *that's true. But why answer loss with loss, insult with years and decades of reinsults, the hater the loser? Why punish, and make everyone worse off,* the economist thought, *the punisher worst punished? As we forgive those who trespass against us.*

And yet, I have sinned, thought the novice Christian. Her head ached with the complexities. *Mine was the first leaving. We sin against our lovers. The cost of love is sorrow, because it must end in death, literal or figurative. Yet one must love, because "from love one can only escape at the price of life itself,"* wrote Freya Stark. *Are my former wife and my children damaging their lives by their unloving escape? Love is risky, yes, for the endgame is sorrow. But "no lessening of sorrow is worth exile from that stream of all things human and divine."*

And, the professor would think, *it has politics. On a small scale. I didn't do my duty in the civil rights movement of the early 1960s or the antiwar movement of the late 1960s or the gay movement of the 1970s. It would be shameful,* secular stoicism declared, *not to stand up this time.* The rhetoric of the families of the cross-gendered or homosexual or Buddhist or whatever is one of victims, but victims not because they are beaten or starved or unloved but because they cannot *bear* the shame. In 1945 a Jew marries a Lutheran and both families say, "Why have you done this to us?" Done this. In 1955 a white man marries a black woman and the families say, "Why have you done this to us?" To us.

In 1995 a lesbian marries her lover in a ceremony in the redwoods, described in Ellen Lewin's book on gay and lesbian marriages, *Recognizing Ourselves: Ceremonies of Lesbian and Gay Commitment.* Muriel's daughter is loving, but her two sons will not bring their families:

my older son called and said he and his wife didn't feel that their children should be exposed to that kind of thing. But he himself would be glad to come.... And then followed an hour or so later by my other son with a similar story.... I called them both back the next day and told both of them I didn't want either one of them at the ceremony if that's the way they felt.

Lewin continues: "Muriel reminded her sons that...as a young white woman marrying a black man in the 1950s she...had not given in.... She thus found her sons' conventional attitudes particularly ironic."

Deirdre listened, touched, to Lewin telling the story in a public reading at Prairie Lights bookstore. A month later she heard on the radio the story of Billy Tipton, the jazz musician born Dorothy, who from 1928 lived as a man, five times married, adopted children, no one knowing, not even his wives. His wives forgave him when they learned, much later: Billy was a pretty good husband, though with a roving eye. But his son was *angry* hurt. Because Billy had been a bad father? No, because he had been Dorothy. Huh?

And finally, prudence and politics aside: *Let it go, Deirdre. Grow up.* Secular stoicism spoke, or in more sophisticated form her new Christianity. The world contains evil, as the widow learns or the unloved wife learns or the spurned father learns. Deliver us from evil. The evil's there. Donald's wife learned this, and her children did, her sister did, and Deirdre learned it too. *For thine is the kingdom,* Deirdre prayed, *thou God of grown-ups.*

THE WOMAN
I WAS NOT BORN TO BE

Aleshia Brevard

2001

Following her 1962 surgery, Aleshia Brevard worked as a film and television actress and as a Playboy bunny. She continues to be active in theater as an actress and director.

from Chapter 3

IN THOSE days—after Lane but before surgery—I was disillusioned but far from world-weary. Somewhere, something was waiting for me. Every day in San Francisco was an adventure, and I didn't dare stay home for fear I'd miss something. Who knew what might be around the next corner? I intended to find out. Lane Erstane was yesterday's B-grade movie, and it was time to get on with the theater of life.

My fascination with Marilyn Monroe seemed a natural foundation for creating a new me. I, along with the rest of the world, was spellbound by the siren's vulnerability. I didn't want to create a tawdry drag impersonation of Marilyn Monroe; I wanted to find myself. Still, while I was waiting for my real persona to jell, it was time to create a specialty act for Finocchio's. Okay, instead of applying protective layers, like traditional drag queens, I would strip them away. I'd allow my vulnerable self to show through. In college, I'd been told that coeds saw me not as a gay male but rather as a deer caught in oncoming headlights. Most of my life I'd felt almost paralyzed by fear. Why not put that poor-little-match-girl quality to work for me?

While Stormy and I were doing the weekly grocery shopping, we'd practice dance steps behind our shopping cart. Doing the dishes, we prattled about new lyrics. Making the beds, we'd chatter about wardrobe. We were energetic, creative, and in love with show business. One thing was certain: if I wanted to live like a star, I needed to become one.

"My Heart Belongs to Daddy" was introduced at Finocchio's on a Tuesday night. My act in a red knit sweater, slowly removed to reveal a red lace merry widow, was an instant triumph. Thanks to Marilyn's musical performance in *Let's Make Love*, I'd found my routine. I also had found my following. "Daddy" was a hit. By the following Monday, my salary was increased to headliner status.

Life consisted of work, shopping, and developing a bond with Stormy that was to continue our entire lives. In many ways, we felt closer than real sisters. We shared a special understanding. We had a common covenant.

One night after work, we were together at the bathroom sink removing our makeup. Stormy took down a pill bottle and took a purple capsule.

"What's that?" I asked.

"Premarin," she answered.

"What's it for?" I queried.

"They make your boobies grow," was her answer.

"Give me one," I said, sticking out my hand.

It felt like the right thing to do. I could never go back to being Buddy Crenshaw; I'd come too far. Standing by the bathroom sink in a basement apartment at 860 Gary Street, I made a commitment to becoming myself, fully, as I took my first female hormone. Early the next day, Stormy introduced me to her physician, Dr. Harry S. Benjamin. After a physical examination, he accepted me as his newest transsexual patient.

I was slightly disconcerted by the famous doctor's initial excitement over my pubic hair. He found the growth pattern very female in appearance, and for his studies that held great significance. I was sorry to disappoint him, but I shaved the pubic area for just that appearance.

The year that followed meeting Harry Benjamin represents the zenith of my gender quest. It was a period of transition, both on- and offstage.

Generally, for several years prior to surgery, male gender-reassignment patients are required to live their daily lives as women, but this testing period was waived for me. I was not able to live full-time as a woman. Due to my professional status at Finocchio's, I was too recognizable in San Francisco. It was professionally necessary that on the street I continue to appear in the despised male garb and the hated skullcap I wore to cover my long hair. My doctor, believing I was learning the fine art of feminine mystique onstage, made an exception in my transitioning process. Nightly audiences did pay to judge my femininity, but my doctor had overlooked the fact that customers were applauding a theatrical illusion. Ultimately, his decision to waive my daily, comprehensive experience as a woman made my transition much more difficult. "Passing" for female was not my dilemma. Ensuring a comfortable passage into the real world of women could come only with exposure to their daily experience. The world of most genetic women is made up of the little things, not the glamour. While my daytime "real girl" sisters toiled for unequal pay, rocked society's cradle, and struggled for complete emancipation, I waited impatiently for twilight hours when I could pose and preen.

Now that I knew I had a surgical way out, I was no longer content in the gay bars and restaurants of the city. I wanted to live my life as a woman. On those nights when I felt I could no longer tolerate my male persona, I'd remove *most* of my makeup after my last show, powder my face, stick my shoulder-length hair up under a navy knit skullcap, and hail a cab. I was off to dance with the merchant marines at a notorious club called the Streets of Paris.

The name did not do this after-hours, smoke-filled, low-rent establishment justice. The *Sewers* of Paris would have been more apt. I loved the joint. I convinced myself that here I was living life as a true girl.

I carried with me at all times, in case of arrest, a letter of medical explanation from my doctor. Letter or no letter, had the men with whom I danced and flirted suspected that I was technically male, there would have been no time for clarification. That, as they say, would have been that. Splat! Smeared all over the tawdry Streets of Paris. The danger was part of the intrigue. I was testing my wings of wax.

Legally, at that time, one was required to wear at least three gender-appropriate articles of clothing. Otherwise you were subject to arrest. Few heterosexuals were aware of the law. The archaic ruling was of major consequence only for the queens of the queer community. For my late-night forays, I generally wore two socks and a silky, if male, tank top under my very feminine slacks and top.

My outer garments had for years been very nongender specific: velvet tops over stovepipe-cut slacks; oversize shirts over tight, tight jeans. I did not, however, hit the streets in cute little skirts and cashmere sweaters. I was conscious of the dress code and the fact that I was known to every cop on our block.

The city's finest were often found kibitzing with the owners at the club. In the years leading up to San Francisco's "gay-ola" scandal of the early 1960s, it was common practice for the owners of gay clubs to "grease" the legal system. Financial consideration in the right blue pockets allowed talented "fairies" to work and play without constant police harassment. The cops on Broadway knew who I was, and I knew them for what they were. Like everyone familiar with gay life, I carried a healthy fear of our law-enforcement officials. I played by the rules and only slightly bent the dictate that you arrive and exit the club . . . male.

"I know you think you're real, girl," Stormy would fret, "but you're still almost six feet tall and bear a striking resemblance to that popular drag queen Lee Shaw. Don't think you're invisible to the police."

My friend was concerned for my safety, but her primary fear was not of the men with whom I danced at the Streets of

Paris. She knew how badly I would be treated if picked up by the police. I would be unceremoniously tossed into jail, if not worse.

Frustrated by the limitations of my maleness, I increased my oral doses of both Premarin and Provera. I also doubled my injections of estrogen.

Stormy had not lied when she told me the little purple Premarin pill would make my "boobies grow." Lee Shaw quickly became an impressionist with impressive cleavage. My body softened in contour as the weekly ingestion of estrogen layered an extra padding of protective fat beneath my skin. The physical changes could not happen fast enough for me. Nausea, emotional fluctuations, and hot flashes were minor side effects, considering the physical results. A sore, burgeoning bosom was a wonderful daily reminder of the miraculous changes occurring in my body. Rounded hips and pubescent breasts, however, were difficult to conceal under the male clothing I was still forced to wear on public outings. In the 1950s and early 1960s, a well-dressed woman in San Francisco did not appear downtown without her hat and gloves. I hated being forced to stuff my developing body into jeans and sweatshirts. Being caught between genders was, at best, an embarrassment.

I wasn't the only one disturbed by my public appearance. A tax audit of Alfred Brevard Crenshaw caused one federal employee more consternation than *his* summons had caused *me*. As later reported in a *San Francisco Examiner* article focusing on unusual tax audits, the IRS agent said my gender was more perplexing than my 1959 tax return. I was in his office with my habitual skullcap hiding my long hair, no makeup, and wearing a man's sweatshirt. It was my untethered bosom that caused the interrogator's confusion. He couldn't take his eyes off my tits. After an awkward interview, he allowed my claim for sequin and lace deductions. He was more concerned that Alfred B. Crenshaw had perky little breasts.

Although I was committed to my physical development, I sometimes lagged far behind emotionally. I still fully believed anyone who indicated that my very existence was shameful.

When Stormy and Michael decided to move to a lovely Victorian on Steiner Street, they asked me to join them. Stormy and I would continue to split all expenses down the middle.

After work, Stormy and I stayed up all night packing, and on the actual day of the move, we certainly did not look or feel our best. We were tired, dirty, and more than a little disheveled. Michael's concern, however, was that a moving man might think we were less than feminine. The man of our house was tense with fear that a stevedore might question his mate's and her best friend's gender. That could prove the ultimate blow to his masculinity. The two paying members of the household were not at their glamorous best; ergo we were not acceptable.

Neither Stormy nor I was shocked when Michael suggested we hide in the closet while movers were in the house. We were programmed to accept such homophobic reactions. We accepted that our existence was a legitimate cause for shame, so when the movers arrived, we willingly hid. We lived our lives in the shadow of society, and now we shut ourselves away rather than prove an embarrassment to anyone. It's hard to disappear much deeper into shadows than when hiding in a closet.

The dreams, the hormones, the surgery were all a desperate attempt at an acceptable life. The journey is a serious one. We joke. We sometimes cavort outlandishly. Each transsexual follows his or her own ritualistic path, but finally, we all try to desensitize the pain. Ultimately, ours is a journey born of anguish. We make that journey in order to live as we are . . . without having to hide from anyone.

from Chapter 5

"IS IT all over?" I asked the recovery room nurse.

"You're fine," she answered. The woman was a mistress of understatement. I was groggy and disjointed, but I recognized this moment as the milestone of my life. My life began at Westlake Clinic on that day in 1962. Gone was my "birth defect." From this day forward I could react to life emotionally, pursue my own feminine dreams of success, and live as an equal partner with the man I loved. I had been reborn woman. I was free.

That I believed to be true.

My idealized existence was based on my skewed perception of a woman's status in America. I trusted that as a female I would be instantly creditable, acceptable, and understood. Automatically, doors would be opened for me, and society would rush forward to reward my femininity with an honored position in heterosexual society. Why not? I was complete. At long last, my excessively submissive nature would earn me respect. By being emotionally fragile, I would now be universally desired, and for being a nurturer, I would be cherished. Surgery was behind me, and so were my years of not belonging. I'd been granted a second chance at life—I could now make a life in the social mainstream.

That I also believed.

Presented with a clean slate, I immediately began to mar it. In those first moments of womanhood, all I wanted was Hank. I hadn't been complete for an hour, and already I was attaching my lifeline to a man. I had no notion of my folly, and the women in my world did not see my error. In the early 1960s, the majority of American women were still perpetuating the archaic myth that without a man, a woman is worthless. Few women had found their stronger voice—and so I was striving desperately to soften mine. I was eager to recline on a chaise and wait for that special man who would peel me a grape. It would be more than ten years before a feminist friend would inform me, "A woman without a man is like a fish without a bicycle." I did not believe her.

———

MOTHER WAS waiting in my room when I returned from surgery. I was blessed by being born to such a strong, nurturing, and loving woman. I don't believe that she ever consciously let me down. If, unwittingly, she at times let me flounder, it was because even she did not realize she had a right to her own power. Mozelle Gillentine Crenshaw had a great zest for life and expressed it freely. She was beautiful and smart. She was also strong—but in spurts. I believe she was very unhappy in her marriage but terrified of living a life on her own. She was, nonetheless, always threatening to leave.

"Leave! If you want out, go!" Daddy would yell. "But don't think you're taking anything with you."

Mother would continue to sputter, rant, and rave, but she always knuckled under to Daddy's intimidation. The threat of being left to her own devices shook my mother. She could not accept the thought of a life without her home, furnishings, or position.

Mother was often peevish and querulous. Daddy was withdrawn from day-to-day family interaction, but you could always sense his overriding disapproval. The threat of his loud and disruptive outbursts bubbled just beneath the surface of our lives. To survive in our household was to tiptoe across a minefield. Fear of a strident male voice and a habit of buckling upon hearing intimidating male tones grew as I matured. I brought that cowering response with me into my new life. I also came to womanhood mimicking my mother's fear of abandonment. I believed I was starting life over with a clean slate. I was not. All the baggage I had previously accumulated was shipped ahead, COD.

When the anesthesia initially wore off, I came back to the immediate moment with a lurch. I was in agony. There was no escaping the pain. Morphine was prescribed every four hours, but it didn't touch the deep, visceral ache. Nevertheless, I quickly became an avid clock watcher. The morphine made me care less that I hurt, but I had not expected such excruciating pain. In my history there was nothing that could have prepared me for the goddamn mind-numbing agony of ripped tissue and muscle as it attempted to heal—only to be ripped open again by the vaginal dilator that I had to wear. Three times daily the vagina had to be enlarged—after first ripping the cotton gauze padding from the vaginal wall. My surgeon's intention was to create vaginal depth; my raw vagina's objective was to snap shut and heal over. As the doctor packed and repacked my new vagina, they crammed enough cotton padding inside me to resurrect the plantation system in at least two Delta states! The Old South might rise again, but I never would.

In creating vaginal depth, Dr. Elmer Belt skinned the penis, took a skin graft from the bottom of each foot, and removed a six-inch square from the back of my left thigh. The sweltering midsummer heat of Los Angeles added to my misery, and open wounds on my feet and thigh oozed onto rumpled hospital sheets. I gave up and surrendered to my agony.

Hank and my mother were always available during my recovery. Their comforting presence made me feel safe and secure. My pride in Hank hit a new high when, soon after my transition, he took a Westlake Clinic nurse to task for repeatedly expressing her moral objection to "that kind of surgery."

"Don't ever let me hear you say 'that kind of surgery' again," he seethed. "This procedure was not a matter of choice, you know. To those of us who love Aleshia, this surgery was no more elective than an emergency appendectomy." Mozelle echoed his sentiments.

That my mother was staunchly on my side was a tremendous relief. I was aware she'd suffered misgivings concerning my gender transformation. Mother was afraid she'd never be able to refer to her son as "she."

"But, James," my mother wailed over and over as she and Daddy crossed the country to lend support for my surgery, "what if I slip and call him—her Buddy?"

She didn't slip. Not once. From the moment she first spotted me, in my skirt and blouse, waiting at the station to greet them, my mother responded as though I'd always been her daughter.

Before surgery, my total focus had been on my emotional turmoil and the impending surgical changes. After the transformation, I still had emotional and psychological work to do. Surgery did not make me a secure woman. It merely opened the door for me to become one.

Not all my concerns, however, were earth-shattering. For one thing, I was curious about the appearance of my vagina. I'd never seen one—and now I had my own. In fact, I had a brand-new one! I'd bought the darn thing sight unseen. I wanted to see exactly what it looked like.

The day after surgery, I asked for a hand mirror and tenderly positioned myself for my first peek at a vagina.

"*Good God!*" I shrieked. "What have they done to me? This looks like something you'd hang in your smokehouse . . . after a hog killing."

I'd never seen anything so gross. It was swollen, red, and *wrinkled.* The wrinkles looked as though they'd been left behind . . . deliberately. This thing needed to be ironed. Over eleven hours of surgery, pure agony as an aftermath, and I had to be left with a wrinkled vagina? Swelling was expected. I might even accept that it would look a bit beat-up and trampled on—but not like this! *This* was a disaster! This was no little pink rosebud! This was no delicate scalloped shell from the seashore. *This* was a red, wrinkled Venus flytrap! I started to cry, which only made matters worse.

Mother rang for the nurse.

"You're perfectly normal," they both assured me. "That's how you're supposed to look."

Who did they think they were fooling? I was having none of it.

"Like *this*?" I keened.

I'd seen my share of nude female statuary. I hadn't been totally lacking in pubescent curiosity. I even had a fair idea of a vagina's function. This wrinkled thing wasn't going to make it on any countenance. I wanted a neat little split. Something that would translate well in Italian marble or, perhaps, alabaster. I wanted something aesthetically pleasing. This thing had folds! I was suddenly reminded of that unattractive rear view as I herded home the cows.

I was truly upset.

"We'll show you," my mother volunteered.

My mother and Westlake Clinic's charge nurse both lifted their skirts, presenting me a view of not one but two naturally born vaginas. By golly, they did have folds. There were four outer labial folds on each vagina. Satisfied that I was normal, I drifted off to sleep.

My mother had made a long, uphill journey to be standing there, displaying her private parts. The trip couldn't have been easy for her. In Mozelle's world, anything smacking of deviant behavior had always been swept under the rug. To digress from the sexually permissible was to be queer. She, like most of the nation, held homosexuals in very low esteem. They were perverts and child molesters. Mother didn't know any homosexuals, but she knew they were repulsive. I'd seen her in action.

At age eleven, I joined Mother on a bus for a shopping spree in Nashville. As we waited for our return bus trip home, we sat on a wooden bench watching people pass through the Greyhound bus terminal. People watching was a favored pastime, and we generally conducted a running dialogue as the world paraded past. One person, a flamboyant black queen, noticeably stood out from this crowd. Flamboyant didn't cover it. This queen didn't pass through a space; he flounced through, making a grotesque statement about his life in transit.

"Would you look at that?" my mother clucked. "He's so sissy, I bet he squats to pee."

I was mortified. I felt as though my protective cover had been ripped to shreds. I couldn't think of anything to say and sat in silent embarrassment, hating that black queen. I reacted at eleven as so many adult closeted homosexuals have since reacted to the transgendered.

"Don't put that spotlight on me!" I screamed inside my head.

I didn't want to believe I was like that outrageous, disgusting person prancing around the bus station, yet I knew there was somehow a link between that "sissy" and me. It felt like a shameful link. That terrible person was in some way distantly related to me, and I knew it. I'd been called a sissy all my life, and now I knew what one looked like. Surely everyone in the bus station was aware of our relationship. I couldn't believe that my mother, who knew me so well, could not see the sissy in me. If she ever allowed herself really to look at me, could she still love me?

How could anyone love me? There was the basis for the fear. Because I was not like other boys, I felt I must be despicable. Daddy recognized it. I was sure he saw my difference. In response, I consciously tried to create a boy child who might be worthy of love. Painstakingly, I tried to mimic the acceptable traits of other males around me. I knew, and so did my daddy, that the mimicry was a sham. The child of my creation, the boy child, was not real.

All children fear abandonment by their parents. That is one of our fundamental fears. One of the differences for transsexual children is feeling we have already been abandoned. The person we are is not good enough. To be loved, we must create another person, an acceptable substitute. We do not grow up and change into women. We grow up and change back into what we originally started out to be.

People had never heard of a transsexual until the media created a furor over Christine Jorgensen's gender reassignment. Prior to those shocking headlines, everyone different was labeled *queer*. *Queer* meant you were a degenerate. *Queer* meant you were so sissy you squatted to pee.

Mother had indeed come a long way from rural Tennessee.

———

THAT SUMMER of 1962, while everyone was dancing the Watusi, I was in Westlake Clinic doing the Transsexual Twist.

After the packing was removed from the vagina, the next step in my recovery process was the insertion of a full-time plastic dilator. The heavy little torture device was approximately seven inches in length and the circumference of a very healthy cucumber. I called my companion Fred. Getting the dilator out at night was no problem. Cape Canaveral missiles have been launched with less velocity. Coaxing Fred back into his dark, dank home was another story. That was an ordeal. Once he was painfully in place, the trick was keeping him there. A dance belt, Kotex pad, plus elasticized panties were poor restraints for an escape artist like my Fred. To sit was excruciating. As scar tissue attempted to form, Fred's job was to rip it apart.

As I improved, Hank took over my mother's all-night vigils. She would slip away to the Hollywood duplex to bathe, rest, and collect herself; Hank would block my hospital-room door and crawl in bed with me. Having lost forty pounds in two weeks, I was an emaciated, unkempt mess, and far from anyone's sexual fantasy. Hank never acted as though he saw a difference. Not once. He would lie down and hold me on those rumpled, sticky, stinking hospital sheets in the sweltering summer heat.

I adored him for the gesture . . . but couldn't wait for him to go home.

Even after Dr. Belt's suggestion that penetration of the vagina would be a good idea, sex was still not a viable consideration. Every time the doctor brought up the subject, I laughed in his face. *He* was outside, looking into my puffy, painful receptacle—*I* knew the feeling from the inside looking out! Even my daily saltwater douches made me think I was being ripped apart. I could imagine nothing worse than intercourse. Even generally randy Hank seemed less than aroused by the prospect.

After almost two grueling weeks in Westlake Clinic, I was discharged. The sweaty little hospital room was behind me, but home was merely a change of scenery. The non-air-conditioned bungalow was just another steam bath. I still sweated, watched the clock, waited for my medication, and squirmed, trying to find a position that would offer a bit of relief. Slowly moving back and forth from bed to living-room couch, I dragged a catheter bag, tubes, and bottles behind me. I was a walking, sweating, smelly zombie.

Physically, my recovery period at home consisted of two daily excruciating exercises. First was the continuous and careful dilating of the vagina. Second, but of no less importance, were the sessions designed to encourage my newly positioned urethra to void properly. Three times daily I sat in an empty bathtub and turned on the faucet. The sound of running water created an urgency and overcame my involuntary muscles' fear of voiding. What little physical or emotional strength I had was directed daily toward the proper functioning of my new genitalia. Never tell me I don't know the pain of being a woman.

In the past thirty-nine years, reconstructive surgeons have bettered their surgical techniques and have become more mindful of postoperative pain control. Now, when I hear of a relatively painless transition made by a newly born transsexual sister, I cannot help feeling a twinge of jealousy. In today's world, it is common to hear that a sister has experienced only mild physical discomfort. In response, I feel like an antique who suffered for her gender conversion and then trudged thirty miles through the snow to reach a log schoolhouse!

It was a hard summer for goddesses.

While I suffered my postsurgical hell in a small bungalow off Sunset and Western, across town, in Beverly Hills, my idol Marilyn Monroe struggled with and succumbed to her own demons on August 5, 1962. When she died, I felt as though I'd lost a close, personal friend. In my distress, I also managed to convince myself that Hank no longer wanted to be around me. He never left my side except to go to work, but I concluded that his devotion was all an act. Why would he want to be with someone in my lousy condition? I didn't want to be around myself! An odor trailed after me. I could smell it. I couldn't get away from it. I was having a heavy, fetid discharge from the surgery. I felt ugly, and I took my frustration out on the man closest to me.

"Aleshia, don't be so hard on Hank. Are you trying to drive the boy away?" Mother scolded, preaching the standard Appalachian female line. "You have to give a man some breathing space."

My mother the nurse never lost sight of her goal to get me physically and emotionally strong again. She'd always possessed a gentle, magical touch but had waited until my sister and I were grown before pursuing her interest in nursing. Mother was a very focused and persuasive lady. Now, finding herself in the role of both nurse and mother, she convinced me that if I hoped to save my relationship with Hank, I should return with her to Tennessee.

I did go home again, despite Thomas Wolfe's famous admonition that such a trip was an implausible notion. I flew to Tennessee to recuperate and landed in another dimension. No one outside the family was to know I'd returned home, and except for the minister, no one in town was privy to my surgical transition. As far as the town folk were concerned, Buddy Crenshaw was still a sissy chorus boy in San Francisco. We'd keep it that way. Nothing could be worse than the truth. I'd stay sequestered on our farm, recuperate, and return to Hank without anyone being the wiser.

Miss Minnie Lee, my grandmother, squelched that plan. Although she would have welcomed Alfred Brevard home with open arms, Gran was not happy with the return of Aleshia.

"I believe, Mozelle," she confided, "that this is an impostor. This person is trying to pass herself off as Alfred Brevard."

"For what possible reason?" Mother laughed, trying to dispel Gran's notion.

"For the inheritance," Gran whispered.

My mother never spoke to her mother-in-law again. That didn't keep my grandmother from "outing" me at her beauty shop.

"I needed to share this burden with those who care most about me," Gran later grumbled to Daddy.

The story ignited like a barn burning. Our phone would ring at all hours, and an unidentified voice would ask, "Is Buddy there?" Our seldom-traveled country road became a curiosity seeker's thoroughfare. Cars would idle by, toot, and speed off. The more brazen country sightseers parked by the side of the road, waiting for a glimpse of the homegrown oddity. I could have sold picnic lunches—the rednecks would have eaten that up. The insensitive invasion was hard on the entire family.

Mama and Granddaddy Gillentine, Mother's parents, drove three hundred miles from east Tennessee just to lend their support. By the time they arrived, my nerves were frayed. When my grandparents pulled into the curved driveway at Twin Elm Place, I was in the upstairs bathroom, nervously applying layer after layer of mascara to false eyelashes. I was scared witless.

"Where's Rosy?" Granddaddy's voice boomed as he came through the front door. "Where's Rosy?"

"Rosy" was upstairs pearling her lashes.

I'd earned the nickname when I was about three years of age. My mother had again run home to her parents, and the grandparents were playing babysitters while my feuding parents slipped away to a movie. All went well until baby Buddy woke up. When I found my parents gone, nothing would quiet me. I was inconsolable. I squalled until Granddaddy dressed me in Aunt Bobby Jean's skirt, put a red hair ribbon in my curls, and called me Rosy. When my parents returned from the movie, they found their three-year-old "Rosy" dancing up and down the stairs. I was entertaining the entire family.

"Where's Rosy?" Granddaddy now boomed as he came through the door. I don't know that I ever properly thanked him for that kindness.

MARK 947

Calpernia Sarah Addams

2003

Calpernia Sarah Addams is an actress, author, and artist living in Hollywood, California. She spent four years in the navy and marines and was a field combat medical specialist during Operation Desert Storm.

WHEN I stepped off the plane it was raining. A light mist, really, but coherent enough to call rain, and I laughed aloud. Here was the desert, I thought. I was stiff from numberless hours in the transport aircraft, sitting on cargo nets with hundreds of others, all of us wearing pale desert camouflage and black boots. There had been a shortage of the suede camel-colored ones, and only a few people with rank or connections had them. Likewise the soft desert hats were scarce, and I only managed to grab one after the whole war was over, just before we got on the plane back home. So there I was, bareheaded and black-booted, gas mask clipped to my belt and a little pack of medical supplies slung over one shoulder. My seabag was on my back and in its center, padded by all my uniforms, was the hard-shell case containing my old fiddle.

We staged on planks of plywood over pallets on the sand beside the runway, separating into our little companies in preparation for loading up and driving to various duty stations. Overall I knew remarkably little about this war or much of anything that was going on. People were loading and unloading crates and pallets of supplies, organizing groups of people with subdued commands in the new dawn's sleepy light. I didn't know exactly what any of the things were for. I didn't know what kind of plane we had just stepped off of or even really why we were here. Something about Saddam Hussein. He was forcing his will on Iraq or something, which threatened U.S. oil interests. I didn't know. Everyone was talking about it every day with their own little opinions, but I just wanted to get through my classes, read my books and try not to think about sex with men too much. The officers had the knowing, superior looks of low-level insiders, and the NCOs had their gritty, in-the-trenches ideas that were oh-so-much more in touch with reality. It all bored me. I looked out across the sand on the other side from the airport and thought about Aladdin and Indiana Jones.

I was assigned to Charlie Company, 1st Medical Battalion, 1st Field Service Support group. This resulted in a long ride through residential-looking neighborhoods of Al-Jubail to a barricaded hospital that we were to rehabilitate from its current abandoned state into a functioning medical facility. I wondered briefly if it had been abandoned all along or just conveniently when the war started. But ultimately it was nothing to me. It was so easy to coast in the military. . . . As long as I completed my assigned tasks and stayed quiet, everything else was taken care of. Food. Housing. My life in general. The navy was my dad and I was safely asleep in his arms.

We were admitted past sentries into a courtyard delineated by huge blocks of concrete rubble and sandbags, a place that I would come to know well as the war progressed. We walked up a decorative-looking sidewalk to the front door of the hospital and got into formation for our first briefing.

The air was crisp and had an entirely different smell than I was used to, expectably. It was similar to that of California, but very clean and surprisingly damp that morning. I supposed it was the dew burning off and the last of that unusual rain. Tropical-looking plants and trees grew in the same places that hedges and oaks held residential court in my own neighborhood back home. There were no other cars on the streets and no people. The neighborhood was quiet. Watching. Some officer checked names off a list, assigning people to various duty sections, and then excused us to go find beds among the unused hospital rooms inside. Finally released, I clopped in my boots past a stripped grand entry and down the echoing halls where normally patients recovered under the practiced care of nurses. Now bored sentries sat at the nurse's stations, reading or making log entries as repetitive as write-offs:

> 1100 Made rounds. No suspicious activity noted.
> 1200 Made rounds. No suspicious activity noted.
> 1300 Made rounds. No suspicious activity noted.

Everything seemed empty, staged for an event no one had bothered attending. A few televisions had been rigged up to play CNN in darkened hallways, on top of boxes or furniture dragged out of some unused room. I walked through their islands of radiated blue and static to the area set aside for enlisted men in the back of the hospital. I took a room where I saw a free bed and laid my seabag on its uncovered mattress. A handsome marine was asleep in the next bunk, his gear set up neatly on the rolling bedside table. They were here to protect us, and the hospital. The bed was an old-fashioned kind, with crank handles that lowered and raised it into the various positions, Fowlers, Shock and Trendelenburg. I cranked mine flat and lay down for a moment. It felt surreally homey, to be on a mattress beneath fluorescent lights, and I had to remind myself I was on the other side of the world in a war. "You might even die," I thought. Finally.

from Chapter 21

IN PREPARATION for a pageant, a girl must have three basic things: a presentation, a talent and an evening gown. Some variants involve swimsuits or sportswear, different spreads of points for the categories, but those three things will get most girls through any system. I focused on the Entertainer of the

Year, or EOY, system, which awarded the most points to the talent category and required that evening wear be creative, as opposed to the basic beads-and-rhinestones theme. Never feeling particularly beautiful, I decided that a system rewarding talent and creativity was my best bet and concentrated on building a reputation amongst its community of judges, admirers, contestants and past winners.

My ability to play the violin was fairly unique in our wasteland of Whitney and Britney, sure to bring extra points in an EOY competition, so I centered my reputation on this skill. In the world of drag, the center of which was pop, dance and R & B music, I hadn't at first seen a place for my home-grown talent. My fiddle had been a friend since childhood, and I found it opened doors for me, started conversations I did not have the courage to initiate, and gave me the feeling that I was special in some way. That I possessed a talent others envied.

My first pageant successes came from playing my family's traditional bluegrass folk style, dressed in a red-and-white-checked gingham square-dancing dress. At the end of the live fiddling, I clogged to a dance mix of "Cotton-Eyed Joe." The vibrant, organic sound of live music spilling from the club speakers caused heads to snap around to the stage. When I handed off my gleaming instrument and the first strains of the newly popular dance song began, people stirred from their stunned paralysis and began to cheer. The crowd screamed and I clogged with all my heart, feeling the first flush of excitement expand in my chest. Then the stage went dark except for black light and strobe. My white crinolines glowed, expanding and contracting like a blue jellyfish, seeming to float in the light. I would hear for years afterward how people had never seen anything so bizarre in their lives, and the image proved an indelible one. From pigtails and gingham, clogging and playing the fiddle I managed to build the beginnings of a reputation.

For talent in this year's Tennessee EOY I planned to lip-synch Sinead O'Connor's ethereal recording of "Don't Cry for Me, Argentina," playing my violin as expressively and sweetly as possible over the instrumental portions that came throughout the song. This would be what was known as a "clean" talent: simple, elegant and with little room for mistakes.

My style had become smoother, more sophisticated, but still included as much mockery of convention as I could slip in. I sought a reminiscence of dark fairy tales and Disney witches gone glamorous. I was finally becoming incarnate the dark angel I had visualized inside for so many years.

"Why *dark angel*?" some talent-night girl had asked once, when I shared this image in an unguarded moment. I could not explain to her what it was to fall from out of the fold to which I had once belonged, into this new role. To nonetheless claim some cutting shards of the broken belief in God, salvaged because I knew them to be true among the many lies. That person had a face, and a body, shaped in strength and perseverance. My face. My body. To my silence she said, "Is that why you always wear that cross?"

"This cross is a scar. I'll always wear it."

She backed away and left. I looked up from the mirror, done with applying mascara, and blessed the empty room.

———

AT NOON on the Sunday of the pageant, contestants began arriving, some from far outside Nashville and a few locals everyone knew. Some girls had an entourage consisting of sponsors and dancers and some kind of manager. Being creatures of the night, we all looked disheveled and grumpy. McDonald's coffee and bottled water were scattered on the round bar tables in the theater. I had worked in that very room every week for many years, but in the daylight it seemed unfamiliar, bleached out and skeletal, cracks and scuffs newly visible in a harsh mix of fluorescent light and sun filtered through the vents in the ceiling. We girls were similarly unflattered by the sun and time of day. Weave tracks showed through hair pulled back in messy ponytails. Exotic bodies were concealed in loose T-shirts and sweatpants. We knew that tonight our appearances would count for everything, so energy was not wasted on the morning. When the pageant owner arrived, we gathered around to receive instructions, turn in last-minute applications and fees, and finally to draw numbers for contestant order. "One" was the dreaded position for superstitious and practical reasons, and any girl arriving late for the meeting (there was always one) was immediately assigned this number, moving everyone back a space. Each draw from a turned-up ball cap was met with expressions of relief or comic dismay. Laughter and camaraderie prevailed among the relaxed group, lower numbers met with ahhs and ohs from supporters or joking detractors of the girls. There was immediate bargaining among the holders for preferred positioning. I pushed in to take my turn, and when I pulled a folded bit of torn-off notebook paper from the hat, I opened it to reveal lucky number seven. A good sign, I thought. Aside from its usual magical properties, seven guaranteed that I would have plenty of time to get ready for each category and relax, unlike the hapless number one, who would rush through the entire night. I ran across the stage and upstairs, two at a time as always, to lay out supplies in my dressing room and prepare for the evening. The out-of-town girls gathered in our guest room downstairs off the side of the stage, their crew stringing racks of clothing along pipes hung from exposed rafters. Each girl claimed her area at the long mirrored table along the wall by laying out an ancient towel stained with countless nights of base and powder, lipstick and glitter, patterns of stage makeup as individual as fingerprints. Most everyone bought their makeup mirrors at thrift stores, rotating ovals, rectangles and circles glowing with dusty fluorescence in this circumstance their owners of a previous era could never have predicted. Suitcases were unzipped to reveal glorious scintillations from heavily beaded silk gowns, light flashing from mirrored costumes and slick patent leather. Racks of foam heads crowned with wigs of every conceivable style and color were balanced on chairs, piles of shoes beneath. Drag slaves, as they were lovingly called, scurried everywhere polishing oversize rhinestone jewelry, sorting through cases of music. And the backstage manager, who had not yet given up or gotten too drunk, provided direction and gossip to anyone paying attention.

Upstairs, I had the unchallenged benefit of being an employee of the club with my own dressing room. The bar was rented that night by whoever owned the pageant, but its employees were still allowed to use their resources, and I was grateful for the relative sanctuary. Special guest entertainers were booked to fill time between contestant changes and categories, usually former winners and whoever was locally popular at the moment. These girls got ready upstairs, cast members opening their rooms to share space and enjoy socializing with old friends. The ubiquitous dressers and drag slaves ran in and out, fetching cocktails and delivering messages with a look of urgent purpose that contrasted with the easy, festive demeanor of their respective divas. The narrow scuffed halls rang with laughter and gleefully gossipy outbursts of, "Girl, *no!*" and "Bitch!" from rows of dressing room doors propped open spilling loud music and suitcases of drag. With close to eight hours until the start of the pageant, I put on a CD of bluegrass gospel and began to clean my room, hanging gowns, capes, suits and unclassifiable costumes on the bar of clothing that filled one entire wall. On the opposite side I piled thigh-high boots in red, white, black, lavender and school-bus yellow beneath a wall of spiky heels in leather and silk. I straightened leaning stacks of CDs and hung my seventeen wigs back on their nails beside the shoes. A table ran the length of the center wall, various large mismatched looking-glasses pushed back to allow room for my own yellowing plastic makeup mirror and array of cosmetics. Creamy foundation in "fair." Two Tupperware bowls resting on top of their airtight lids filled with fragrant Coty air-spun powder in shades designed to high- and lowlight my face. Ragged brushes in need of washing. Circular disks of pigment were grouped by use: sienna for contour, rose for blush, subtle pink and Egyptian gold for eyes. Large black eyelashes to be attached with rubbery weave glue waited next to pots of glitter, eyeliners in black, gold and white, mascara standing next to a palette of lipsticks dark red and blackish purple. Pencils in brown and black filled with color soft as butter waited to outline lips and brows, and over everything a thin layer of settled powder. I was ready.

Barry and I had discussed his coming down for the pageant again earlier that day, in a phone call.

"Hello? Barry?"

"Hey, babe, what are you doin'?"

I was in bed, as I always was until two or three P.M. "Just awakening from my coma." I looked at the clock and winced. "Oooh, I shoulda been up at noon, I've still gotta go throw some more money away on this pageant."

"You want me to come? I can help you backstage or something."

"Well, it's the Fourth of July. . . . I thought you had a carnival and keg and all that up there?"

"Yeah, but I wanted you to come to the carnival with me. . . ."

I wasn't anywhere near comfortable enough with my look to attend a carnival on base, but I couldn't admit that to him. Anyway, we had just spent four of his days off in a row together the previous week, part of the weird schedule they had him on, and honestly, after being together that entire time I kind of wanted the next two days solo. It wasn't that I didn't want to see him, but there was so much to do. And during the pageant my dressing room would be crazy. I didn't want him sitting around backstage through the interminable hours of stress, including my own. Surely he would have more fun at a carnival and keg party with his friends.

"Mmm, I *know.* But I have to do this pageant or my spon-sters will withdraw the other half of my prize money from Miss Nashville." *Spon-ster* was my combination of the words *sponsor* and *monster.* "Honey, just stay up there and do your friends thing. We'll see each other next week, and if I win I'll wear the crown for you. *Heh, heh.*"

"OK . . . yeah, I have to take care of Nasty tonight anyway. Duty."

"That's the dog?"

"Our mascot. I wish we didn't have that damn hour drive between us." He sounded so cute.

"I know. Trust me, if we didn't we'd be having French toast in about ten minutes. But hey, I'd better get up and get crackin' on this stuff or I'll end up in bed all day."

"You sleep too damn much."

"Twenty-four-seven if I could."

"Quit your drag-assin' then and get up. I gotta go; some-body's yelling at me."

"Are you at work? That's my tax money you're wastin', slacker."

"Bye, Sarah. I'll call you tonight, see how you did."

"OK. Wish me luck. . . . Bye, Barry."

"I love you."

"I love you too."

———

BIANCA STRAINED to read the handwritten sheet with the pageant's outcome in the shifting vagaries of light onstage. Everyone was waiting. The girl next to me dropped my hand to smooth her gown and then reached for it again. Bianca found what she was looking for and moved the hand with the microphone and list up to her mouth. The other hand simultaneously held a cigarette and cocktail. Her trademark voice poured like gravel from the sound system, eliciting a chorus of imitators bleating, "*Heyyy!*"

"*Heyyyyy,* yourself, motherfuckers." There was a smile in her voice, an innocence in the raspy laugh she made as she took a quick sip from her cocktail. That little laugh had traveled intact over a long course of years and experiences. She tipped the plastic cup toward the audience and took another sip, a drag from her cigarette, and then smacked her lips with a wet-sounding, *Ahhh!* Aside from her voice, and obvious talent, she was famous for a close attachment to the physical vices.

"Do y'all want to know which one of these bitches won?" There was the expected uproar. I was excited to note that more voices were yelling my name than the other girls'. "Well . . ." Bianca looked at the page again. "Hey, have I told y'all about the time me and Stephanie Wells drove up to Fort Campbell?"

"Yeah, yeah," someone yelled out. "If Rita Ross had been with you, you coulda saved the Lincoln Continental!" The crowd was frenzied for results. Chaos boiled at her feet. Bianca laughed over the noise.

"OK, OK. The winner is . . . Y'all give me a drumroll. . . ." Everyone banged on their tables.

It was killing me. "Shut up and say it, whore! Get this over with!" I thought.

"*. . . contestant number seven, Calpernia Addams!*"

When my name was announced the first time I won a pageant, I jumped up and down and screamed like a game-show contestant. That's what it was to me then, and the prize had been validation. With that first crown, I had physical claim to a bit of pride and the status of a professional showgirl. Now winning was more of a relief than anything. The money spent competing was ridiculous. I couldn't afford to lose it. And losing is more and more embarrassing the more established and "famous" one becomes. So when I accepted the roses and knelt down to have the massive thirteen-inch rhinestone crown pinned to my head, my mood was light. I smiled and was excited and grateful, but mostly I was just relieved. Chelsey put on music for my crowning walk down the runway. Usually winners got Whitney Houston, but she knew me better. It was an ethereal, urgent performance of "Ave Maria" by Sinead O'Connor, from my talent CD. When I listened to it at home it was so beautiful it made me feel light, entranced, as if I were flying. They finished pinning and I stood. I walked. I floated down the runway. It felt nice to win, after such a long fight even to be there at all.

————

SIXTY MILES to the northwest, Barry lay sleeping on an army cot beside the barracks mascot, a dog named Nasty. The keg party was over and they were both exhausted. The cot was on the landing outside his room because it was Barry's duty to watch the dog, but his roommate, Justin, did not want the animal inside. As Barry slept and Nasty watched, a private named Calvin Glover moved past him and into the room. There was talk, and then Justin gave him a baseball bat. The door was opened again. At about the same time a glittering crown was lowered onto my head, Calvin swung the bat at Barry's sleeping face, again and again, until the man I knew was no more.

———

WHEN IT was done, all I wanted was to go home and wash my face. Stage makeup is so heavy. I posed for a few pictures. Took off the ridiculously huge crown. I signed some papers. Took a stack of twenties and counted them to make sure the full five hundred was there. This was solitary work, people's attention directed elsewhere once the pageant was over. At the announcement of winner, there is a polite congratulation, and then everyone scatters to dissect whatever result through the prism of their own involvement. I changed from the heavy beaded gown into jeans and my Reese's Peanut Butter Cup T-shirt, skipping a bra. Alone in my dressing room I looked at the crown, tracing its fiery lines of rhinestones. It really was beautiful. And this time I had won a scepter, too. My first. I was prouder of these things than I had realized. I decided to take the crown home with me and sleep with it beside my bed, so that I could see it twinkle in the semidark. I wanted to show it to Barry tomorrow. I knew he would get a kick out of it.

Outside the night was humid and warm. Tennessee summers seemed to get hotter every year. I hefted my huge bag into the cab of my truck and then carefully nestled the crown into the paper trash in my floorboard. I laid the scepter beside me on the seat, so that I could play with it as I drove. It was tipped with a bright star of crystals and reminded me of a magic wand.

The Link was situated amongst factories and warehouses down by the Cumberland River. The area itself was safe, if a bit industrial-looking, but the interstate home could be reached only through the edge of the projects. Here there were haggard streetwalkers and bums minding their outposts on poorly lit streets. Corpses of Happy Meals flapped in the wake of trucks entering and leaving the highway. As I prepared to merge onto the ramp toward home, I felt a lurch and looked with dismay at my gas gauge, fallen well below empty. I let out a frustrated moan, knowing my truck well enough to realize that I had about five blocks of mobility left. Why did I always *do* stuff like this? I made an instant decision to continue into the seedy neighborhood toward a gas station I remembered and passed under the interstate. Run-down homes and midnight wanderers passed by my anxious gaze, but I could see the gas station in the distance. It looked dark, and I remembered it was the Fourth of July. Perhaps there would be another one down a little farther. . . .

By now I didn't have enough gas even to consider going back to the club. My engine began to stutter and I was able to continue forward only by riding the clutch and barely pressing on the gas. I passed two more closed stations and just managed to coast my Chevy into a brightly lit Krystal parking lot with the last wisps of fuel in my tank. It felt as if I had come to a stop on a darkened movie set, soundless and empty. Outside the restaurant's stark halogen lights, the neighborhood looked to be assembled entirely from shadows. An understanding of my situation coalesced like the gently materializing fog on my windows. My face was painted with exaggerated stage makeup sure to appear shocking to anyone I might ask for help. Sure to draw attention from people when I needed to go unnoticed in this place. Half an hour ago I had been the center of attention in a room of five hundred people. Now I was alone in what passed for Nashville's ghetto. In my pocket was a fat roll of twenty-dollar bills, and beside me lay a piece of jewelry bigger than my head. The makeup was industrial, designed to withstand sweat and hours of exertion, so there was no way to get it off without making a smudged mess. The money could be hidden, and I slipped it under my seat. I covered over the crown and scepter with fast-food sacks and newspapers. Then I steeled myself for whatever might come and exited the safety of the cab. There was a phone booth a block away, and I walked with a tired expression that I hoped said, "I really don't wanna be bothered with kickin' your ass." As if I could have. There was no one else on the street.

I reached the phone booth without incident and called the club, feeling foolish as I described my situation. I secured a promise of rescue as soon as the registers were counted down.

I passed another forty-five minutes in the truck, listening to 98.7 and being wryly amused at myself. The Krystal was closed, so I couldn't even order a soggy little square burger. There was no one on the street, and I relaxed enough to push aside the paper and look at my crown again. "Yay, I won!" I thought, in a gently self-mocking voice. I think I was embarrassed to allow myself the pleasure, but I grew more and more excited as I thought about the title. The money. That was pretty nifty.

I was rescued from these thoughts by the arrival of my manager with a can of gas. We laughed a little at how stupid I was, but we were both terribly tired and little was said. He made sure my truck would start and drove away into the dark. "Home," I thought. "I must get home."

———

THE FIRST step back toward myself was a long, hot shower. Being Calpernia fed something inside me, starved for so many years that it would never be completely full, but the exhaustion that followed could not be denied. The house was empty, quiet, and I let the water lay down my gel-stiffened curls and play over my face. I always peeked into the swing-out medicine cabinet mirror beside the shower after that, to see the immaculately painted face beaded with water. The only thing that ran was my mascara, in messy black rivulets down my cheeks. I imagined I looked like Ophelia, all wet and crying dark tears. I smiled into the mirror and leaned back into the shower. A handful of baby oil and my filthy drag rag was all it took to scrub away the face, and then I washed my hair twice to get rid of the crunchiness. Then the body; then I brushed my teeth. The same ritual, same order, every night for years and years. I found myself wishing Barry were there, waiting for me in bed. My own fault, I thought. He had asked.

I dried off and went into my room, where the muted television was playing a rebroadcast of the ten-o'clock news. The remote was not in its usual place beside my bed and I spent an annoyed minute looking for it. I would rather look for the remote than walk over and turn the channel manually, and I finally gave up and just put on some panties so I could walk around the house. One never knew if a window shade might be open a crack or someone might knock at the door. "I suppose to some people, being caught in their panties would be devastating too, though . . ." I said aloud to no one in particular. The crown glittered on my bed. "I'm a winner." I laughed at myself.

In the kitchen I took one from a stack of ninety-nine-cent Kroger pizzas in the freezer and crammed it into my toaster oven. It didn't quite fit while frozen and was tilted up where one edge stuck out the mostly closed door, but as it softened in the heat the door curled it back into itself. A sweating phalanx of Dr Pepper cans filled the lower half of the refrigerator, and I relocated one to the freezer to chill further.

I hated the telephone and used it as seldom as possible. Because of this, I simply hit redial and the only number I had been calling recently began to ring. Barry had his phone turned on just for me, I thought. Just for me. It rang and rang and there was no answer. "Hey, Barry, guess what? I won!" I said into the rings. Ha, ha. I hung up.

———

WITH EVERYTHING balanced on a tray, I went to my room and settled in. The cheap pizza smelled so good. I sat on the bed and the buried remote clicked on the volume.

". . . Fort Campbell soldier dead . . ." Something reaching from far away crossed miles of gray nothing and hooked into delicate internal organs I hadn't known were there. It tugged, on the edge of tearing something out. I was afraid to move. I dug out the control and turned the TV all the way up. It couldn't be. A tingling numbness was beginning in my heart and stomach, around the hooks. No way. My brain had cleared, and its empty page buzzed to be filled with information. "Barry is going to call me. I'm going to call him, right now. He's there waiting for me, and always will be there. Don't be stupid. This can't happen to us. Can't." The woman continued speaking in her flat, informative voice, and a photo of Barry Winchell appeared over her left shoulder. There was a dropping of pressure around my head, as if I had been rocketed to a great height, and then in one ripping withdrawal my entire insides were torn from me and carried away beyond the horizon, into the lightning and fire that had always lived there. Much, much later I would remember the words I could not hear at that moment, from inside the storm. "This was never meant to be yours and never will be. Stupid. Never was. Never will be." I fell from the bed. Some sounds must have bled from the cracks in my skin, some moaning and tears. I can't remember very well. Those hours are lost to me.

I lived the next week on my best friend Oscar's couch. Other friends came and went, the best ones somehow knowing without my having to tell anyone. I wanted nothing but sleep and could not bear to be touched. When I could move, it was to make phone calls, to the base and the hospital, looking for information. I knew from working at a hospital myself that they could tell me nothing over the phone. Family members only. A memorial service was to be held on base. I did not dare go. Calls began to come from work, the relaying of messages from the first wave of media seeking me out. My only real source for discovering what had happened was the television news, and I watched every broadcast for details. The phone kept ringing. I slept. Alone. Why hadn't I called him? Why hadn't I brought him down?

Chapter 22

THE HEAT was so thick that summer. It fell onto me like molasses or tar and broke down whatever makeup I tried to wear into its powerless components of grease and pigment. I hadn't realized the inadequacy of my wardrobe until I tried to dress for court. I was expecting my ride in less than an hour and scrabbled through the clothes on my floor with trembling hands. Nothing was right. Low-rise jeans, little T-shirts that said things like "Meow" and "Reese's Peanut Butter Cups—Two Great Tastes that Taste Great Together!" right across the breasts. I had to look right, so that they could understand. I wanted them to see me and know why Barry had liked me. I was going to see the people who had killed him. I had to see their faces, hear what they had to say for themselves.

"*That's* what he got killed for? Now that's a prime grade-A example of a faggot there."

Don't look at me. I know. I already know what you're thinking. A crazy thought, Carrie's mother, popped into my head: "They're all gonna laugh at you. They're all gonna laugh at you." A laugh pushed up past the tension like a bubble surfacing in slime. I hated myself.

I finally settled on a navy suit with white piping that one of my talent-night girls had given me. It was a size too small and decades out of fashion, but I jammed it on anyway. I pulled on a pair of sheer stockings (was I supposed to wear these in the summer? I didn't know ...) and dropped to my knees in front of the closet to dig for shoes. I quickly realized I had only stilettos from work and tennis shoes. Everyone was going to be looking at me. Alone. What Barry and I had was private; they had no right to stare and pry and ask and judge, but they would. "It's not..." But I couldn't even allow myself to use the word *fair*. The concept was a joke. A huge balloon of emotion began to expand inside me, humming as if filled with bees, and I knew I could not let it explode, or whatever was inside would destroy me. I leaned forward, knuckles white around some fabric at hand, and I could feel my face clench in a silent rictus. A hot, damp exhalation escaped against the cigarette-scented jeans beneath my face and I realized I was lying down in the pile of clothing. My open eyes were rimmed with moisture but no tears gathered or ran. "You're gonna make this suit look worse than it already does," I said aloud. My voice quavered. "Get up and get ready, you stupid idiot."

In the bathroom I rinsed my face with cold water and retrieved a boutique's worth of cosmetics. My hands trembled slightly, and a sticky film of sweat reappeared at my lip and hairline. I desperately wanted to get in the shower and scrub myself, but there was no time. I began dabbing on concealer, my face getting closer and closer to the mirror as I looked for any flaw that might be covered, until my nose bumped the cold glass. I jerked back in frustration. "Stupid!" The sweat was diluting the makeup, and blotting only left a mottled, ineffective patch of color. "You look like a man. Everybody's gonna throw up when they see you. A man in a dress. A stupid freak." I was talking out loud, whispering, hissing the words. I stared into the mirror, hypnotized, moving more and more slowly till my whole body tingled, bloodless. "Dammit." I shook it off and got my fan from the bedroom to set it up beside the bathroom mirror. The light breeze it provided seemed to help. I would remain in control. Precious seconds melted away in the heat.

I finished with powder and mascara, then struggled with whether or not to wear lipstick. Finally I settled for plain old cherry ChapStick. "You're worried about your stupid face and he's layin' there dead." I raked my hair back into a chignon, secured it with chopsticks and resolutely took out the lowest heels I had in my closet, which were unfortunately clear Lucite open-toes. It was either that or four-inch black pumps. They looked impossibly frivolous to me then. Humiliating. As I slipped them on, over my hose, I closed my eyes and whispered, "Dammit, dammit, dammit. Fuck." I packed the makeup into my purse and a washrag for sweating, and when I was done I went back toward the bathroom.

I paused at the door. I wanted to look in the mirror again. "You look like a man. You may as well know it for sure than go around stupid.

"No, I look as good as I can, and there's no use starin' at myself and makin' it worse." But still I wanted to go. All my armaments were ready for hating what I would see, and I needed only to sight the target. I almost started forward again and put out a hand to catch the doorway. The need was a physical force, invisible as magnetism but completely real. I laughed a little at myself, feeling crazy. "I am not gonna do it. I'm not."

I went into the kitchen and poured a glass of water, of which I had exactly one sip before the honking of my ride called me out into the blinding sunlight.

––––––

THE TRIAL was held in prefabricated structures like school portables or trailers, easily lost among hundreds of other similar buildings if not for the reporters and their attendant crews in satellite vans and rental cars. Many of these were faces I had watched for years covering local tragedies and scandals, now incarnate outside the glowing screen and looking at me. Everyone had an attitude of routine seriousness. The military personnel all in green camouflage, the newspeople and gay groups in suits. A serious army spokeswoman named Pamela wore a different kind of detachable bun every day, which I dispassionately noted and cataloged without mention to anyone.

I watched the trial on a large projection screen with the media and activist groups in a building across the street from the one serving as courtroom. Correspondents were seated at a horseshoe table directly in front, and I watched uncomfortably among other people in rows of chairs behind them. It felt like church somehow, with the pews and formality and horror. The military personnel must have been well schooled on dealing with my presence, because not one person in uniform looked at me or spoke to me directly during the entire trial. I was a ghost.

"Do you know which person is Calpernia Addams?" It was the first day of the trial, and a woman I recognized from the local news stood beside me. She held a doughnut wrapped in a napkin and a cup of coffee.

"Yes . . . That's me."

"So here it starts," I thought. I told her our story, part there, part outside in front of a camera. We waited for the trial to begin, for the screen to light up and show me faces, friendly

and deadly and impartial as every person involved took his
turn in the chair. I sat in my chair cold as stone and learned of
things I had not known. Barry had never told me. I had never
asked. Weeks of harassment and cruelty, mocking and hateful
words Barry had endured every day when he left my soft
rooms of light and air to return here to his death. Face after
face filled the screen, uncomfortable, sad, guilty, telling of particular taunts they had overheard, moments of humiliation.
"But he was your top gun," I said to myself. "He was your
brother. Why didn't you stop this? Why?" Day after day
passed, and at the end of each one I learned another way to
hate myself for sleeping through the ringing of my phone, forever letting him go.

Cardboard trays of fat yellow doughnuts and government-
issued coffee became my sole diet, something to fill my sick
stomach. I watched the screen, unrolling the digest of a stolen
life, desperate for details, details of his daily life and last day
alive. I wanted to see Fisher. Glover. I had to hear them speak.
I wanted to know why, and how, and how could they. When
they finally came, it explained nothing, and I wanted only to
leave.

In between sessions I went outside, walking up and down
the lot in the mesmerizing pneumatic drone of industrial air
conditioners. People left me alone, in my suits and heels and
patched-up face. I didn't care anymore. This very white sky,
hot and centered by the burning yellow sun, had been his sky.
He had walked or driven these very roads, maybe thinking of
me and counting the hours until he could leave and come back
to my pale arms, my soft kisses. They had called him *faggot*,
and other names almost too stupid to be offensive to my mind,
with its hard-won catalog of endured insults. I wished I had
known. I could have helped him, defended him. I played in
my mind again and again a fantasy: my hand catching the bat,
as light as foam against my fingers, and plucking it from the

boy who would be a killer. "Wake up, Barry. Wake up. Let's go." I would have taken him from there. I had wished I were dead so often anyway, I would have taken the blow if I could have. Easy to think, impossible to know, but I imagined it. The force against my flesh, the wood striking and taking away life. If I could lie down there in his place, I believe I still would. It was my fault it ever happened anyway, I told myself, and the tears came finally. "It's all my fault."

"Calpernia?" It was a reporter. "Have you been watching all this? What do you think? Could I get a statement from you?"

"It's . . . horrible. Too horrible. I can't right now, I'm sorry. I'll be back." I turned and walked away, into the heat and the sun. No one could follow me now. It seemed easier to cry in the light.

Chapter 23

IT'S THE Fourth of July 2001, and I'm in my old Chevy truck on the way to Clarksville, Tennessee. Earlier in the day I was sweating under its hood to replace a worn-out alternator, the fairly simple task interrupted by offers of help in the parking lot of Nashville's Mexican AutoZone. Now, at 10:15 P.M., I pray that nothing else will go wrong with the put-upon engine as I prepare to cross forty-odd miles of nothing from city to city.

Deciding to go back was an impulse. I spent the day mostly alone, eating, walking, wordless. The Tennessee humidity was like a hot, damp cloth pressed against my face, and looking any kind of decent was just about impossible. I usually kicked around town in jeans and some little top, purple tennis shoes and my hair a Medusa-like mass of curls. After an hour of scraping sweat-glued bangs from my eyes, I decided I had to get into some air-conditioning more effective than the diffuse whisper leaking out of my truck's open dash. I passed a theater in my wandering and spun the steering wheel a hard right into its shimmering asphalt lot. Perfect.

"Two?" he asked, after I requested a seat. The ticket sellers always seem surprised I'm alone. I guess most girls don't go by themselves. I wasn't there to be with anyone, though. In the darkness of a theater the throbbing tentacles of worry could detach and slip away into blackness for a little while. There was only the bright image of another world filling my vision.

I felt drugged after the movie. I'd hardly spoken to anyone all day, and the passage of hours made words harder to grasp, like melting ice cubes slipping from my fingers. In two years the experience of Barry's murder had coalesced into a heavy stone, a stack of memories preserved in the acrid atmosphere of a just-missed gunshot or strike of lightning. But on the Fourth of July I call up the ghosts of possibility and guilt, wonder what might have been. I try to look across from this line of events to alternate realities, where the lives have not been entangled and then broken by clumsy hands unable to figure the knots. Driving the emptying streets, I had no plan but to listen to the familiar thoughts play themselves out. Then a voice from the radio announced a carnival to be held tonight, in Clarksville. On base. To celebrate the Fourth of July.

The sky is already darkening with an infusion of night and stars. I pull into a gas station and walk back out with containers of oil and gasoline additives and a candy bar. An indeterminate perimeter of scrubby grass and weeds reaches out from the backdrop of woods toward the station's lot, advance scouts already penetrating cracks throughout the blacktop. As I pop my hood, a thick clerk pushes open the door to ask if I need any help. I can't fault Southern manners, so I only smile and say, "No, thanks." A moment's work and my poor engine is as lubricated and optimized as ten dollars of chemical science can make it. I wipe my hands on the dark denim of my jeans, swipe at my rebellious hair, and I am on the road.

The drive from Nashville to Clarksville is not a terribly long one, in physical miles. Close to forty of them, a passage that cuts through limestone hills like a cross section through layer cake fossilized and iced with verdant deciduous forest. In Tennessee every horizon is shaped by the roll of a hill covered in trees, something I appreciated more after traveling flatter and more urban landscapes. I can see the occasional light of a house or, yes, even trailer out in the woods. Otherwise it is a storybook scene of green and mist and ever-deepening sky. Silent fireworks appear at random intervals, launched from some humble country porch to coruscate and twinkle a moment before spent dust and sticks fall invisibly back to earth. Any sound is lost in the rumble of my truck, hypnotic drone for the miles to unroll in with changeless regularity.

Alone, I give myself dispensation for self-pity. With no one to see, I conjure scenarios and ideas marked as off-limits for public viewing. The tears come. Not only for what could have been with Barry, but also for other new sorrows laid up in waiting for these moments of release. I suppress my cynical ego just long enough to ask, "Will I ever be loved?" It is a gentle cry, easily hidden if some observer should enter the scene. What if I had called? What if they hadn't known my secret? What flaw in me allowed this possibility to solidify into a burning moment of anger and death? Selfish of me, to take the blame, but that is the luxury of private thought.

As I come nearer to my exit, the lights on either side of the interstate are brighter. From here it all looks like a waterlogged Polaroid, colors bleeding out into gray from blurred outlines. Small-town pit stops sprawl, nothing taller than a story or two, everything seeming long resigned to a modest existence. When the off-ramp finally comes, I feel unexpectedly cavalier about the possible dangers this town holds for me. I slide into the first gas station, a huge truck-stop combination, and pop out of my truck with a flourish of hair and arching back. In a way I almost wish someone *would* figure me out, that the sheer stunning insolence of my existence would punch a button marked "destroy" deep inside them and I'd be done in with a flare of quick liberating violence. But these thoughts are without substance, and besides, my walk across the immense lot to the cashier is unremarkable to anyone. When I catch a glance from a cute boy pumping gas, I know I'm glad to be alive. There is so much more to see. Dying can be had any day.

I remember the route to the base because I drove it so many times to the improvised courthouse during the trial. I had dropped Barry off once a long time ago, at some obscure back entrance, but the main gate had been a new experience. Now, past eleven at night, the landmarks are cast in reflected neon from dark-hour haunts. Street lamps divide the lots into dissipating circles of electric white while other buildings hide invisibly in their absence. I follow the signs to Fort Campbell Army Base, past the lamprey pawnshops and loan-shark shacks that always ride alongside military bases. Gate four is stark in its halogen glare, venous flow of red taillights queuing in and white headlights streaming out. Tonight is the carnival, everyone is welcome, and the sentries give me a stiff-handed salute as I pass.

Fort Campbell is laid out in an intentionally bewildering manner. I heard somewhere that bases were designed to be difficult targets for invasion, so being a ways off the interstate and hard to navigate were protective measures, I suppose. I remember the summer when I rode in past media vehicles encrusted with antennae and satellite dishes, past the following eyes of anyone who understood what our army escort meant. It was so hot that summer; I will always remember that feeling. My face was melting, cracking off in front of everyone's judging eyes. Tonight I hardly need any makeup, and the air has cooled to a tolerable degree. I am free in the comfort of favorite jeans and cotton. During the trial a soldier had recognized me resting during lunch break and shouted a question across the walk as he held the paper with Barry's murder in his hands. "Hey! *You* wanna be in the papers?!" Then he and his friends were laughing. No one is looking at me tonight. Maybe now, two years later, he is at home asleep next to his wife, his girlfriend . . . his boyfriend, for all I know. I begin to doubt there is any kind of carnival left at this late hour, but I follow the signs around the dark base and finally come to what I am looking for.

There is always a sense of majesty in the sight of a Ferris wheel. It is simply a matter of size. However complex a video game, or however exciting a movie, they cannot loom so bright and graceful in the vegetable-scented air of a limitless country night. Spotty lines of leftover cars sprawl out in patterns like a partially filled-in crossword, and families roam among them looking for their own. I park immediately, despite the sure availability of spaces closer, because I know I will need the walk to calm increasing nervousness that buzzes just below my heart. A moment away is the luminous, simple carnival. Crowds of young people move through and around its attractions, none of them aware of who I am, what it means to me to be here on this night. My shoes whisper through the cool grass; voices come close and pass by. Music blares from a large open tent, rowdy and coarse, unsettling to me despite its happy intent. The last night Barry was alive he was supposed to go to this carnival. He went to bed instead.

"No charge for a pretty girl!" A heavy man with black mustache and beard looks disturbingly like my dad. He offers a handful of darts from inside the little stall, slow, uninterested. "No charge, you pop five balloons I give you a big one." The stuffed animals, I assume. I remember them from childhood. Available only at fairs and carnivals, they were full of pinhead-sized Styrofoam granules that leaked from the clumsy seams after a few hours of play. I wearily hold out my hand for the darts, wondering at the same time when everything had become so cynical, so postmodern ironic. Neither of us wants to be, at that particular second, in a rickety balloon stall, but what the hell. . . . I throw a dart, aware that I am young and shapely and probably attractive to this dirty, sweating man. My awareness shows in the way my arm moves, my back turned at the waist, the way I smile. I know I am doing it, don't even care what it means, and pop two of five balloons. "Three more tries for the big one, two dollars."

"No, no, just give me what I earned with those two."

"That's just a little one; you don't want that. . . ."

"Hand it over." I smile, hand out, flirting for no reason by being demanding. He wants to argue, I can tell, but some animation in his face goes out and he digs a minuscule Chihuahua doll from a battered cardboard boxful. A knockoff of the Taco Bell dog, and just about a year late at that. "Thanks!" I walk away feeling accomplished. In a tragic, perverse way it means something to me that someone finds me attractive here, in the very place where my guy was murdered for doing the same thing. I know it is pathetic, but tonight's my night. I allow it.

After a few circles of the carnival and a corn dog I am ready to go. I had been watching with melancholy desperation for signs that someone had figured me out, that I am something more exotic than they might have guessed at first glance. I wanted to walk away feeling I had passed completely, and the only way I could do so was if I detected no negative attention. Always realistic to the point of self-punishment, I was completely ready to be discovered and chased out like Frankenstein with torches and pitchforks. But nothing had happened, for whatever reason. I feel like I have stolen something rare, and thus follows the urge to flee. My earlier attitude has evaporated and now I am only bored and uncomfortable in a crowd of people I don't know. I begin to make my way toward the path leading back to the cars. As I leave, I pass a group of young soldiers who yell for me to come over. I smile and continue walking, but one detaches and runs after me to nervously offer his phone number. "You don't wanna date me . . . I'm *poison.*" I wink, trying to be mysterious, the worldly older woman to this nineteen-year-old boy. When he insists, I take him by the shoulders and place a maternal kiss on his cheek before gently turning him around and back toward his group with a little shove. How could he not *know*? I ask myself. On some level it still surprises me. I walk on with his buddies cheering at my back.

A bit farther down another group calls out to me. As I get closer to my truck my desire to be inside it and leaving here grows more intense, and I do not even turn around. The voice comes again, mean this time. "We don't want your ho ass anyway!" I keep my pace but break off the path, across the grass and back to my truck and safety. "Never forget," I tell myself, "you are always a stranger here, always carry a smoldering, deadly secret. Never fully relax; never completely let go."

The ride back to Nashville is as quiet as the one coming. No one even knew that I'd left. No one to worry, to call or ask questions. I am tired with the thrill of danger departed, and unsure of what I am coming away with. I do know now that I could have gone there and not been hated. And if so, if I hadn't sparked the fire, then it wasn't my fault. I will try to believe this, I tell myself, starting the engine.

In spite of the hour, I still feel hot, and crank down the window to let in some of the night air that rushes by. It is steeped in the scent of damp woods, and cold at this great speed. Above is only stars. I sail up and down the rolling hills like dark waves in a whispering sea, completely alone. But I have my memories. And I know what it feels like to be loved.

WRAPPED IN BLUE

Donna Rose

2003

Prior to her surgery, Donna Rose was a world-class college wrestler and built a successful computer consultancy. She lives in Texas with her son and two dogs.

HOW DOES a father tell his son that he is really a woman? What kind of a reaction should he expect? Why should it be so hard? Those questions had paralyzed me during my previous attempt to transition. This time I had no hesitation in telling him. The only question was how.

I had discussed it with my psychologist, who felt that kids are far more aware and accepting than we give them credit for. She said that I needed to have faith in our relationship, in our bond, and in our love. I told her that's how I tried to approach this when I first told Elizabeth, and look where that got me.

I had hoped that Elizabeth and I could tell him together, but that was obviously my own fantasy. I had come to the conclusion that he could either learn the truth from me, with compassion and love, or he could learn from Elizabeth, out of anger and bitterness. Either way, it wouldn't change the plans I was making, or the decisions that needed to be made.

At the time, Matt was taking tae kwon do lessons. The drive from our house to the studio usually took about a half hour. It was during these drives that I started, little by little, to set the stage.

One day, as we drove, I asked if he wanted to know why things had been so unhappy in our house lately. Why Mom and I couldn't stand to be in the same room, why Mom had wanted to divorce me. What she meant when she said that my family was all fucked up. I asked him if he wanted to know the big secret that we had been hiding.

"Yes, of course," he said, suddenly interested.

I told him that before I could actually tell him, I needed to explain a few things.

He was curious, and eager to listen.

I asked him whether he felt that people who were born with birth defects really *wanted* to be that way. If someone was born blind or deaf, or had a hole in their heart, or was mentally retarded . . . was that their fault?

He said, "No. Of course not."

I explained that the things that caused those birth defects happened while the baby was developing inside the mommy.

"There are many things that can go wrong while a baby is being made," I explained, "some of which you can see as soon as the baby is born, and some that you can't see until the child gets older."

On a subsequent drive, we talked about boys and girls, and what actually makes a boy a boy, and a girl a girl. Are you a boy because you have a penis, or because you *feel* like a boy? Did you ever think that maybe it was both? What happens if a person has a birth defect where they have a penis, but they don't feel like a boy? Is that their fault?

He said, "Of course not."

Just because a person wears a dress, or has long hair, or likes the color pink, does that make them a girl?

"Of course not."

I explained that being a boy or a girl was partly based on your body, but also based on your brain. Some girls like boy things, and some boys like girl things. That doesn't mean that they want to be the other sex; it's just the way they are. But there was a birth defect where a person's body could develop into a boy, but their brain felt that it should be a girl.

Here we were. We were on the brink. It was time to push us over the edge.

I told him that *that* was my problem. I had been born with that birth defect. I was born with the body of a boy, but I didn't feel like a boy. I had tried my best to be a boy, but it just wasn't working for me. I needed to figure out if I could be a girl, and the only way to do that was to try to live like a girl and see how that felt.

He thought about it for a few seconds, and said words that I will never forget as long as I live. "Does this mean that you're going to have your *schlong* cut off?" he asked.

I told him I really didn't know.

I told him that his mom did not think it was a birth defect. I told him that she felt it was sick, and wrong. I told him that she felt I was choosing to do this, and would try to make him think that I was selfish. I told him that, no matter what, I loved him and wanted to be with him and hoped he could understand.

"Are you going to get divorced?" he asked.

I told him I didn't know. I told him that I still loved his mother, and that she still loved me, but that it was a possibility. I told him that she wanted me to fight the birth defect, but that I couldn't fight it any longer. I told him that she would say things about me that might or might not be true because she was angry, so if he had any question to feel free to ask me *anything*.

We talked about treatment for people who have this birth defect, and some of the things I was planning to do. I asked him if he thought he would have a problem with any of it.

"I don't really care," he said.

We drove silently for a few minutes. I could tell Matt was thinking.

"I think you'll make an ugly girl."

I smiled. I had a picture, and asked if he wanted to see it. I watched his eyes as he studied it, looking for some reaction.

He really didn't have one. Then he asked another historic question.

"Where did you get those boobs?" he asked.

———————

OF COURSE, Elizabeth was absolutely furious that I had disobeyed her order that Matt not know about my problem. At that point, there was nothing she could really do about it.

After yelling at me for a while, she immediately went to quiz him. . . .

JOURNAL ENTRY

Sometimes things happen in this whole mess that really catch me by surprise. They are truly defining moments, and today was one of those times.

Apparently, after Elizabeth and I had our little "chat," she ran right off to interrogate Matt. Based on what I've heard so far, the conversation went something like this. . . .

ELIZABETH: So, I understand Dad told you all about his "problem."

MATT: Yep.

ELIZABETH: It's really sick, don't you think?

MATT: No, not really.

ELIZABETH: What do you mean, no? It's really pretty sick.

MATT: No, it's not. It's not his fault. It's the way he was born. Kinda like when I talk too fast. I was just born that way. I don't want to do it, but I can't help it, and he can't help it either.

ELIZABETH: I heard he showed you a picture.

MATT: Yep.

ELIZABETH: I'll bet he looked ridiculous.

MATT: No, not really.

His support would not last.

[. . .]

We put on a pretty good *happy* face for our friends and family. Nobody would know that we were absolutely devastated, and that our marriage and our lives were hanging by a thread. We had gotten far too good at giving the outward appearance of marital bliss despite all the inner upheaval we were both feeling.

The highlight of my trip was finally disclosing my situation to my mom.

The thing I felt most awkward about was timing. Between my dad dying, and my sister having a baby with birth defects, our family had been through some very difficult things over the previous several months. If it's true that bad things happen in threes, then my little revelation would just be icing on the cake.

I think that, no matter how well we think we know our parents, who can say for sure what their reaction to news like this will be? I have known gals whose parents have completely disowned them as a result of this news. Although I did not expect outright and total rejection, I did not expect the news to be greeted with welcome arms, either. That left a whole lot of room in between.

My sister knew about my plans to disclose my situation to Mom, and was ready to do damage control. "If she does go off the deep end, I'll do my best to help her get back to shore."

That reassured me, and as the day that I planned to tell her arrived I felt as ready as I would ever be.

————

I HAD arranged for the two of us to go out to breakfast on Saturday morning. We sat down, ordered, and started to chat. She could tell that I had something important to talk about. I had dropped subtle hints that we needed to have a talk for several weeks, and I'm sure she was curious about what I had to say. I wasted very little time before I started right in.

I spent a half hour doing my best to explain. I talked about the difference in physical gender and mental gender. I explained what happens when there is incongruence. I explained about treatment options and my plans for the future. I explained my feelings since early childhood. Somehow, I think I got it all out.

She listened carefully, mumbling an occasional "Uh-huh" from time to time. I scanned her face for reaction as I talked, but was both relieved and concerned that I really didn't notice one.

Once I had finished, I asked her if she understood what I was trying to tell her.

She thought for a second, and then replied: "Are you telling me that you're gay?"

"No!" I said. I explained that this had *nothing* to do with sexuality. So I tried again, using a more in-depth explanation. When I was done, I asked her if she understood.

She replied, "So are you telling me that you are bisexual?"

With that, I knew that I could not give her all the information she would need to comprehend my situation. Perhaps her generation sees these things through a sexuality-tinted lens. Luckily, I had brought a copy of *True Selves* with me, so I gave it to her. I asked her to read it, and perhaps then she would understand. I assured her that she'd have questions, and I told her to feel free to ask me anything.

As we sipped our coffee, I could see that my mom's mind was churning.

"What are you thinking about?" I asked.

"I'm just searching for clues that I might have missed that should have indicated this to me a long time ago," she replied.

"I doubt you'll find any," I told her. "I was very good at being a guy, and there were very few chinks in my armor. Elizabeth didn't know. Judy didn't know. And although I can tell you a few times where things happened that were related to this, if you didn't know the entire story you'd never be able to put two and two together."

We sat a few more minutes.

I spoke. "It's not your fault, you know. It's nothing that you did, or didn't do. It's the way I was born."

She was silent.

"I looked for reasons for years and years, racking my brain why this should happen to me. I am comfortable now not needing to find the reason or the cause. I just know that it is, and I'll deal with it."

As we left breakfast that morning, I knew she would be okay. I was relieved that another burden had been removed from my shoulders. I knew that, despite my awkward attempts to explain, she would eventually understand. Granted, it was not easy, and it took a bit of time, but I felt incredibly proud.

from Chapter 28

I HAD not had any sort of contact with my son in nearly seven months, and out of everything that I had endured, that one issue was the most consistent and persistent source of pain. Here he was, growing up without me. What was he thinking? What was he feeling? I would have given anything to be able to sit with him again. I felt helpless to do anything about it other than send him e-mails on a regular basis, telling him that I loved him and missed him and hoping that he actually read them. Elizabeth screened all the calls to the house to avoid having to talk to me, so I had no confidence at all that any messages I asked her to relay to him actually got passed.

My frustration in their rejection boiled over a couple of times. For example, one afternoon I got a very nasty phone call from Elizabeth, who was angry that I had changed the message on my voice mail at work. Initially, I recorded a generic message, but I had gotten tired of people asking for Donna and having to explain that I was Donna, so I eventually changed it to, "You have reached the desk of Donna Rose. I'm sorry I'm not here to answer your call, but if you'll leave your name and number . . ." Elizabeth had called and heard the new message, and it had made her angry. She called to yell at me.

"You are not now, nor will you ever be Donna!" she yelled. "I'll never call you by that name. I can't believe you changed it, and neither can Matt. It's all just so ridiculous and pathetic! You've gone way too far now! What if there's an emergency with Matt, and the school calls?"

I yelled right back at her. "That name is who I am now! If you'd take your head out of the sand and see me you'd know! You can be in denial all you want, but that doesn't change the fact that I am who and what I am!"

"Well," she replied, regaining her composure, "you can keep deluding yourself all you want. But until you stop being so selfish and start thinking of Matt and me, we won't have anything to do with you." Click. She hung up on me.

Something inside me snapped. Who the heck did she think she was talking to? The only reason that I hadn't seen her or Matt over those long months was because I had honored her wish for me to stay away. But this was too much. It was time for her to face reality. I was going to *force* the two of them to see me.

I left work and jumped into my car, heading up to the house to confront her. All logic and common sense were drowned by the blinding outburst of my pent-up anger and frustration. Luckily, rush-hour traffic slowed my trip, and the realization that this probably wasn't a good idea had time to seep in. As time passed and I calmed down, logic and reason regained control. What did I hope to accomplish? How would a major confrontation make things better? Eventually I turned around and went to my apartment to reconsider.

Rather than force myself on them, I decided to offer them the opportunity to see me. I decided to wait until it was dark, to avoid having to explain to nosy neighbors, and then pay them a visit. So, with a clearer mind and a calmer demeanor, I drove to my house after dinner. I had not been there in many months, and the drive north through the Sonoran desert was strangely relaxing.

As I pulled into the driveway of the house that was still technically half mine, I saw that although the shutters were closed, the light in Matt's bedroom was on. He was probably in there doing homework or watching television. I walked up to the front door and pushed the doorbell. I could hear the dogs barking, but nobody came to answer the door. I rang it again, and to my surprise, the light in Matt's bedroom went off. They had obviously peeked through the shutters, recognized my car, and gone into the bedroom to hide.

This was so pathetic. Here I was, less than twenty feet from Elizabeth and Matt, separated by only a wall and some shutters, and we still had to play this silly game.

I walked around to the back of the house, unlatched the gate, and went into the backyard. One of the dogs was out there, and greeted me warmly, his tail wagging enthusiastically. He remembered me, and it was so good to see him. As I peeked through the kitchen window, I saw the other dog inside. I noticed that Elizabeth must have been balancing her checkbook on the kitchen table, and had hurriedly left to go and barricade herself in the bedroom with Matt when I rang the doorbell.

I checked the doorknob on the back door. It was unlocked. I opened the door and took a half step inside. All I needed to do was to go into the house, and go to Matt's room, or wait for them to come out eventually. I wasn't breaking any law. As far as I was concerned, I wasn't doing anything wrong.

Or was I? Would this really make things better? What did I think she'd do if I entered her house and forced myself upon them? Did I need her acceptance that badly? Was that the kind of person I had become? It only took an instant for me to answer. No.

"Hey! I know you're in Matt's room!" I shouted, loud enough so that they'd hear. "I had hoped that we could spend a little time face-to-face, but apparently you're not ready yet. I just want you to know that I love both of you, and I won't bother you here again. I'm leaving now, so you can come out."

I got in my car and drove home.

[. . .]

JOURNAL ENTRY

I called home and talked to Matt yesterday. He sounded good. I was feeling him out to see if he wanted to spend some time with me during his spring break, but he answered "Maybe" to most of my questions, which all parents know actually means no. He's not ready yet. It was a nice chat, though.

Elizabeth and I had talked about arranging for me to spend some time with Matt again, and the importance of maintaining at least some semblance of a relationship at this critical juncture. I think she had mentally come to terms with the fact that I wasn't coming home, so it was time to consider the nature of our relationships as we moved forward. She seemed to be supportive of my efforts to spend time with him, and we worked out the details in late April.

We arranged that I would pick him up at the house, and we could spend an evening together. It would be our first significant time together in over eight months.

My plans for the evening were pretty low-key, as I wanted to avoid any possibility of making him more uncomfortable than necessary. I thought perhaps I would bring him back to my apartment, we could order a pizza, and maybe we could watch a movie together.

As I drove to the house to pick him up, I was nervous. I had butterflies in my stomach. How would this go? Would it be awkward? Elizabeth had suggested that I try to look as much like Dave as possible, but that just showed how out-of-touch she was with things at that point. The goal was to get him comfortable with my new direction in life, not some ridiculous charade that I had left behind long ago.

As he walked out to my car, it was great to see him. He had a bag full of stuff to show me. He brought his most valuable sports cards. He had a baseball that was autographed by Barry Bonds. He had a bunch of CDs to play for me. It was almost like show-and-tell.

We had both changed so much in those eight months. He had grown quite a bit, and was very much the young man. I, on the other hand, had feminized tremendously, and although his changes were significant, mine were much more so. He seemed to take things in stride, and that was very comforting to me.

In fact, he told me he wanted to go to his favorite pizzeria for dinner. They didn't deliver, so I offered to order it, pick it up, and take it back to my apartment to eat if he didn't want to be seen out with me. But Matt seemed hell-bent on eating it there, so I agreed. "This should be interesting," I thought to myself.

As we parked out front, and collected our things to bring into the restaurant, I waited for Matt to get out of the car, but he seemed to be waiting for me to get out first.

"You can get out," I said. "I'll be right there."

"Nah," he replied. "I'll wait for you."

"Are you sure?" I questioned. "If you want to get out, I'll only be a second. . . ."

"What are you going to do?" he asked.

I paused for a second, not quite sure how to put this. "Well, to tell you the truth, I'm going to put on some lipstick, so if you really want to stay here and watch me do that, you're more than welcome. I just thought you might be more comfortable if I did it by myself at this point."

"You're probably right," he said, getting out of the car and waiting for me at the door as I adjusted the car mirror, applied my lipstick, checked my makeup, and got out to join him.

As we entered the restaurant, the hostess greeted us. "Good evening, ma'am. Table for two?"

I thought Matt would split a gut right there. Here I was, his father, but to the rest of the world I was a woman. And as the evening progressed, he saw firsthand that I was totally and unquestioningly accepted as a woman everywhere we went. There was no awkwardness. There was no staring and pointing. Things appeared totally normal, and Matt quickly seemed to get comfortable with me. It was a very special evening.

Once we finished dinner, Matt didn't really want to spend time at the apartment, which was certainly fine by me. Instead, he wanted to run some errands, and I happily agreed, pleased that he seemed to feel so comfortable so quickly.

The last stop of the evening was at a bicycle shop; I had a question to ask one of the salespeople. As we entered the store

Matt went off to browse some of the bikes there while I went to the back to find some help.

As I stood, waiting to chat with the sales guy, who was busy with another customer, Matt saw something that interested him.

"Hey, Dad!" he yelled. "C'mere when you're done!"

As soon as he said it, he realized just how odd it was. He covered his mouth as though trying to recapture the words that had just gotten out.

After we got outside, we laughed about it. "I'm going to have to find something else to call you," he said.

"You're probably right," I agreed, glad that it was he who brought it up. "You can call me whatever you want. If you want to call me Donna, that's fine. If you want to call me Dad, that's fine too. But my mom and my brother are having the same problem you are, and they both call me 'Dee.' It's kind of in-between Dave and Donna. 'D' for Dave. 'D' for Donna. 'D' for Dad."

After the success of the evening, we started to see each other a little more regularly. It gave a tremendous boost to my spirits.

SHE'S NOT THERE

Jennifer Finney Boylan

2003

Jennifer Finney Boylan is cochair of the English department at Colby College, where she was voted Professor of the Year in 2000. As James Finney Boylan, she wrote several critically praised novels, including The Planets.

The Ice Storm
(WINTER 2000)

BACK IN Maine again, our family stood on the banks of Great Pond, watching fireworks, as the millennium came to a close. In the house behind us were the voices of our friends, the music of Jimmy Durante: *Don't you know that it's worth, / Every treasure on earth, / To be young at heart....* Corks popped off of champagne bottles. Couples slow-danced, their arms wrapped around each other.

Our children looked up at the night, their breath coming out in frozen clouds. Rockets exploded in the sky above us. Fiery blue streamers fell toward earth.

A few days later, I dropped Patrick off at day care and drove back through the snow toward home. I passed through the Colby campus, where a woman was doing a figure eight on the ice of Johnson Pond. Across the street, the Colby Woodsmen's Team was throwing hatchets at a large wooden bull's-eye. An ax struck the center of the circle as I drove past. *Thunk.*

I drove down the icy hill on Rices Rips Road and crossed the Messalonskee Stream, its small waterfalls frozen into cascading stalactites. As I approached the railroad tracks, the lights began to flash at the crossing. A long freight train lumbered past, and I stopped and looked and listened. The boxcars were covered with various legends: *Bangor and Aroostook, Georgia Pacific, Chessie System, Southern Serves the South.*

I reached for the radio and turned it on. From Blue Hill came the sounds of the Zombies on WERU, "She's Not There."

I turned off the radio. There were all sorts of sounds already—the squeaking of the wheels of the freight train, the idling of my engine, the caboose rolling into the distance. The soft dinging of the crossing bell ceased. Horns honked from behind me; engines gunned angrily. People shouted as they drove around the Audi: *Hey, what's the matter with you? Why are you just sitting there?* Snow fell on my windshield. The wind howled.

I pulled the emergency brake. I stayed in the car, motionless, for a long time.

Okay, I said. *Okay, okay, okay. Enough.*

———

THAT NIGHT I said to Grace, "Listen, would you mind if I got back into therapy again?"

She looked perplexed. "How could I mind it if you went into therapy?"

"I know," I said. "It's just that I feel like I'm being crushed, with the whole gender thing. I'm beginning to wonder if maybe what I need is to be a woman full-time. But even just thinking about that makes me crazy, all the losses it would mean for us. All I know is, I can't do this alone anymore. I need to talk to someone."

Grace looked pale. "If you need therapy," she said softly, "you should get it."

———

I SAW a therapist not far from my home who claimed to specialize in gender issues. He had an office in a building that more than anything else resembled the Island of Misfit Toys. Beneath a single roof was a massage therapist, an aromatherapist, a polarity therapist, and a numerologist. And then there was my advocate, a concerned-looking man I called Dr. Strange.

Strange listened to my story for six weeks, twice a week, two hours a shot. He took a lot of notes, talked about Greek mythology, lectured me on the nature of the soul, and asked me how I felt about my penis.

At the end of our sessions, I got a hug.

He gave me dozens of diagnostic tests. Some of them were relatively straightforward; others seemed completely obscure. Later, he asked me to find archetypal images of masculinity and femininity and to bring them in and talk about them. I brought in prints of twenty Impressionist paintings, including *After the Bath* by Degas.

"Very interesting," said Dr. Strange.

He asked me to talk about the differences between male and female and how I imagined that these were distinct from the differences between masculine and feminine. He asked me to trace my entire history as a transgendered person, from my earliest memory to the moment when I froze at the railroad crossing. We talked about sexuality, about marginality, about culture and archetype, about the difference between reality and fantasy. He researched my medical history, inquired about any history of abuse or neglect, searched my life in vain for symptoms of pathology.

I tried to comply with all of this and told him the truth, as best I knew it. He seemed startled by how well-adjusted I was. There didn't seem to be any explanation for it.

At the beginning of March he sat me down and said, "All right, look. We've been talking for a while now, and I think I have a pretty good sense of where you fall along the scale." He looked out the window. "You want to know what I think?"

"Okay," I said.

"First of all, let's agree on what you're *not*. You aren't a cross-dresser, or gay, or intersexed, or suffering from any other condition, like multiple personality disorder, or dissociative disorder. You operate at a strangely high level of functionality, actually, considering what you've been dealing with."

Dr. Strange cleared his throat.

"I would consider you a strong, positive candidate," he said, "for gender shift."

It was snowing outside, and the flakes ticked against the windowpanes. The radiator pipes clanked and hissed.

"Are you surprised?" he asked.

"No," I said.

"You're familiar with the Benjamin Standards of Care?"

"Yes, I know about them." The winter wind shook the windows.

"Well, the standards provide you with a safe and cautious manner of proceeding, if proceeding is what you want to do."

"If proceeding is what I want to do," I said. I felt like punching him. "How can I know if *proceeding is what I want to do*?"

"Do you doubt that this is what you want?"

"Of course it's what I want. But that's not the point. If I do this, I'm going to lose everything, don't you understand that? *Everything.*"

Dr. Strange reached forward and squeezed my hand. I snapped it back from him. I didn't want to be squeezed.

"Listen, Jim. You can start by doing what the standards suggest, which is talking the situation over in a therapeutic setting. You need to understand what you need to do, and the consequences. You can, if you so decide, start taking bigger and bigger steps out into the world as female, monitoring your reaction to that experience, and observing whether being female in the world is what you expect it to be. You don't have to do everything at once."

"Doing everything at once isn't the problem," I said. "The problem is doing anything at all."

"You need to talk this over with Grace," he said.

"You're telling me."

"It seems, from everything you've said, that you want to stay with Grace. And yet, you should know that most couples don't survive this. The ones that do aren't exactly *couples* after transition. They're more like friends, or sisters."

"I don't want to be sisters with her."

"Well, that's not a choice that's necessarily yours to make." He looked sad. "You also should be prepared for this to be the thing that others most misunderstand about transsexuality. People generally have a hard time distinguishing between sexual orientation and gender identity. But as it turns out, gay and lesbian people don't necessarily have that much in common with transsexuals."

"Yeah," I said. "Except for the fact that we get beaten up by the same people."

"You should be ready for people who don't get this to say, 'Oh, well, he was really just gay and couldn't deal with it.' "

"I know."

"Let me ask you. If you weren't married to Grace—if you didn't know her—and you were female . . . whom would you be attracted to, men or women?"

"I can't imagine not knowing her."

"Humor me."

"I don't know. I mean, my world has always revolved around women. I've never thought about men that way. I mean, it's never even crossed my mind."

"Well, be prepared for it to cross your mind. Once you start on hormones, it's likely you'll see the world in a different way. Of the previously heterosexual male-to-female transsexuals I've known, about a third of them remain attracted to women after transition, another third make the leap to men, and another third become kind of asexual. The best thing you can do is to just keep an open mind."

"I'm not sure I want an open mind," I said, "if it means destroying my relationship with Grace."

"Well. The very first thing you have to do, as far as I can see, is to begin including Grace in your transition. From the little work I have done with you already, I can tell you with absolute certainty that if you and Grace split up, the results will be *atomic*."

"Atomic," I said. "Yeah, that's a pretty good word for it."

"And you should start thinking about talking to a larger circle of people about your being transgendered. Not everyone has to know at first, and the people you tell first need not be the most important people in your life. But slowly, you need to start bringing this thing that has always been secret into the light of day, and sharing it with the people you love."

I nodded. "Uh-huh."

"After a few months, we can start to prescribe hormones for you, if that's what you want. Most people going from male to female start out on Premarin, usually a low dosage, increased gradually over time. You might also want to start in on an antiandrogen, to bring your testosterone down. I have an endocrinologist I work with I can recommend; or you can consult your own family doctor. In any case, hormones are dangerous, and you should make sure that you take them in consultation with someone who knows what they're talking about. You know what hormones will do, don't you?"

"I have a pretty good sense of it."

"Well, I'm going to say this anyway, just so I know you heard it. Your skin will soften. Your hair will get thicker and fluffier. The hair on your arms and legs and chest will grow finer. Your breasts will start to grow, gradually reverting you to the genetic shape you've inherited from your mother and grandmother. A general rule of thumb is that you'll be about a cup smaller than your female relatives."

I nodded again. I came from a family of large-busted, slim-hipped women.

Dr. Strange continued. "You'll experience something called 'fat migration.' The fat in your body right now is centered in the male places—on your cheeks, in your neck, and on your belly. Over time it will move away from those places toward the female places—your bust, your buttocks, and especially your hips. Your overall weight will probably remain the same, but people will think you're losing weight since your features, and your face in particular, will change.

"People who have taken hormones report that the most dramatic effect of all that estrogen is on your brain. There is said to be a distinctly different way that your brain will function, and in which you experience the world. I don't know if this is true or not, but you will probably want to keep a journal and monitor those changes."

"I'm going to be writing," I said quietly.

"Your voice may soften over time, more from culture than biology, but you might want to talk to a voice specialist. There is a woman at Bates College who works with transsexuals. Here's her card."

I took it. "Tania Vaclava," I said.

"She's Hungarian," he explained.

"Great," I said. "So I'll talk like a Hungarian woman."

He smiled. "When you've been on hormones for a year, the standards require you to seek a second opinion from another mental health care professional. You are specifically required to see someone with a medical degree, either an MD or a PhD. When you have two letters of recommendation from your therapists, you can schedule surgery, which usually takes place a year or two after that. People in Maine tend to go to Drs. Menard and Bressard in Montreal, but other top surgeons include Schrang in Wisconsin, Meltzer in Oregon, Biber in Colorado, and Alter in Los Angeles. There are others, too. You should research each of the available doctors and see whom you're most comfortable with. Maybe you'd like to go to Thailand. There are a lot of good surgeons in Bangkok."

I shook my head. "Bangkok," I said.

"Anyway, before you can have the gender-reassignment surgery—or GRS—you are required to live full-time as a woman for a minimum of one year. During that period you may not go back to being a man at any time. You are expected to be psychologically preparing for your new gender. If you have any reservations or second thoughts, the time of your real-life experience, or RLE, is the time to learn of them, not after surgery, which is permanent and irreversible."

"I know," I said.

"Okay," said Dr. Strange. "Now the first thing you want to do is sit down with Grace tonight and talk this over with her. You are going to need her every step of the way. My own opinion is, you cannot get to where you need to go without her support and her love."

"But Doc, how can I expect her to participate in a process that by its very definition will take the man she loves away from her? That will destroy the life we have lived?"

"You can't expect it," Dr. Strange said. "But you can ask for it."

"I can't do this to her," I said to him.

"Listen," he said. "You aren't 'doing' anything. You are a transsexual. Amazingly, you have managed to carry this burden all these years. It is time for you to get help. You need to turn to the people you love to help you. You can't keep carrying this burden alone."

"I'd rather keep carrying it alone," I said, "than cause all this grief to the people I love."

"Well," Dr. Strange said, "that's your choice, I guess. Do you really think you can keep on the way you've been going? How much farther do you think you can go?"

"I can't go any farther at all," I said to him.

"Then what you have to do is clear," he said.

"No, what I have to do is completely *unclear*," I said. "Just because I can't go any farther as a man doesn't mean I can just pick up and start on the road to being female. I don't know how to do that. I *can't* do that."

"Maybe Grace will help you," he said.

"Maybe Grace will want to suffocate me with a pillow."

"Jim," Dr. Strange said, "do you really think that's what's going to happen?"

"No," I said, "probably not. Actually, she'll probably want to suffocate *herself* with a pillow."

"Jim, Grace is a social worker. These aren't new issues to her. I'll bet she has more of a sense of how this works than you think. She does love you, no matter what else is true. She is going to want you to be happy."

"You really do live on your own little planet," I said, "don't you?"

Dr. Strange stood up and spread his arms. "Have a hug," he said.

That evening just before sundown, Grace was in tears, her heart broken in two.

———

THE BURDEN that had been mine alone for all these years was now Grace's, and in the weeks that followed she walked through her days broken and crushed.

I had spent most of my life hearing the refrain of our culture, which says that truth is always better than lies, that we shouldn't have secrets, that the truth will set us free.

Now that I had told the truth, I felt anything but free. Every time I looked at my family, I thought, *Remind me again what's so terrible about mendacity.*

Of course, our lives continued, in spite of the atom bomb that had gone off in our midst. Luke continued to board the bus for first grade each day, and Patrick was taken over to day care several mornings a week. We would all get home at the end of the day, and the boys would eat macaroni and cheese and get their baths, and Grace or I would make dinner and we'd sit down and eat it while the children watched *Rugrats* on television.

I made salmon on the grill, marinated in jerk sauce. Actually, *jerk sauce* began to feel like the house brand.

"So how are you doing?" The children were watching television in the sunroom.

"Oh, I'm terrific," Grace said. She drank her chardonnay. "Never better."

"Have you been thinking any more about . . . you know, the *issues*?"

Something in the next room broke into hundreds of pieces.

"What was that?" Grace shouted.

"Nothing," Luke and Patrick said in unison.

"I mean," I continued, "I'm trying to think about the issues. . . ."

Grace's eyes filled with tears. "Jim, what do you want me to say?"

"I don't know," I said. "I just want to know if you're, like—"

"Stop it," said Luke. "Mommy! Patrick's annoying me!"

"Luke," I shouted. "Patrick. If you can't play nice together, I'm going to have to separate you."

Grace looked down at her salmon. "I feel like you're on a runaway train," she said.

"What do you mean?"

"I mean, you see this Dr. Strange, this maniac, for, like, six weeks, and all of a sudden it's, like, that's it, you're going to—"

"Luuuuke," Patrick said angrily. "I'm warning you! Don't make me *bite* you!"

"*There's no biting!*" I shouted.

Grace sipped her wine.

"I'm not on a runaway train," I said. "I've been thinking about this stuff for years, for decades. I've tried negotiating with it every way I can think of. I have to do something now, or I'm going to go crazy."

"Well, I haven't been thinking about it for decades. I've been thinking about it for what seems like five minutes."

"*Ow!*" Luke yelled. He came running to the table. "Daddy, Patrick bit me!"

"I'm sorry, Luke. But did you do anything to *make* him bite you?"

"He *said* he was going to bite you," Grace said.

"He was *annoying* me!"

Patrick came into the room. "Paddy," Grace said, "we don't bite people in our family." She looked at me. "No matter how much we want to."

"That's right," I said. "That's not how we express ourselves. Not if we can help it."

"I want a cheese stick," said Patrick.

"Okay," Grace said.

"I'll get it," I said, and went to the refrigerator.

Grace finished her wine. Luke went back into the sunroom. Patrick grabbed the cheese stick as if it were the Olympic torch and ran as fast as he could toward the television.

"What do you think we should do, Grace?" I said.

"We?" she said. "What do you mean, we?"

"I want to include you in this," I said. "I want for this to be something that we do together."

"Together? How is it going to be something we do together?"

"I don't know. By sharing what we're going through—or . . ."

Grace didn't say anything. "Can I get you anything?" I said. "While I'm up?"

Grace wiped her eyes. "I want what I had," she said.

Drunken Noodles

I ASKED Grace how she felt about the year to come. She was eating drunken noodles and spicy chili fish, along with a side dish of plad mun.

Grace looked at me and said, "I know you always ask me how I feel, but there are times when I think it doesn't matter."

"Of course it matters," I said.

"Jenny, shhh," she said. "This time you listen."

She poured herself some tea.

"You're good at asking me how I feel, Jenny, about trying to have a conversation about your transition, but you know what I think sometimes? I think, What's the difference? Since day one you've pretty much had an idea in your head of exactly what you wanted to do, and when you'd do it. All I've ever said all along was, Wait, please, stop, slow down, and to that you've responded with all sorts of words about your suffering, about what you've been through, about how you don't have any choice, about how this is mostly a medical issue and all that. It seems like no matter what I say it doesn't matter, because it's all been decided a long time ago. You've just been on a freight train for two years now. You're going where you feel like you need to go. For me, it's just like I'm standing here watching."

Tears filled Grace's eyes, dripped down her face, and fell into her drunken noodles.

"Do you believe," I asked her slowly, "that all of this is necessary for me?"

She wiped her eyes.

"Yes, I suppose so," she said. "But you can't expect me to feel the way you do about this. I can't imagine what it's like for you, even now. I'm not the one who's trapped in the wrong body, in the wrong life, in the wrong place. At least, I didn't used to be. No matter what happens from here on out, I lose."

Her lower lip trembled.

"I'm sorry," I said.

"I know you're sorry," Grace said. "But what can I say to you? You don't want to be the person I married." She shrugged. "I do love you. But this isn't what I signed up for. This isn't what I had in mind when I spent the last twelve years building something."

"It was something I built, too," I said.

We both sat there for a long time then, not saying anything.

"For all that," Grace said, "I still believe that being together is better than being apart. I still want to be with you."

I said quietly, "No, Grace. What you want is to be with Jim."

"No," she said. "What I want is to be with *you*."

We were silent again for a little while.

"But being with you can't mean what it used to mean. I'm always going to miss my boyfriend, the person I married, the person I love. The fact that all of this is necessary for you doesn't make that any less hard for me. But I know I want us to be together. I know I will always be close to you, Jenny. I'm just not sure . . . how near."

"Do you want me to move into the guest room?" I asked. "Do you want me to move out of the house?"

"No," she said. "I don't."

We were silent again for a long while.

"But," I said, "that doesn't mean you ever want to have a relationship with me again? That just means we're like *sisters*, for the rest of our lives?"

"I don't know what it means, Jenny. I'm not sure what we are. It's like you get to be happy, and me—well, we all just wait for me to get over it. But I can't get over it. I'm always going to feel betrayed by you, abandoned, like our little family was not enough. You know how I feel? Gypped.

"You asked me if I thought this was necessary, and yes, I do. I think it's taken incredible bravery and courage for you to be the person you need to be, and I'm not going to stand in the way of that. I would never keep the person I love from being who she needs to be. But I can't be glad for you, Jenny. Every success you've had as a woman is also a loss for me. I mean, I'm proud of you—you're a beautiful woman, you've come so far. But all of that success for you just feels like failure to me. I can't feel the way about your transition that you do; I'll never feel that way. All of the good things that have happened to you—your acceptance at Colby, with the band, with the school—to me, they all just mean one more thing I've lost.

"And I didn't get to participate in this at all. I didn't get to choose when you started hormones, or when you went full-time, or when you'll have surgery. I mean, you consulted me, you included me, and we talked about it all again and again and again—but it didn't *really* matter what I said about any of it, did it? I mean, really?"

The waitress came by and asked if there was anything she could get for us.

We said that we were fine.

The Yankee-Doodle Girl

ON THE Fourth of July, Grace and I were in Boothbay Harbor, attending the wedding of our friend Frank's daughter. The ceremony was performed down by the water, as yachts and lobster boats sailed by.

There we were, two women in our early forties, wearing our summer dresses, watching our friends and their children walk down the aisle as a man in a white tuxedo played Pachelbel's Canon in D. Wind blew across a microphone. The sound of the ocean was picked up by the PA system. Gulls flew in circles over our heads.

The groom, a sweet-faced young man, came down the aisle in his white jacket and bow tie. The bride followed, on her father's arm. In one hand she held a bouquet of white tulips.

The ceremony combined the two families' Jewish and Christian traditions; a minister officiated, but the vows were exchanged beneath a chuppah, and a glass was broken. "We do this," explained a rabbi by the minister's side, "to remind us of the destruction of the temple, to remind us that even in the midst of joy there is sorrow." As if this were something we could ever possibly forget.

Those two young people looked in each other's eyes and shyly, softly, promised to love each other "as you are, and as you shall be." They promised to make each other's needs their own.

After the ceremony, we sat inside a rustic lodge that overlooked the harbor, eating salmon and drinking champagne. Our friend Frank, a tall, burly, elegant man, stood before the gathered crowd at the side of the woman he had divorced twenty years earlier and toasted his daughter and his new son-in-law. His eyes filled with tears as he raised his glass, and as the big man cried, so did everyone else.

Between the two of us, Grace and I had only one napkin, and we kept snatching it back from each other in order to dab at our eyes. After a few minutes we got up, still crying, and went outside. Salt air was blowing in across the harbor, and the moon was rising above the sea.

Throughout that evening, I had felt the eyes of strangers upon us, silently asking the question for which we ourselves still had no answer: *What are you two?* Clearly we were not husband and wife; on just that much we could all agree. But neither, by any stretch of the imagination, were we a lesbian couple. We were parents, yes, of two remarkable and resilient children, both of whom had apparently inherited the unsink-able optimism and faith of their grandmother, the woman whose motto was "Love will prevail." Were Grace and I "sisters," then, two siblings somehow born to different parents? Was that what we had become?

We were still legally married and could remain so even though I was now female. Although we could not legally have *gotten* married now, if we were to meet and fall in love for the first time, we were allowed under the law to *remain* married, for as long as that suited us both. If we chose to divorce and remarry, however, I could legally marry only a man. If I then divorced that man and Grace married him, then Grace's ex-husband and her husband's ex-wife would both be the same person. I smiled as I tried to make sense of all this and thought of the song I used to sing my children, "I'm My Own Grampa."

What were we? For her part, Grace was still a beautiful woman, still able to whistle with two fingers in her mouth as her eyes crinkled with devilish laughter. Even now, men still looked at her as she passed through a crowd and thought, just as I had twenty-five years earlier, *Whoa. Who was that?*

As for myself, I had begun, to my own shock, to see men through different eyes. Dr. Schrang's hope that I would be orgasmic postsurgery had been fulfilled. The sensation— which I'd cautiously, curiously, produced all on my own— was like nothing I'd experienced, and yet, sure, it was familiar. The Greek prophet Tiresias, who was said to have lived as both a man and a woman, claimed that "the pleasure for a woman is ten times that of the man." To this, all I can add is that what it reminds me of, more than anything else, is the difference between Spanish and Italian.

I had always imagined that posttransition my sexuality would remain constant, that I would remain fascinated by women no matter what form my own body took. Yet somehow, without any conscious thought, the object of my desire was gently shifting. Now, looking around at the world, I would occasionally think, *Jeez. Look at all these* men. *Surely they haven't been here all this time? Where did they all* come from?

Occasionally a man would give me a hug, and the sensation of his stubbly face against my soft neck and cheek made the hairs on my arm stand on end. Women no longer struck me as creatures of such wonder. Their world seemed like the one I knew, like the one into which I woke each morning. Men, on the other hand—to me they now seemed like a mystery.

It was inevitable, I suppose, that one or the other of us, at some point, would take a first tentative step in a new direction. Yet that time was not upon us, and it was impossible to know whether it would come months from now, or years, or never. In some sense, I think we both dreaded that moment as much as we hoped for it. Where on earth would either of us find men that we adored as much as we had adored each other? How could we want, even after all these losses, to ever wake up beneath a roof that did not cover the other as well?

We knew what we were *not*—we were not husband and wife; we were not lesbians; we were not merely friends. We knew that we were not all these things. But what were we?

"Are you all right?" I said to Grace.

"I'll be fine," she said. "What about you?"

I nodded. "I'm okay."

Grace turned to me.

"Jenny," she said softly.

"Grace."

I had no idea what it was she was going to say next. It could have been anything—*I want you to move out. . . . I want a divorce. . . . I want you to climb a mountain in Nova Scotia and allow yourself to be blown off a cliff by the wind.* Nothing would have surprised me, I thought, with the exception, perhaps, of the one thing Grace did say to me then, the thing she said after all these years together.

"So, Jenny," she said. "Do you want to dance?"

Acknowledgments

I would like to thank the Kinsey Library at Indiana University for its resources, Edward Kastenmeier for his patience, Rosalie Siegel for her perseverance, and Thomas Jones for helping me photocopy and select a good deal of the text as we sat there for many hours in the fluorescently lit Kinsey reading room. Most of all, I want to thank Brian McMullen who did all the real work on this book.

Caroline Cossey: Excerpt from "Betrayal," "A Dream of a Wedding," and "News of the World Nightmare" from *My Story* by Caroline Cossey, copyright © 1991 by Caroline Cossey. Reprinted by permission of Faber and Faber, Inc., an affiliate of Farrar, Straus and Giroux, LLC.

Lili Elbe: Excerpts from *Man into Woman* by Lili Elbe, edited by Niels Hoyer, translated by H. J. Stennings, Intro by Norman Haire, copyright © 1933, renewed 1961 by E. P. Dutton. Reprinted by permission of Dutton, a division of Penguin Group (USA) Inc.

Christine Jorgensen: Excerpt from *Christine Jorgensen: A Personal Autobiography* by Christine Jorgensen, copyright © 1967 by Christine Jorgensen, copyright © 2000 by Motion Picture and Television Fund. Reprinted by permission of Cleis Press.

Deirdre McCloskey: Excerpts from *Crossing: A Memoir* by Deirdre McCloskey, copyright © 1999 by The University of Chicago. Reprinted by permission of The University of Chicago Press and the author.

Mario Martino with harriet: Excerpts from *Emergence: A Transsexual Autobiography* by Mario Martino with harriet, copyright © 1977 by Mario Martino and harriet. Reprinted by permission of Crown Publishers, a division of Random House, Inc.

Jan Morris: Excerpts from *Conundrum* by Jan Morris. Reprinted by permission of International Management Group, Julian Bach Literary Agency.

Mark Rees: Excerpts from *Dear Sir or Madam: The Autobiography of a Female-to-Male Transsexual* by Mark Rees, copyright © 1996 by Mark Rees. Reprinted by permission of The Continuum International Publishing Group.

Renée Richards: Excerpts from "Renée Richards/Richard Reborn" from *Second Serve* by Renée Richards (Stein and Day, 1983). Reprinted by permission of Stein and Day, an imprint of Taylor Trade Publishing, a division of the Rowman & Littlefield Publishing Group.

Donna Rose: Excerpts from *Wrapped in Blue* by Donna Rose, copyright © 2003 by Donna Rose. Reprinted by permission of the author.